Useful Illegality

Stefan Kühl is professor of sociology at the University of Bielefeld in Germany and works as a consultant for Metaplan, a consulting firm based in Princeton, Hamburg, Shanghai, Singapore, Versailles and Zurich. He studied sociology and history at the University of Bielefeld (Germany), Johns Hopkins University in Baltimore (USA), Université Paris-X-Nanterre (France) and the University of Oxford (UK)

Other Books by Stefan Kühl:

Organizations: A Short Introduction
(Organizational Dialogue Press 2021)
Sisyphus in Management: The Futile Search for the Optimal Organizational Structure
(Organizational Dialogue Press 2020)
The Rainmaker Effect: Contradictions of the Learning Organization
(Organizational Dialogue Press 2019)
Work: Marxist and Systems-Theoretical Approaches
(Routledge 2019)
Ordinary Organizations: Why Normal Men Carried Out the Holocaust
(Polity 2017)

To contact us:

Metaplan
Goethestraße 16
D-25451 Quickborn
Germany
Phone: +49 41 06 61 70
info@organizationaldialoguepress.com
www.metaplan.com

Stefan Kühl

Useful Illegality

The Benefits of Breaking the Rules in Organizations

Organizational Dialogue Press
Princeton, Hamburg, Shanghai, Singapore, Versailles, Zurich

ISBN (Print) 978-1-7349619-4-2
ISBN (EPUB) 978-1-7349619-5-9

Translation of Stefan Kühl's work Brauchbare Illegalität: Vom Nutzen des Regelbruchs in Organisationen (Frankfurt/New York: Campus Verlag, 2020).

Translated by: Jessica Spengler
Cover Design: Guido Klütsch
Typesetting: Thomas Auer
Project Management: Tabea Koepp
www.organizationaldialoguepress.com

Contents

Dealing with Rule Violations in Organizations: An Introduction

Whenever an organization comes under public fire for an environmental violation, bribery scandal, or financial manipulation, it is worth thinking about *Prince Friedrich von Homburg*, a classic play by the German dramatist Heinrich von Kleist concerning the refusal to follow orders.[1] In this play, Kleist—who had served as a lieutenant in the Prussian army when he was young—confronts his hero with all the pitfalls of successful rule deviance.[2]

The story is straightforward enough. The Prince of Homburg is serving as a general of the cavalry in the army of Friedrich Wilhelm, Elector of Brandenburg. Before a battle against Swedish troops, the Elector orders his generals to attack the enemy only after being explicitly instructed to do so—the Prince "is not to move from the place assigned to him, whatever course the battle takes" (Kleist 1996, 528). The head of the military organization recognizes that the situation is critical to the army, and he demands that all serving members of the organization strictly adhere to the official chain of command.

But the Prince of Homburg acts as if he hadn't heard the order—or perhaps he really didn't. He tells his cavalry to attack, despite the lack of a command to do so, and despite the explicit warning of his first officer. He insists on unconditional allegiance from his subordinates: "A soldier who does not follow his general into battle is a cowardly scoundrel!" He also

---

1   Horst Bosetzky (2019, 37ff.) was the first to make this connection with his description of the "Prince of Homburg effect." According to Bosetzky, rule deviance is only tolerated when it is successful and the deviant individual subsequently pledges himself unconditionally to the formal order.

2   Kleist's aversion to his military service is apparent from his letters: "The greatest wonders of military discipline, while objects of awe to all the experts, became objects of my own most heartfelt contempt; the officers I regarded as so many drillmasters, the soldiers as so many slaves, and when the whole regiment was performing its tricks, it seemed to me a living monument to tyranny." (quoted in Miller 1982, 22)

takes responsibility: "Let it be upon my head. Follow me, my brothers!" (Kleist 1978, 31f.) The prince thus reveals himself to be a shining example of a proactive, risk- and responsibility-taking transformational leader.[3]

This willingness to take risks pays off, as does the element of surprise. The prince's courageous intervention wins the battle for the army of Brandenburg-Prussia. But his success does not change the fact that this is a clear case of insubordination. The Elector of Brandenburg is furious: "Whoever it was who led the cavalry on the day of battle and arbitrarily advanced before I gave him orders to attack [...], he has incurred the penalty of death" (Kleist 1978, 42). The Elector has the prince arrested and sentences the insubordinate general to execution.

Granted, Kleist's play is not about common behavioral patterns exhibited by many different people; it revolves around individuals and their conflicts, as theatrical works typically do. Nonetheless, it addresses nearly all the questions organizations face when dealing with rule deviance and legal violations. A rule has clearly been broken, but does the success of the rule-breaker not justify his actions after the fact? And who is to judge whether the rule-breaking was ultimately successful? The battle was won, but most of the Swedish army was able to escape. Was this not just a Pyrrhic victory with dire consequences for the next confrontation? Would it have been smarter to wait until the opposing army was destroyed, thus ensuring victory not just in this battle but perhaps the entire war?[4] And what drives the rule-breaker to do what he does? At first glance, he seems to act solely for the sake of the organization. But does the pursuit of individual glory also play a role? Did the prince rationally calculate the costs and benefits of insubordination—for both himself and the army as a whole—or did he act intuitively? And, last but not least, how should the organization deal with what appears at first glance

---

3 This is a selection of adjectives for leaders that are particularly hyped in management literature. Regarding "transformational leadership," see Bass 1990; regarding "proactive personality," see Bateman and Crant 1993; regarding "risk-taking propensity," see Howell and Higgins 1990.

4 This question has been addressed in literary terms by Wolf Kittler (1994, 76f.), as noted by Bernd Eckstein (2018), who has written a worthwhile analysis of the play from the perspective of organizational sociology.

to be a successful breach of the rules? Should the violator be punished—as announced by the Elector—despite his potentially good intentions and his success, or should he be celebrated as an exemplary organizational rebel and pattern-breaker?

Functional Rule Deviance and Useful Illegalities

Kleist's play teaches us that while organizations must ensure the effectiveness of their official policy, they also count on their members to frequently deviate from rules and ignore instructions for the sake of the organization (Bosetzky 2019, 37ff.). This is because formal rules are often too rigid to fit every situation, so organizations must be willing to tolerate deviance—as long as it does not fundamentally call the existence of the formal order into question.[5]

In the social sciences, rule deviance that is functional for an organization is known as useful illegality. The concept pertains not only to behavior that breaches state laws, but also to behavior that violates an organization's formal expectations, meaning the laws of the organization (Luhmann 1964b, 304).[6] Disregarding occupational safety laws, exceeding state-mandated rest periods for truck drivers, or bribing customers to win a contract can all be considered cases of useful illegality, as can ignoring official channels or flouting internal procedural

---

5   This approach to rule deviance (namely, from the aspect of its functionality) has been much more sociologically productive than the research conducted into white-collar criminality. The concept of white-collar crime, which was introduced by Edwin H. Sutherland (see Sutherland 1945, 1949, 1983), significantly influenced the discussion of rule deviance, but it also caused great confusion due to its murky definition (see Punch 2008, 102). One problem was the original focus on middle- and upper-class individuals as criminals, which meant that rule deviance among organization members who did not wear "white collars" to work was overlooked (see the critique by Reiss and Tonry 1993, 6).

6   Luhmann writes: "We refer to behavior as illegal when it violates formal expectations. Nonetheless, such actions can be useful." This acknowledgment of functionality for an organization is the key difference between the functionalism of systems theory and the functionalism of early American organizational sociology, which often refers to rule deviance as being functional even when it only benefits individuals, sub-groups within an organization, or interest groups outside of an organization. In my view, the pioneering work by Philip Selznick (1949) about the Tennessee Valley Authority must be read with this aspect in mind. Regarding this, also see Schrager and Short 1978, 411.

guidelines—incidents that violate the formal expectations in an organization but do not break state laws.[7]

Rules are broken remarkably often in organizations. Rule deviance is so deeply entrenched in organizations that if members do not participate in or at least tolerate such deviance, they will fail to meet the organization's informal expectations. Rule deviance is a central aspect of the culture of organizations.

For all of the outrage usually generated by broken rules and laws, it is widely acknowledged that, in practice, rule deviance is functional for organizations. It is not for nothing that "working to rule" is considered the most effective form of labor strike for paralyzing an organization. When all rules and instructions are followed to the letter, even a well-planned organization will grind to a halt. The organization will be broken by the rigidity of its formal structures and done in by its mania for order and ordinances, its frenzy for regulations, and its fetish for rules (for an early analysis of this, see Crozier 1963, 247ff.).

Anyone who doubts this could conduct a kind of breaching experiment and spend several days doing only precisely what their organization requires.[8] This would largely bring the work process to a halt. The person in question would be written off as a "bureaucratic virtuoso" who could never let a single rule go, an "insistent formalist" incapable of occasionally "letting things slide," or a "rule-obsessed nitpicker" who doesn't know how organizations actually function. Co-workers and superiors would increasingly pressure the individual not to overdo their "bureaucratism," or their strict adherence to the formal order.[9]

---

7   The concept of "useful illegality" indicates that Luhmann considers the formal order of organizations to be equivalent to the legal order of a state. However, by using the term "illegality" to refer to deviance from both an organization's formal expectations and from the legally enshrined expectations of the state, Luhmann squanders the opportunity to differentiate more systematically between violations against an organization's formal order in which no laws are broken, and violations against an organization's formal order which are also legal violations.

8   Regarding the concept of the breaching experiment, see Garfinkel 1967. It is unfortunate that Garfinkel developed breaching experiments primarily for face-to-face interactions in families and between acquaintances, because organizations are the ideal place for highlighting self-evident expectations by means of such experiments.

9   Regarding the figure of the "bureaucratic virtuoso," see Merton 1940, 563.

Unsuccessful and Successful Useful Illegality

The insight that occasional rule deviance is functional for organizations is complicated by a particular phenomenon, namely, that rule deviance is only ever publicly discussed when something has gone fundamentally wrong.[10] The spectacular bankruptcy of a US energy company led to condemnation of the tricks used to report its finances rather than praise for the company's creative accounting (see, e.g., McBarnet 2006). The revelation that emissions values were manipulated by a German automobile manufacturer led to public demands for compliance with the law. This phenomenon clouds public understanding of the fact that companies have to break the rules now and again.

These examples alone show the extent to which our view of rule deviance is distorted by the public failure of these organizations. Once a scandalous story has taken hold in the mass media, it is very difficult to bring in more nuanced alternative interpretations. Put simply, the media's inevitable dramatization and trivialization of a case inhibits a more balanced assessment of the situation from the perspective of organizational studies.[11]

Granted, many people may quickly come to view the spectacular failure of an energy corporation as the epitome of a botched criminal undertaking. But they would be disregarding the fact that, just a few months before the bankruptcy, corporate consultants had—euphorically and without opposition—declared the company to be a prime example of enduring profitable development thanks to ongoing "creative destruction."[12] Similarly, after manipulating emissions values, an automotive company would not only be forced to pay fines and damages in the millions, it would also have to battle the reputation of being

10 For example, for his book on corporate social responsibility, Ronald R. Sims (2003) chose the subtitle *Why Giants Fall,* thus suggesting that unethical behavior causes companies to fail. Regarding the "restructuring [of] alternative horizons" after being caught, see Luhmann 1984, 403.

11 Regarding the logic of the mass media, see in particular Luhmann 2000.

12 Regarding Enron, see Foster and Kaplan 2001. It is a typical risk for corporate consultants to praise their star clients as exemplary companies only to be surprised by the sudden downfall of the organizations they had advised so intensively over the years.

a criminal association that deceives its customers. The public would soon forget that the same corporation had been nearly unanimously lauded for its exemplary engineering skills and high profitability shortly before the disclosure of the scandal in the business press.[13] It is evident that the revelation of an organization's rule-breaking or legal violations can have financial consequences that make the organization's behavior seem irrational in retrospect (see, e.g., Reichert et al. 1996; Baucus and Baucus 1997). But what is often overlooked here is that the financial balance would have been very different had the rule-breaking and legal violations not been discovered.

Whether actions are subsequently deemed successful or not is often a matter of chance. In hindsight, an energy corporation's accounting tricks may appear to be the reason for the company's demise, but the tricks would probably not have been revealed had a financial bubble not burst—meaning it is not out of the question that the company ultimately could have earned "real money" by monopolizing the gas and energy market.[14] Likewise, the revelation that an automotive concern was manipulating its emissions figures might be accepted as a key reason for the corporation's problems, but without this chance revelation, the company could have continued to vaunt its engineering feats in emissions control until more economical control solutions were available.[15] After all, the professional management of an organization's display side is the basis of success for many political, religious, and business organizations.[16]

As a contrast to cases of rule deviance that have failed on a grand scale, it would be necessary to carefully analyze organizations that are deemed successful in order to determine how much of their success

---

13   Regarding enthusiasm for Volkswagen prior to the scandal, see, e.g., Rhodes 2016, 1501.

14   Regarding this strategy, see Bartlett and Glinska 2001.

15   For a detailed analysis, see Ewing 2017, 204–5. In connection with this, it would be worth considering a previous case of exhaust emissions manipulation, namely, the submission of manipulated emissions figures by General Motors to the Environmental Protection Agency in the USA in the early 1990s. This is not to say that, despite the discovery of the deception, the overall outcome could have been positive for General Motors a few years later. Regarding this case, see, e.g., Green 2006, 250.

16   "Fake it until you make it" is the phrase that applies here. Regarding this strategy among venture capital-funded companies in exit capitalism, see Kühl 2003.

can be traced back to practices of useful illegality.[17] It would probably come as a surprise to discover that quite a few of these organizations maneuver just within the limits of what is allowed, engage in deliberate, minor legal violations, or have tolerated rule deviance for many years—but since these activities have not become the focus of public scandal, the organizations in question have not been plunged in a crisis of legitimacy.[18]

Decisions in organizations are always made under conditions of uncertainty and are therefore unavoidably risky. After all, it is always possible for a different decision to have been made (see Luhmann 1984 and Luhmann 2009). Developing a jumbo jet is risky because it is impossible to know whether it will be a market success or a flop. Introducing new administrative software is a gamble because there is no way to know if it will be more efficient than other software or only lead to further complications.

Admittedly, one central feature of functional rule deviance is the uncertainty regarding its costs (according to Luhmann 1964b, 314). But an organization's decision to violate laws or rules is fundamentally no different, in terms of risk, than any of its other decisions. Regardless of whether rule deviance proves, in hindsight, to be a shortcut to efficiency and customer satisfaction or a fatal step toward catastrophe, this is simply the normal risk arising from any organizational decision, and indeed from the very existence of an organization. Whenever organizations come into the world, they are immediately faced with risky matters such as market monitoring and influence, the payment and use of tax money, and the formulation and observance of laws. Instead of looking at public scandals and subsequently declaring all functional rule deviance or legal violations to be useless for organizations, we must develop a sense for the existence of both successful and failed cases of useful illegality in organizations.

---

17 Even organizations that have been forced to pledge themselves to compliance following a rule-deviance scandal may continue to be successful because of ongoing systematic rule deviance in other areas.

18 Some attempts at such an analysis have been made in historical studies of the "robber barons"; see Josephson 1995.

The Problem with Focusing on Individual Cases

Every time an organization attracts public criticism for a bribery scandal, breach of environmental protection laws, or financial manipulation, the same scenario plays out. Media commentators express outrage about the legal violations, politicians claim to be baffled by how brazenly the rules could be broken, and the accused organizations appear to be shocked by the decisions made in their name and promise to do better. Over the course of weeks and sometimes months, there is a general state of excitement—until interest gradually wanes and the case fades into obscurity.

Granted, some cases are not forgotten and instead become part of a global collective memory. We need look no further than the My Lai massacre, in which US soldiers in Vietnam killed hundreds of civilians (Jones 2019); the burglary of the offices of the Democratic National Committee at the Watergate Hotel in Washington, which ultimately led to the resignation of US President Richard Nixon (Bernstein and Woodward 1974); or the leak at a Union Carbide plant in Bhopal, India, which took thousands of lives (Shrivastava 1987). But who still remembers the bribery of government officials in dozens of countries by the aircraft manufacturer Lockheed (Bolton 1977); the manipulation of quiz shows on US television in the 1950s (Stone and Yohn 1992); the attempt by the now-defunct US pharmacy chain Revco to defraud state welfare authorities (Vaughan 1980); or the financial support provided to terrorist organizations such as the Islamic State by the French cement company Lafarge (Belhoste and Nivet 2018)?[19]

Admittedly, the detailed description of an individual case satisfies the desire for a "good story"—and stories are considered especially good when they deal with something bad. The accounts of organizational law-breaking found in newspapers and books often read like thrillers

---

19 Anyone interested in these largely forgotten incidents may be intrigued by others as well, such as the fact that automobile manufacturers allow for a certain number of vehicular deaths (Nader, 1965).

in which a few upright individuals defy the odds to uncover and fight the wrongs of the evildoers.[20] Movies that reconstruct the background to a scandal are more exciting than many murder mysteries.[21] But these accounts often leave us feeling dissatisfied because the elaborate depiction of an isolated case tells us little about how organizations function on a general level.[22] We are entertained but not given much food for thought.

In this book, I am interested not so much in individual cases as in fundamental patterns of rule violations in organizations.[23] That is not to say that isolated incidents of rule deviance play no role. I reference them to illustrate fundamental patterns of such deviance and clarify central problem areas. Some of these incidents are still remembered today on account of the media uproar they generated, while others flew below the radar of public attention but still have something to teach us.

Rule Deviance in Different Types of Organizations

I am concerned with rule deviance in companies, government departments, and administrative bodies as well as universities and schools, armies and police forces, political parties and non-governmental organizations.[24] Granted, when it comes to the details, there is a difference

---

20 One very accomplished recent example is the analysis by John Carreyrou (2018) of the manipulation carried out at the blood-testing startup Theranos.

21 For example, see the cinematic treatment of the rise and fall of Theranos by Gibney 2019, or the podcast on the same topic by Jarvis 2018.

22 This was the criticism of Ermann and Lundman 1982, viii–ix.; Shapiro 1983, 306; and Reiss and Tonry 1993, 6.

23 I am focusing specifically on the period in which organizations have emerged as independent social systems. Glancing at the discussions from antiquity, the Middle Ages, and even the early modern period, we find that such discussions revolved mainly around market behaviors that deviated from the norms, or around the moral infractions of rulers; for a brief historical overview, see Geis 2007b, 49ff.

24 The discussion that was kicked off by the concept of white-collar crime initially focused on companies. It was a lengthy process to discover that the concept of rule deviance could be applied equally to companies, administrations, armies, police forces, universities, schools, hospitals, and NGOs; see Ermann and Lundman 1982. Similarly, see Szwajkowski (1986, 124), who recommends using the term "organizational misconduct" in an attempt to move away from the narrow focus on companies.

between the rule deviance of government ministries under the Nazis, prison officials in the USA, political parties in the Philippines, and water and sanitation authorities in Jordan. But for all that the practices of very different types of organizations are influenced by various forms of government, economic market processes, cultural characteristics, and even technical developments, rule deviance in every organization is ultimately driven by similar processes.

In this book, I want to transcend the narrow focus on rule deviance in companies. Though there is no systematic justification for it, companies are the prototype generally used to play through questions of rule deviance and legal violations in organizations.[25] This results in a tendency to attribute rule deviance not to the characteristics of organizations in general, but rather to the special conditions of companies in a capitalist economic order. Corporate rule violations and law-breaking are thus explained away as the consequence of either not enough or too much capitalism, depending on the political sympathies of the observer.

Proponents of a neoliberal economic order attribute corporate breaches of law to state interference in economic organizations. If a state-owned public transportation company obtained subsidies by fraud, these proponents would argue that it was because the company was not subject to the same market pressure as privately owned transportation companies. Meanwhile, an environmental scandal at an automotive corporation would be attributed not to the rationality of a company attempting to circumvent environmental regulations wherever possible, but rather to excessive state influence on the company. The thrust of this argument is that if organizations were less influenced by state, they would follow the law.

Critics of a neoliberal economic order, by contrast, say that organizations are almost forced to become "criminogenic" because they are embedded in a capitalist economic order (according to Farberman

---

25 Even when it came to identifying white-collar criminals, the first people to spring to mind were generally corporate executives; see Sutherland 1983. For a general overview of the erroneous assumption that companies are the prototype of organizations, see Kette 2012; for a detailed analysis, see Kette 2017.

1975, 438; Punch 1996, 213). Tampering with emissions values, bribing civil servants to win contracts, and manipulating balance sheets
are thus seen as expressions of rational corporate behavior in light
of the tendency of profit rates to fall in capitalism. The most radical
conclusion here is that the only way to reduce legal violations and rule
deviance is by overcoming the capitalist economic order (regarding this
approach, see, e.g., Barnett 1981).[26]

There is little empirical basis for these restrictive interpretations,
however. We know that rule deviance and legal violations are just as
widespread in companies in a planned economy as they are in capitalist companies. Furthermore, due to increased bureaucratization,
companies in planned economies and market economies alike rely on
distinct cultures of rule deviance to be able to function at all (for a
pertinent early analysis of this, see Berliner 1952; also see Meirovich
et al. 2000). We know that even though state organizations may function as "law makers" and "law monitors," they can still occasionally
become "law breakers" as well, and that rule deviance is therefore at
least as prevalent in armies, police forces, and public administration
as it is in companies.[27]

Rule deviance and legal violations are not primarily the result of an
economic order that is too capitalist or not capitalist enough, they are
the consequence of the complex demands facing any organization. The
social world of organizations is so varied, surprising and contradictory
that it cannot be adequately mastered with a fixed set of rules or laws.

---

26 Also see the study by Snider (2000) of the legalization of corporate illegality enabled by
neoliberalism. Such theories are based on more or less well-conducted analyses showing
that for-profit nursing homes break the law more frequently than non-profit ones (Jenkins
and Braithwaite 1993), and that students in the economic sciences tend more toward corrupt behavior than their fellow students in other disciplines (Frank and Schulze 2000).

27 This is according to Ermann and Lundman 1978, as well as Ermann and Lundman 1982;
other very readable studies have been produced by Turk 1982; Anechiarico and Jacobs
1996; Snook 2002; and Ross 2003. In connection with this, it is also interesting to see the
growing resemblance between "left-wing criticism" of corruption which is oriented on the
concept of civil society and "right-wing criticism" of corruption oriented more on neoliberal ideas; see the illuminating analysis by Engels 2019, 146f. For a general discussion of
the fusion of "left-wing" and "right-wing" paradigms since the post-war period, see, e.g.,
Boltanski and Chiapello 1999, or Reckwitz 2019.

Toward a Systems-Sensitive Theory of Rule Deviance

This book deliberately focuses on rule deviance in organizations. It thus stands apart from traditional sociological and philosophical works that string together very different kinds of rule deviance in a largely unordered way (see, e.g., Popitz 1968; Williams 1970; Ortmann 2003). These studies are fascinated by the omnipresence of rule deviance, and they use the same analytical apparatus to explore everything from the violation of tacit conventions in the literary industry to the lulls in combat during World War II and the selective anarchy of the Venice Carnival.[28]

In contrast to this expansive treatment of the subject, one key benefit of a systems theory approach is that it heightens awareness of the unique aspects of rule deviance in very different social situations. The strength of systems theory is that—if you will excuse the tautology—it can make the different logics in diverse social systems comprehensible and put them to use for its own analyses. Organizations have different rules, and thus different forms of rule-breaking, than families, groups, or protest movements. Individual functional systems such as law, religion, and politics have their own specific logics and programs and produce their own forms of deviance.

In light of these different logics, systems theory views law-breaking as a rule violation that is fundamentally different from simply neglecting to maintain target quantities in a warehouse, for example. This is why rape is different from violating the generally accepted rules of tact at a party, and why if a celebrity is caught visiting a prostitute, the situation will be dealt with differently in the person's own family than in the media. All of these cases involve violations of norms, but the

---

28 This is particularly clear in the work by Günther Ortmann (2003, 100 and 103f.), who suggests taking a quote from Jorge Luis Borges—"Literature is a game with tacit conventions; to violate them partially or totally is one of the many joys (one of the many obligations) of the game, whose limits are unknown"—and simply replacing the word "literature" with "organization"; then you are right at the heart of things. This recalls a certain postmodern arbitrariness that seems to have made its way into some parts of systems theory as well. The importance of encountering the object under analysis retreats into the background, replaced by elegant formulations and theoretical constructions.

way these deviations are labeled and handled follows fundamentally different logics depending on the type of system.

The advantage of a systems theory perspective is that it enables us to define organizations—and thus their rule violations—very precisely. Organizations differ from other membership-based systems in that their membership is predicated on following carefully specified rules. Only in organizations do we find such a stark contrast between formal structures and the informal, or cultural, organizational norms that often deviate from them.

Looking at Gray Zones

The goal of this book is to explore the fundamental questions raised by rule-breaking and legal violations in organizations. Why are rules broken in organizations in the first place (chapter 1)? What is the difference between violating state laws or an organization's internal rules (chapter 2)? How does rule-breaking that is useful for an entire organization differ from rule-breaking that only benefits individual members of an organization (chapter 3)? What distinguishes rule violations that are contained by formal structures in many organizations from the uncontrolled, epidemic rule violations found in organizations in some African, Asian, American, and European countries (chapter 4)? How do rule deviance and legal violations emerge in organizations, how do organization members learn to use these violations, and how are they internally enforced (chapter 5)? What happens in organizations when they find themselves in a crisis of legitimacy after a rule violation has been revealed (chapter 6)? What effects are produced by an organization's attempts to encourage its members to behave with more integrity by means of moralization (chapter 7)? What options are available to organizations for dealing with functional rule deviance and useful illegalities (chapter 8)?

Focusing on fundamental questions of rule deviance and legal violations in organizations makes it possible to step back from the black-and-white view that almost inevitably emerges when we look at individual cases alone. When we analyze isolated incidents, we are driven to identify the "bad guys" who initiated or tolerated an organization's rule deviance out of negligence, greed, or narcissism, as well as the "good guys" who warned others of the violations early on, pointed out their potential consequences, and often faced significant opposition from the organization for doing so.

I want to move past this black-and-white view and illuminate the gray zones in organizational rule deviance and legal violations. If all organizations struggle to get by in a world that continually surprises and overwhelms them, then dichotomous distinctions such as "permitted and prohibited behavior," "useful and non-useful legal violations," and "known and unknown rule-breaking" might be helpful for initially categorizing these behaviors, but they ultimately reduce the complexity too quickly into clearly defined classes (see Luhmann 1972, 124f.). After all, the survival of organizations depends above all on their ability to move flexibly in the spaces between apparently distinct poles.

It is certainly not the case that organizational researchers have been unaware of these gray zones between rule compliance and rule violation.[29] It is clear that, when it comes to examining organizations, it is necessary to abandon the approach of coarsely characterizing every action as either legal or illegal (Luhmann 1964b, 311). However, it is also obvious that no close attention has been paid to exploring these gray zones.[30]

The problem with gray zones is that their peculiar ambivalence makes it difficult to discern their contours. Anyone hoping to define gray tones as precisely as black or white will inevitably be disappointed. But gray zones can be illuminated to better understand the shading within them. Highlighting these gray zones may make some organizational practitioners nervous. If you are used to the typical management

---

29   See, e.g., Luhmann 1964b, 304; Land et al. 2014, 234; Soltes 2016, 189ff.
30   In some cases, entire thematic complexes have been defined out of existence because gray zones are so hard to illuminate. For example, some scholars argue against making a systematic distinction between self-serving rule deviance in organizations and rule deviance for the benefit of the organization because the boundaries between the two are often fluid (such as Palmer 2012, 26).

literature with its impressive heroic tales, dazzling model organizations, and simple recommendations, it may be difficult to grasp any descriptions that go beyond this simple contrast. Unfortunately, however, life in organizations is more complex than the simplified recommendations, colorful charts, and spectacular success stories found in consultant self-help books, executive autobiographies, and articles in the business press would suggest.

A Text for Practitioners and Theorists

It is relatively easy for researchers to write a text either only for fellow researchers or only for practitioners. Articles intended for an academic audience have become so heavily standardized in their style that— assuming they have something new to say and are backed up by interesting empirical evidence—they almost write themselves. Articles by researchers that are aimed exclusively at practitioners are subject to fundamentally different requirements, but they are no less standardized. We need look no further than the insistence with which leading management journals demand that their authors submit texts with the same structure, consisting of practical tips, examples of best practices, and at least a suggestion of empiricism.

Difficulties always arise when an author hopes the same text will both influence an academic debate and contribute to a discussion among practitioners. A text that strives to be rooted in scholarly discourse while remaining accessible and comprehensible to practitioners will inevitably be criticized by both sides. Practitioners can get the impression that theoretical figures are unnecessary complications, and that relatively straightforward issues are being cloaked in scholarly jargon. Theorists, in turn, can justifiably complain that too many concessions have been made to practitioners regarding comprehensibility and entertainment value.

In this respect, the book at hand demands a degree of tolerance from its readers. Practitioners will have to accept that the text is not quite as catchy as the usual management literature. It offers no formulas for managing rule deviance in a better way, no profiles of model organizations, and no central ideas summed up in bullet points. Instead, practitioners will have to grapple with scholarly categorizations, supplemental footnotes, and an extensive bibliography. Specialists, in turn, will have to put up with the fact that the book's theoretical positions are not presented in the usual compact, shorthand way, that there are perhaps a few too many illustrative examples for their liking, and that the empirical foundations are not described in as much detail as they would be in a purely academic work.

1.

Functional Rule Violations and Useful Illegality: Why Rule Deviance in Organizations Is Unavoidable

"The best way to fight bureaucrats is
to follow their instructions precisely."
*(Attributed to British historian and sociologist
Cyril Northcote Parkinson)*[31]

Rule deviance and legal violations in organizations are generally viewed as a problem. They are referred to as "misconduct" and "misbehavior" (Wardi and Weitz 2004), as "antisocial behavior" (Giacalone and Greenberg 1997), as "morally objectionable" or even as a "crime" (Greve et al. 2010). Companies are said to do "dirty business" (Punch 1996), and organizations are accused of "wrongdoing" (Palmer 2012) or having "dark sides" (Vardi and Wiener 1996). Organizations with excessive rule deviance and legal violations are called "uncivilized" (Andersson and Pearson 1999) or "shadow organizations" (Allen and Pilnick 1973).[32]

The organizations criticized in this way can exhibit very different kinds of rule deviance. Banks might manipulate their financial reports, electronics firms might bribe contracting authorities, and automotive companies might violate environmental protection requirements. We find rule deviance in the everyday manipulation carried out in universities forcing student achievements to fit into an increasingly complex set of rules, the little tricks used in the computer-based documen-

---

31 This saying is repeatedly attributed to Cyril Northcote Parkinson, a critic of bureaucracy, but I have not been able to identify an original source for the quote.
32 This view of rule deviance as a scandal emerged relatively early on; for example, see Filler 1975 regarding the "muckraker" movement in the USA in the early twentieth century.

tation of care services in nursing homes, and in the ruses employed by government departments and companies to get around bidding guidelines. Such deviance can also take the form of the abuse of minors by priests in the Catholic church, the manipulation of patient data so that a hospital can transplant as many donor organs as possible, the violent initiation rituals in armies, and the bribes paid to athletes so they deliberately lose games.

If the management literature is to be believed, then the solutions for dealing with legal violations and rule deviance are obvious. Managers should proactively make it clear to their employees that illegal conduct is never in the interest of the organization. Employees should be encouraged to "disobey" if their superiors demand things that go against the organization's internal rules (Brief et al. 2001, 491ff.). If difficulties arise in an organization's everyday work, the "concerns and fears of employees" should be escalated so that employees have no need to resort to violating the rules in order to achieve their goals. And to avoid rule deviance, even "upper-level management decisions" should be "constructively questioned" (Müthel 2017, 35). The aim here is to create a culture in which employees are encouraged to comply with the rules even in difficult situations (Anand et al. 2005, 17ff.).

These relatively simple suggestions are based on a certain interpretation of how organizations work. What is this interpretation, and how plausible is it?

1.1 The Personalization of Responsibility

When rule violations are made public, the affected organizations react in similar ways. They try to show that just a few isolated individuals were responsible for the violations and acted without the knowledge of the rest of the organization. They also try to paint themselves as the victim. Fingers will be pointed at a chief financial officer who—supposedly unbeknownst to other executives and the supervisory board—used accounting tricks and ultimately brought down the entire organization (regarding Enron, see McLean and Elkind 2004). Development engineers whose superiors instructed them to break environmental laws will not only be convicted in court, they will consequently be fired by their employer for damaging the company (regarding VW, see Ewing 2017). And banks will pass off a tax scandal as the act of lone traders who deceived financial authorities by claiming multiple refunds for capital gains taxes without the bank's knowledge, causing the bank as a whole to suffer from the transgressions of a few individuals (regarding Deutsche Bank, see Laabs 2018).

Personalistic Explanatory Models

A personalistic approach attempts to explain rule deviance by looking at the personal traits of the individuals who broke the rules or laws (see Vardi and Wiener 1996, 159). Deviance is blamed on the weak moral development of criminal characters or the sociopathic tendencies of toxic employees.[33] The explanation proposed here is that employees with bonding issues struggle to identify with an organization, so they do not view the organization's formal norms as binding. Proponents of this model claim that organization members who find themselves in difficult social situations tend to deviate from the rules and must therefore be identified as risk factors early on. Another explanation is that the personal needs of the rule-breakers were not sufficiently met by the organization, so they resorted to illegal activities instead.

The tendency to deviate from rules or violate laws can be correlated with any number of personal traits. Rule-breakers are studied for signs of innate or acquired characteristics that could explain their behavior (see Raine et al. 2012). For example, attempts have been made to correlate the propensity to break laws or rules with physical traits and gender (see Soltes 2016). Deviance thus comes to be viewed as the

---

33 The diffusion of the term "toxic" in literature on rule deviance, especially since the turn of the century, is worthy of a separate analysis. It is not out of the question that the song "Toxic" by Britney Spears played a role in this.

result of a pathological need for control, extreme narcissism, or a low tolerance for frustration (see Croall 1991). The excessive individualism of amoral egoists is blamed for their readiness to break the rules (see Gormley 2001). Rule-breakers are said to be highly impulsive, with a strong desire for approval or an inordinate need for recognition (see Alalehto 2003). Some researchers note that emotionally cold people who score particularly high on the Machiavellianism scale tend to deviate from the rules more than people who are not predisposed to play power games (see, e.g., Flynn et al. 1987; Hegarty and Sims 1979; Jones and Kavanagh 1996). However, people with low self-esteem are also said to be more susceptible to violating rules and laws than people who are very self-confident (see, e.g., Treviño 1986; Treviño and Young-blood 1990). Another proposed explanation for rule deviance is that the respective organization members did not pass through all phases in the development of a moral conscience (see works following Kohlberg 1969). Other researchers have said that the propensity for rule deviance is associated with an individual's weak ties to society (see Hirschi 1969). Ultimately, the objectionable behavior of rule-breakers in organizations has been explained using the same approaches applied to the analysis of the behavior of street criminals (see Hirschi and Gottfredson 1987; Gottfredson and Hirschi 1990; Fisse and Braithwaite 1993).[34]

Entire industries have been devoted to solutions based on this personalization of responsibility for rule deviance (regarding the emergence of a compliance industry, see Laufer and Robertson 1997). Law firms offer to gather evidence against suspicious employees so they can eventually be removed from an organization. Accounting firms (which, ironically, are often caught up in rule deviance scandals themselves) have their own forensics departments for tracking down the guilty parties in a scandal. And consulting firms provide psychological tests intended to preventively identify potential rule-breakers.

These personalistic explanations are summed up by the metaphor that one bad apple spoils the bunch. The concern is that other people will see individuals get away with breaking the rules and will emu-

---

34   For a brief overview of deviance theories, see Goode 2007.

late their behavior. In the end, the whole organization would then be infected with this rule deviance. It is therefore critical to quickly identify and remove the rotten apple before it spoils the entire barrel.[35]

Functions of Personalization

From an organization's perspective, it makes sense to try to personalize rule deviance and law-breaking. By blaming single individuals, an organization can contain a scandal. Specific organization members can be publicly condemned so the organization can clearly distance itself from the rule-breakers, thus easing the pressure on it (regarding this effect, see Pinto et al. 2008, 689).

It can be useful to pass off responsibility onto living organization members, since an organization's public separation from them can be staged as an act of purification. According to the rules of Aristotelian dramatic order, the catharsis qua "pity and fear" is followed by a final act of closure which involves separation from the "guilty" (Schütz et al. 2018, 164). But it can also be helpful to pass off responsibility for rule deviance onto organization members who have died. Regardless of whether the deviance entails bribes to win the bid for the soccer world cup, manipulated research findings for the approval of a medication, or even the mass murder of Jews during the Holocaust—responsibility is often assigned to people who are already dead because (for obvious reasons) they can neither be prosecuted nor defend themselves against the accusations.

It is important not to underestimate the function of this approach for an organization. Organizational research shows that, at least to a certain degree, it is useful to attribute failures, transgressions and legal violations to people. When one particular person bears responsibility, it eases pressure on the organization to engage in a search for other causes, which often blocks action (Brunsson 1989, 202f.). The allevi-

---

35 Regarding the debate surrounding the influence of "bad apples," "rotten barrels," and, lately, "bad cellars" as well, see, e.g., Palmer 2012, 7; Ashforth et al. 2008, 672–678; and Muzio et al. 2016, 141ff. The term "bad cellars" refers to how cross-organizational "professional ecological systems" (in fields such as accounting and law) influence "misconduct" in organizations.

ating function of personalization was brought into sharp relief in the repression of the Holocaust after World War II. Asserting that the mass killings were the act of psychopathic and fundamentally evil murderers made it possible for people in Germany to continue living as if nothing had happened (see Waller 2002, 65; Berg 2003, 505ff. and Berg 2015; for a fundamental analysis, see Lübbe 1983).[36]

This function explains why managers who have broken laws, tolerated rule violations, or made grave errors are often dismissed with high severance payments. The personalization of responsibility works particularly well when the organization members in question do not resist the assignment of responsibility. Severance pay is often a more or less imposed reward for an employee who has accepted blame that could just as easily have been attributed to someone else (Kühl 2019b, 81).

But when organizations personalize responsibility, they cloud their own view of the structural reasons for the rule deviance (as pointed out by Schrager and Short 1978, 407; also see Besio 2013, 310). Personalizing an incident offers an apparently convincing explanation that spares the organization from having to delve deeper into why rules were broken in the first place (Luhmann 2014, 43). The organization can thus quickly rid itself of the problem, but it also makes itself more ignorant because it does understand the deeply rooted processes that led to the rule deviance and legal violations.

1.2 Reasons for Rule Deviance

In opposition to this personalization of responsibility, organizational research suggests a fundamentally different explanation for rule deviance and legal violations. Max Weber, a forefather of the social sciences,

---

36 The way in which National Socialism was dealt with demonstrates that personalization functions not only on the level of single political, economic, legal, religious or athletic organizations, but also on the level of entire nations. The analysis by Burleigh (1994, 232f.) of the mass murder of mentally ill and disabled people under the Nazis shows how prominent such personalistic explanatory models have become in academic literature.

not only concisely defined bureaucracies as goal-oriented machines working on the basis of efficiency criteria, he also impressively described how bureaucratic principles can both conflict with and supplement the personal networks in an organization (see Weber 1978, 956ff.). Chester Barnard, a founder of modern organizational studies, not only determined how an organization's formal order functions, he also showed that in order to find their way in an organization, members must first recognize the organization's "invisible government" and understand its "informal society" (see Barnard 1938, 121). And Niklas Luhmann, the most important representative of organizational studies oriented on systems theory, hones this argument further with his concept of "useful illegality" by emphasizing that the informal processes that are functional for organizations are often not compatible with their formal expectations, and in many cases even contradict them (see Luhmann 1964b, 304ff.).[37]

The phenomenon of functional rule deviance has been referred to in many different ways—and sometimes with very different emphases—in the relevant literature.[38] The terminology used here includes "positive deviance" from organizational norms (Spreitzer and Sonenshein 2003), "pro-organizational illegal behavior" (Müthel 2017, 31), "unethical pro-organizational behavior" (Umphress and Bingham 2011), and "illegal corporate behavior" (Baucus and Baucus 1997) that organization members engage in for the benefit of the organization. There is also

---

37 Also see the definition of "organizational deviance" published at almost the same time by Reiss 1966.

38 Also see the dominance of functional analyses of corruption in the period after World War II, such as the very different perspectives offered by Huntington 1968 and Scott 1969b. A key social-scientific controversy lurks behind the specific discussion of the functionality of rule deviance, namely, the debate about the possibilities and limits of a functional analysis. Regarding the debate surrounding the early functional concept by Robert K. Merton, see the elaboration of the concept by Merton 1936 and Merton 1940, as well as the critique by Davis 1959 and Elster 1990, for example. Regarding the equivalence functionalism of Niklas Luhmann, see the deliberations in, e.g., Luhmann 1964a; Luhmann 1969; Luhmann 1970a; Luhmann 1970b; Luhmann 2010a. It is beyond the scope of this book to reflect in detail on the concepts of functional illegality and functional rule deviance against the backdrop of this debate. But it is interesting to note how strongly the loss of focus on useful illegalities correlates with the loss of the importance of functionalist perspectives in the social sciences.

mention of "pro-social rule breaking" (Morrison 2006), "principled organizational dissent" (Graham 1986), "functional disobedience" (Brief et al. 2001), "constructive deviance" (Galperin 2003; Warren 2003; Vadera et al. 2013), the "organizational misbehavior" sometimes exhibited by members to benefit the organization (Vardi and Wiener 1996), and the "necessary evil" that often must be committed for the sake of the organization when formal rules are ignored (Molinsky and Margolis 2005).[39]

But why is rule deviance seemingly inevitable in organizations? Why can't organizations get by if their members always follow the rules?

Contradictory Requirements

Organizations must come to terms with highly contradictory requirements.[40] Even a superficial glance reveals that very different environments are relevant to organizations. An important role is obviously played by the owners of an organization—regardless of whether they are states, shareholders, or founders—who demand efficiency, effectiveness, and innovation. In most cases, a key role is also played by an organization's beneficiaries—be they customers, clients, patients, students or prison inmates—with their price, quality, and load demands. And a non-negligible role is played by the members of an organization, who are interested in appropriate remuneration, meaningful work, and sensible working conditions. Last but not least, organizations must not

---

39 Although a great deal of effort has been put into distinguishing these various terms from one another in the research literature, the concepts have not yet been clearly categorized (see Ilie 2012, 3ff.).

40 This situation has been described from a wide variety of organizational theory perspectives; see, e.g., Selznick 1949; Luhmann 1973; Pfeffer and Salancik 1978; Oliver 1991; Friedland and Alford 1991; Kraatz and Block 2008; Thornton et al. 2012. With concepts like "institutional logics" and "multireferentiality," organizational researchers are continually rediscovering the heterogeneous and indeed contradictory nature of environmental expectations (see Greenwood et al. 2011). However, they frequently overlook the fact that these descriptions apply not only to organizations, but also to other systems such as families, protest movements and small groups.

neglect the demands of their political environment—such as paying taxes, creating jobs or simply obeying the law.[41]

We can look at very different types of organizations to see how they try to cope with the contradictory demands placed on them. Public administrators must make decisions based on the prevailing legal situation, but they also have to take the views of the dominant political parties into account, juggle the expectations of interest groups, and—last but not least—pay heed to the stress limits of their employees (for a detailed analysis, see Luhmann 1973). Associations will pursue what they consider to be ambitious goals—bringing about world peace, achieving gender equality, or preserving ethnic homogeneity—but they must think carefully about whether they want to break laws to achieve these goals. They also have to ensure continual financing through donations or public funding, and they must not lose sight of the sometimes idiosyncratic motivation structures of their volunteer members (Horch 2018, 60ff.). Companies, in turn, must ensure that their shareholders receive attractive dividends, their customers do not feel bamboozled, their employees do not rebel, and laws are not stretched to the breaking point (for a detailed analysis, see Schreyögg 1984).[42]

Limits of Optimization

Quite a few managers harbor the notion that they can handle the problem of contradictory requirements by setting priorities. The concept of "shareholder value" propagates the idea that companies

---

41   I am focusing on just four particularly relevant (sub-)systems found in an organization's environment: the organization's "owners," members, beneficiaries, and political framework. The pressure on organizations is intensified by the fact that the demands from each of these systems themselves can be very contradictory.

42   The formation of contradictory environmental demands for organizations has been explored for different types of organizations in a variety of studies; see, e.g., the study by Scott (1982) of health organizations, by von D'Aunno et al. (1991) of drug abuse treatment units, by Marquis and Lounsbury (2007) of community banks, and by Rottenburg (2009) of development banks.

should feel obligated only to make as much money as possible for their owners, without being distracted by competing goals such as social responsibility (Friedman 1962, 9, 133f.). By contrast, companies that hold up the customer (or client, patient or student) as king focus entirely on the beneficiaries of their services and prioritize them above the needs of employees or state regulators, for example. And in an employee-centered organization, the demands of customers and even owners are subordinate to the well-being of the employees. Furthermore, the demand for absolute compliance with the law is nothing more than an attempt to proclaim a single guiding principle. Ultimately, organizations act as if one goal—meeting the demands of owners, fulfilling customer needs, ensuring employee satisfaction or complying with rules and laws—is the most important and all other goals are secondary to it.

But it would be naïve for an organization to act as if only a single environmental segment were relevant to it. Administrative bodies soon run into problems if they mechanically work through the directives applicable to them while ignoring the demands of ruling parties, key interest groups or their own employees. An association will encounter serious recruitment difficulties if it places the achievement of its goals above all else, because "the end justifies the means" is not an attitude likely to be tolerated by law enforcement officials, and not everyone who sympathizes with a "good cause" is willing to go to jail for it. Governments will face legitimacy issues if they place the health of the population above all else in a pandemic and ignore the economic problems that arise from the closure of key business sectors. And companies will quickly plunge into a crisis if they focus only on shareholder value in the interest of their investors and dismiss other expectations from their environment, such as those of their customers, employees or state legislators (regarding this, see Fiss and Zajac 2004).

One-sided optimization strategies soon lead to adaptation difficulties which can eventually destroy an organization (Luhmann 1964b, 305). The profit margins in drug trafficking, prostitution, and waste management are undoubtedly high, but if this realization leads to a one-sided focus on shareholder value, it will result in considerable problems with the law enforcement authorities in most countries and will thus hamper the recruitment of new organization members (regarding this, see the essays in Heilbroner 1972). Focusing entirely on customers, clients, patients or students will become problematic for an organization if these beneficiaries demand services that are unlawful, that overload the employees responsible for providing them or that challenge the organization's financial viability. An organization that prioritizes its members' welfare will encounter issues if this highly vaunted employee focus is taken as an invitation to ignore the needs of customers or clients, the expectations of the organization's owners or the state's demand for legally compliant behavior. And a one-sided focus on achieving a high degree of political legitimacy by rigidly adhering to the law, willingly paying taxes or embracing social responsibility will reach its limits as soon as it becomes too obvious that this approach has been at the expense of the demands of the organization's owners, customers and clients, or members (see Box 1998, 35).

Systems theorists realized early on (Becker and Luhmann 1963, 13) that it is not possible to "maximally fulfill" an organizational goal such as legal compliance "at the expense of everyone else without endangering the continued existence of the system."[43] "It is the seamless conformity, the absolutely consistency, the perfect loyalty to one's own rules" that endangers the organization. "Unequivocal means one-sided," which is why strict adherence to what is "unequivocally right" is not a sensible strategy from a systems theory perspective (according to Kieserling 2015, 57).[44]

---

43 Also see Schütz et al. 2018, 105; for an early formulation of the concept of white-collar criminality, see Aubert 1952.

44 See Osrecki 2014, 409ff., who applies this thinking to functional systems. He refers to the systems theoretical description of the political system, according to which there is both an official and an unofficial circulation of power (regarding the dual circulation of power, see, e.g., Luhmann 2010b, 130ff.), as well as to the systems theoretical analysis of the scientific system, in which reputation depends not only on scientific brilliance but also on a media presence, political influence or economic success in the form of external funding (see, e.g., Luhmann 1992, 245).

1.3 Between Formal Expectations of Consistency and Contradictory Environmental Demands

Classic organizational theorists have a simple solution to the problem of contradictory requirements. They say organizations must "sort" these requirements in order to establish clear criteria for making decisions. The thinking here is that different demands should be optimally balanced and the respective requirements should then be molded into a consistent formal structure for the organization's members. Once a clear order of preference has been determined, decision-makers can weigh up the consequences of various alternatives and ultimately make the optimal decision for the organization.[45]

Demands for a Consistent Formal Structure

At first glance, this approach seems fairly plausible. After all, an organization's formal structure looks remarkably consistent when it is depicted in organigrams, process manuals, and job descriptions. Communication and decision channels are often laid out in a way that tells members exactly whose instructions they must follow and which ones they can ignore. Programs are arranged so that, in the vast majority of cases, organization members are clear on what constitutes rule compliance and rule deviance. And the qualifications needed for members to carry out tasks are generally explained in a way that leaves no doubt as to who may complete a task and who may not.

An organization's formal structure is consistent because compliance with its formal rules is a condition of membership, so the scope of the rules must be clearly specified. If you want to remain a member, you must at least act as if you are following the rules formulated by the organization. Anyone who openly rebels against the rules must leave

---

45 For a compact summary of this by a proponent of the behavioral theory of decision-making, see March 1991, 97; for a neoinstitutionalist analysis of this approach as just one of many strategies, see Oliver 1991.

(Luhmann 2020, 441ff.). This can be confirmed by conducting a simple crisis experiment: just tell your superior that you have no intention of following an instruction. The palpable tension this creates among everyone involved is a clear signal that such a refusal will lead to a crisis—not because a particular instruction is so important, but because the refusal to follow a rule undermines the fundamental principle upon which organizations are based.[46]

Since membership is contingent upon complying with an organization's formal rules, these rules must be highly consistent (regarding the requirement for consistency in legislation, see the classic analysis by Fuller 1969, 39). If organizations fail to define these formal conditions of membership, or if the conditions are too contradictory, members could do whatever they want. They could follow their manager's instructions or instructions given by someone else, as they saw fit. They could choose to follow one rule, if it were to their taste, or another diametrically opposed one. This would undermine the central principle of organizations for ensuring compliant behavior.

It is certainly not the case that all formal norms are always neatly harmonized in every organization. There are always collisions between these norms. The rules of a newly acquired business unit often deviate considerably from those of the holding company. The details of a university's study regulations will not always be precisely in tune with the rapidly changing accreditation requirements of the responsible agencies. The directives hastily issued by government departments in a sudden crisis often contradict one another. But organizations are under immediate pressure to resolve such contradictory formal expectations. After all, if an employee points out to their manger that the formal instructions for a particular task are contradictory, the manager cannot respond with total indifference.[47]

---

46 This ability to define formal expectations is what fundamentally distinguishes organizations from protest movements or small families, for example. Children know there might be strife if they do not follow their parents' rules, but they usually do not face exclusion from the family for failure to comply with a condition of membership. Just try threatening to send an unruly child to an orphanage; the child will not take the threat seriously because "parents don't do things like that."

47 A similar phenomenon has been discussed in the field of law with reference to the "prohibition of the denial of justice": a court cannot fob off disputing parties by saying that no judicial decision can be made because the contradictory requirements of the existing laws cannot be resolved.

The Pitfall of Contradictory Expectations

The problem, however, is that a formal structure designed for consistency will struggle to cope with the contradictory and changing requirements imposed on an organization from its environment. Formal structures cannot define rules of conduct for every single situation because it is impossible to know every eventuality in advance. Even if it were possible, the rulebook would be so thick as to be unmanageable. If someone did try to tackle this challenge, there would probably still be a delay in adapting the organization's formal structure in response to changing environmental conditions due to the complicated coordination necessary between the different levels and parts of the organization.[48]

Organizations could take the easy way out and tell themselves that their environmental conditions were constant and predictable, meaning that they could be managed with a clearly defined formal structure. But this would be an oversimplification of their actual environment.[49] All of the management literature indicates that the time is long past in which organizations imagined their environmental conditions to be consistent and calculable. The current prevailing diagnosis is that the demands on organizations are increasingly volatile. Surprising, unpredictable, and unfamiliar events are causing ever more uncertainty. And because there are no clear cause-and-effect chains, complexity is growing and organizations are confronted with more and more contradictory requirements.[50]

---

48 Regarding the attempt to address fast-changing environmental conditions through ongoing adjustments to a formal structure, see Robertson 2015.

49 For an example of arguments about rule deviance in organizations from the perspective of contingency theory, see, e.g., Staw and Szwajkowski 1975.

50 Since consultants believe managers can only retain and understand ideas communicated in the form of acronyms, the contradictory requirements facing organizations have been referred to for several years as "VUCA." This stands for the volatility, uncertainty, complexity, and ambiguity that organizations must confront. It is noteworthy that companies have adopted an abbreviation first developed by the US military to describe the changed situation after the end of the Cold War. The suggestion here is that the supposed political stability following the split into NATO and the Warsaw Pact was reflected in stable economic conditions for companies as well. But the notion that a stable, secure, simple, and unambiguous environment previously existed is a fiction. To see this, we need look no further than the

In some cases, an organization may face very contradictory require-ments from a single environmental segment. Troop visits by politicians are obviously subject to the same strict safety requirements that apply to military exercises, but there is also an implicit demand that the pol-iticians be treated to particularly "pretty pictures" in the form of fast, interesting and loud sequences of exercises. For this to be possible, a safety officer might not bother to ensure that the ammunition belt in a machine gun has been fired until empty, he might disable the safety mechanism on a howitzer so it does not always have to shoot at the same target, or he might make a copy of his key for unlocking weap-ons systems so that an exercise can be resumed quickly after the safety system has kicked in. The irony here is that the more prominent the politicians in attendance, the higher the expectation that the formally specified safety mechanisms for a "good shoot" will be (responsibly) circumvented.[51]

If it is true that the expectations facing organizations are becoming more volatile, uncertain, complex, and ambiguous, this increases the likelihood that formal structures will not be suitable for responding to these demands. This puts organizations in an unresolvable bind. On the one hand, their formal structure must meet high standards of consistency because otherwise their members will not be able to gear their behavior toward it. On the other hand, these fast-changing and contradictory requirements make it almost impossible for organizations to be thoroughly formally programmed with a clearly defined purpose in mind.

Organizations have always solved this problem by presenting their members with a formally consistent set of rules while simultaneously tolerating a certain degree of informal deviance (see the early analysis by

---

requirements facing colonial authorities in the late nineteenth century, the first automotive companies in the early twentieth century, or political parties after the end of World Wars I and II. The main reason to proclaim the existence of a "VUCA world" is to conjure up a "VUCA solution" involving the concepts of vision, understanding, clarity, and agility.

51 In the backstage area, soldiers will gripe that the implicit pressure to deviate from the for-mal structure for maneuvers is especially high when the responsible government official is present, even if this official is known for having a zero-tolerance policy towards violations of the formal structure.

Sjoberg 1960, 201; Luhmann 1964b, 304f.).[52] They accept that small and large shortcuts will emerge which cut across official channels (see Friedberg 1997). They endure the continuous redefinition, stretching, and circumvention of their goals, procedures, and guidelines if this eases the rigidity of their formal rules (see Bosetzky 2019, 38). They put up with the fact that when personnel are recruited, transferred, or dismissed, for example, not everything will always take place according to the rules, because otherwise the right people will often not be available at the right time. The option of violating the formal order is practically a condition of the ability of organizations to function in a contradictory environment.[53]

The Lightness and Suppleness of the Organization

Tolerating occasional rule deviance could be viewed as a weakness in organizations—but the opposite is true. The ability to occasionally deviate from their formal rules gives organizations a certain "lightness" (Luhmann 1964b, 246f.). Contradictory demands placed on employees do not necessarily need to be resolved immediately by introducing new formal rules. Instead, organizations can tolerate some deviation from their formal rules in well-justified cases. At the same time, the existence of the formal order prevents organizations from becoming "balkanized" and everyone simply doing what they want (Luhmann 1964b, 247).

A tolerance for rule deviance ultimately strengthens the rules themselves. If strict adherence to the rules were enforced, everyone

---

52 Different theories relevant to organizational research—including behavioral decision theory, strategic organizational analysis, structuration theory, neoinstitutionalism, and systems theory—are all in agreement on this point. For classic case studies, see, e.g., Selznick 1949; Gouldner 1954a; Bensman and Gerver 1963.

53 Tolerating rule deviance is a way of dealing with contradictory environmental requirements on the informal side of an organization. A parallel process takes place on the display side of the organization. The conflict between contradictory environmental expectations and the demand for consistency in an organization's formal structure is resolved by an organization's attempt to placate different environmental segments with abstract value formulations; regarding hypocrisy as a reaction to contradictory environmental expectations, see Brunsson 1989.

would soon realize that they were too rigid and inadaptable for many decision-making situations. Without allowing for some deviance, the pressure to justify the rules would become so great that the rules would be less accepted—precisely because of the pressure to follow them. A limited tolerance of deviance is therefore necessary to maintain the rules in the first place. Put simply, tolerating deviance is the "grease" that keeps the rules functioning.[54]

Everyone in an organization knows that, if necessary, they can put a stop to informal deviations by invoking the organization's formal regulations. Organization members thus carefully weigh up how much they will deviate from the formal rules in justified cases. Deviations from the formal rules might creep into the everyday life of an organization for good reason, but if a conflict arises, members can always play the trump card of harking back to the organization's formal structure.[55]

In practice, therefore, organization members permanently oscillate between basing their actions on formal rules and informal deviations. They debate whether to put critical information "on file," as formally required, or instead go against the regulations and leave no written trace for the time being. They might reject a verbal request from another department and insist on using official channels instead, or they could cooperate and respond informally even though it violates the official rules of procedure. They can formally discuss a matter with their

---

54 For a fundamental analysis of this, see Ortmann 2003, but also Osrecki 2015. Fran Osrecki deserves special credit for having established that the functionality of rule violations applies not only to the organization as a whole, but that rule deviance is also of vital importance to the preservation of rules. There is a certain elegance to identifying the functionality of rule deviance for the rule itself because it definitively solves the classic reference problem of functionalism, namely: "functional for who and what?"

55 This interplay between the enforcement and violation of formal norms can be seen in the tendering process for contracts in organizations. The purpose of the tenders monitored by purchasing departments is to prevent wheeling and dealing in order to acquire a good service for a reasonable price. However, tender procedures can lead to a high degree of inflexibility because the processes are often complex and unpredictable. For this reason, the tender process is often undermined in various ways, such as by formulating tenders so that only a predetermined supplier comes into question, by cutting contracts into small installments that do not need to be put out to tender, or by directly awarding contracts informally while inviting inflated competing offers to formally justify the award of the contract. Despite these many deviations, one could argue that it makes sense to retain the formal tender regulations because they prevent contracts from being awarded arbitrarily.

superior and risk an official refusal, or they can keep the conversation informal so that the issue can be brought up again at a better time (Luhmann 1964b, 117).[56]

Organizational prudence, therefore, does not consist of slavishly following externally imposed or internally defined rules, nor does it entail ignoring these rules altogether. Instead, it is the ability to occasionally deviate from the rules. Ultimately, an organization can only preserve its rules by tolerating a good deal of deviance from them (Luhmann 1983, 190).[57] Rules have to be broken—at least from time to time—in order to remain true to the spirit of the rules (Dalton 2013, 219) and in order for these rules to continue to exist (see Friedberg 1997, 145). It is not "clinical cleanliness" that strengthens an organization's immunity, as Fran Osrecki puts it, but rather the "dirt of systems" (Osrecki 2014, 420).

But how far can an organization take its situational adaptation to changed environmental conditions?

1.4 Gray Zones between Rule Compliance and Rule Violation

It would be overly simplistic to act as though everyone always knows exactly what is allowed and what is not. Granted, the efforts of organizations and states alike to define unambiguous rules must not be underestimated. An organization's rules must be precisely defined if they are to serve as the formal order upon which organization members can and must base their actions. And state laws must have a modicum of clarity if they are to create transparency regarding which behaviors are allowed and which are prohibited.

---

56 This approach is supported by instrumental rationality approaches in organizational research. The concept of scientific management is dominated by the notion that all processes in an organization must be formalized. In this celebration of the formal, anything informal—not to mention illegal—is viewed as a pathology indicative of a failure of management (see Taylor 1967; also see Fayol 1949).

57 There is a parallel here with legislation; the high complexity produced by legislative activity can only be managed by accepting deviations.

This is why, in some cases, it is clear to everyone involved that a rule has (or has not) been broken in an organization. If an employee follows a process manual to the letter and seeks approval from her superior in case of doubt, she can be relatively sure she is acting in compliance with the organization's rules. And if an employee is passed over for a promotion and reacts by mowing down her co-workers with a machine gun (not an uncommon occurrence in the USA), she can be fairly certain that she is not only violating a whole host of the organization's formal rules but also, in all probability, the laws of the state.[58]

But we would be succumbing to formalistic, quasi-juridical thinking if we assumed that all decisions can be fundamentally categorized as either "allowed" or "prohibited." The everyday reality in organizations often makes it rather difficult to determine whether someone has violated a rule or not. Where exactly is the line between intelligent cooperation with one's competitors—extolled in the management literature as "cooptition"—and the illegal formation of cartels between competitors, which harm suppliers and customers (see Benz and Seibel 1992)? Where is the line between the illegal deactivation of emissions scrubbers in automobiles and the legal option to switch them off to protect the engine (regarding the differences, see Jung and Sharon 2019)? Where is the line between barely legal "creative accounting" and the "criminal manipulation" of accounts in order to fabricate success stories for the stock market (see Graham et al. 2005)? What is the difference between the legal use of information about a listed company and illegal insider trading (see Solomon and Soltes 2015)? Where is the line between tax evasion, which can result in criminal prosecution if discovered, and tax avoidance, which enables multinational companies to pay essentially no taxes despite profits in the billions (see McGee 1993)? Is it legal for a publicly traded energy company to shut down multiple power plants due to real or supposed maintenance requirements, thus temporarily tripling or

---

58 Regarding killing sprees as an established but legally prohibited form of identity assertion at US universities, see Braun 2015. For an interesting dramatic interpretation of this phenomenon, see Jacobs-Jenkins 2015.

quadrupling the price of electricity, or does this constitute the illegal exploitation of a monopoly position (regarding the case of Enron, see Eichenwald 2005)?

The Murkiness of Rule Deviance and Rule Compliance

There is a certain "murkiness" that must be accepted when dealing with the question of whether an activity complies with the rules or not (Luhmann 1964b, 304). Just think of how rules can be broadly interpreted, creatively stretched, skillfully undermined, discreetly ignored or tacitly flouted (Ortmann 2003, 33f.). Or think of the practice of "following rules based on impermissible motives or impermissible purposes," or the "right action at the wrong time," or the "deferment of compliance" (see Luhmann 1964b, 304; Luhmann 2014, 212).[59] Despite all attempts to establish clarity, legal norms are not distinct "lines" that must not be crossed, they are "zones" in which organizations negotiate what they will and will not tolerate (Williams 1970, 413).[60]

In the factual dimension, one reason for the existence of gray areas is that even the most well-defined formal rule is open to interpretation. Formal expectations can be formulated extremely carefully, but the real meaning of actual expectations can never precisely be put into words. For example, the official regulations of colleges and universities stipulate that group work must consist of flagged individual contributions from the authors, which are to be graded individually as well. But these

---

59 Unfortunately, even Niklas Luhmann fails to illuminate these interesting gray zones any further. As regards useful illegality, Luhmann is interested in the adaptive strategies that "can help an organization member when he has to wander through stretches of problematic legality." He is not concerned with whether useful illegality "could potentially be saved by good lawyers"; see Luhmann 1964b, 304. From an organizational studies perspective, however, what is interesting are the approaches used in a gray zone to nudge actions in the direction of either rule compliance or rule deviance.

60 Robin M. Williams (1970, 430) references the book *Outsiders* by Howard S. Beckers (1963) to discuss institutionalized norms in general. In my opinion, the same argument applies to formalized or positivized norms. Prechel and Hou (2016) use financial markets as an example to describe attempts to increase the complexity of regulations through lobbying so that the gray zone can be expanded.

regulations have not prevented instructors from sabotaging this intention by giving the members of a group individual but identical grades.
Out of necessity, there are aspects that cannot be factually resolved by
means of an organization's internal rules. Formalized expectations are
therefore always just tendency expectations (Luhmann 1964b, 311).

The social dimension is another reason for the murky zone between
rule compliance and rule deviance. Formalized rules are interpreted in
very different ways from person to person depending on their position
in an organization. For example, departments responsible for rule observance, which are often staffed by lawyers, tend to interpret rules more
restrictively than departments trying to achieve their goals despite being
subject to ever more detailed regulations. The headquarters of a global
organization is often less sensitive to the specifics of the environmental and
occupational safety laws in a given country than the corporate divisions
located in the country itself, which are directly affected by violations of
criminal or civil law. It is therefore not surprising that, despite all attempts
at clarity, there are fierce debates about how rules should be interpreted.

Furthermore, rules and their interpretation permanently change
in the temporal dimension. For example, there may be a delay before
an organization can implement formal changes to its rules. We need
look no further than the use of insider information, which was long
considered not just a legitimate but a legal bonus for managers, and
how it increasingly came to be viewed as a violation of stock corporation law based on new court judgments.[61] Formal rules are always
being interpreted in new ways, so it is often difficult to say whether an
action complies with the rules or deviates from them.

The Expansion and Constriction of Gray Areas

One could argue that organizational rules are created when formal
regulations are issued or a law is implemented in an organization's
programs. This view is very plausible. Reshuffling an organigram rear-

---

61 For a case study of the Celler-Kefauver Act in the 1960s, see Palmer 2012, 247f.

ranges the relations between superiors and subordinates. Changing processes or goals can give rise to new criteria for proper or improper behavior. Appointing or transferring someone to a precisely defined role determines which work this person must do. But all of this is just the starting point for the establishment of formal rules in organizations.

The precise contours of rules do not emerge in organizations until the rules have been interpreted in decision-making processes. When a new organigram is adopted, the relationships between superiors and subordinates that it defines will only slowly propagate through the organization. When processes or goals change, an understanding only gradually develops of how these changes will affect everyday practice. Even when a job description is as detailed as possible, the role will only take shape over time after a new person has been assigned to it. Rules are always the result of the practices that emerge based on the principles that have been decreed.

Rules are honed through their interpretation, a practice that applies not only to the formal rules of an organization but also to the laws of a state. The readings and interpretations laws and regulations that take place in and between organizations can even come to influence the decisions of courts (see the enlightening case study of anti-discrimination laws by Edelman et al. 2011, 911ff.). Ambiguous legal formulations, limits on the scope of measures, and enforcement difficulties give organizations the leeway to construct various interpretations, and these emergent interpretations then serve as the basis for interpretations by courts (see Edelman 1992, 1567).[62]

Granted, internal organizational rules and state laws are binding in different ways. Some regulations broadly specify how organizations should take measures to prevent sexual discrimination, ensure data protection, or guarantee legal compliance, but they leave the organi-

---

62 The innovative studies by the researchers associated with Lauren B. Edelman are concerned primarily with how the practices of organizations influence legal interpretation in fields such as occupational and environmental law. Also see Edelman 1990; Edelman et al. 1991; Edelman and Stryker 2005; Edelman and Suchman 1999; Edelman and Talesh 2011. With slight modifications, their arguments can easily be applied to the emergence of an organization's formal rules through interpretation in everyday practice.

zations a good deal of leeway in the implementation of the measures. Other regulations—such as working time specifications, environmental protection directives and anti-corruption rules—are more binding by comparison (see Edelman and Suchman 1997, 482ff.). But even when rules have been specified relatively precisely, their actual definition only emerges through practice.

The rules issued by organizations are widely visible symbols indicating that the legal or organizational regulations must be taken seriously. Programs are defined in accordance with the regulations, departments are set up to ensure the regulations are observed, and people are hired to oversee their implementation. But the exact meaning of the rules only becomes apparent over the course of time.

2.
Violating "Laws of the State" and "Laws of the Organization"

"If you make 10,000 regulations you destroy all respect for the law."
British Prime Minister Winston Churchill
before the House of Commons in 1949[63]

Committing oneself to rule compliance and law abidance is part of the self-presentation of every organization member. It would cause consternation if the CEO of a company, head of a social welfare department or commander of an infantry battalion publicly announced that compliance with state laws and formal directives was not a serious issue. It would be very surprising if a new employee told her superior that she had always struggled to follow rules and was therefore planning to continue her successful career as a rule-breaker in this organization as well.[64]

A distinction is usually made in organizations between violations of state laws and violations "only" of the laws of the organization itself.[65] Violations of state laws may entail breaches of civil, administrative or criminal law, but they may also involve a failure to comply with regulatory requirements (Clinard and Yeager 1980, 16).[66] Violations of an organization's laws entail small and large deviations from the organization's formal programs, official communication channels, and established rules for hiring, transferring, and dismissing personnel.

---

63 Quoted in Langworth 2008, 17.
64 With respect to this, the ISO 26000 international quality standard demands that companies acknowledge that laws and rules should be followed; see Hahn 2013.
65 I have repeatedly referred to this important distinction in my studies of organizational cultures; see, e.g., Kühl 2013, 123f.
66 See Bergmann 2016, 4. Because these offenses can also include violations of administrative or civil law, the term "criminality," which encompasses only criminal violation, is too imprecise here; see Yeager 2007, 26.

At first glance, this distinction is convincing—after all, it makes a big difference whether organization members violate a law governing working hours or the organization's internal rule for recording their working hours. It clearly makes a difference whether the member of a political party ignores legally binding requirements for reporting large donations from abroad or simply violates internal party guidelines governing coordination between regional associations when drawing up a strategy paper.

But can violations of state law and violations of organizational law really be so clearly separated? What are the similarities and differences between these two types of "laws"? And how do they relate to each other?

2.1 How Expectations Can Be Fixed: The Similarities and Differences between Positivization and Formalization

States and organizations have one main thing in common: they use a very similar mechanism for formulating their expectations. They specify—usually in writing—what is permitted and what is not. Binding expectations do not develop in an evolutionary process; they are established by a decision that is applicable to everyone. In the context of state legislation, this is referred to as the positivization of legal expectations. In organizations, the same process is called the formalization of organizational expectations.[67]

Hidden behind the principle of the positivization of state laws and formalization of organizational expectations is a highly unusual development whose significance to the creation of modern society is impossible to overstate. When expectations are defined in the form of state laws or formal orders, it is possible to make decisions that establish very clearly specified demands with which everyone must comply and

---

67 For an analysis of the mechanism of complexity reduction from the perspective of systems theory, see Luhmann 2020, 440ff.; regarding the field of law, see Luhmann 2005b, 227. In organizations, these expectations are often specified in writing, but they can also be communicated verbally. In states, by contrast, the expectations are always formulated in writing in the form of laws, decrees or directives.

the violation of which can be punished (see Luhmann 2005b, 225).

Furthermore, the expectations enshrined in state laws and formal rules can be changed with the stroke of a pen—but this does not change the requirement that everyone meet these new expectations just as they were obliged to comply with the previous ones. While norms changed slowly in most tribal societies, and even in many early high cultures, they can now be altered from one day to the next through a modified law, a new regulation or a different directive. We can observe this in the constant stream of new instructions, modified rules, and rearranged reporting channels that organization members are expected to officially acknowledge.

The similarity between the mechanisms of positivization through state law and formalization through organizational rules was identified early on by organizational researchers (for example, see Luhmann 1964b, 393).[68] Formal expectations are spoken of as a kind of "secondary law" that develops as a supplement and with reference to the "primary law" of state legislation. In this instance, law is formed not at the state level but at the organizational one, but in both cases the acceptance of normative expectations is assumed (Luhmann 2014, 197).[69] This similarity between positivization and formalization explains why both infringements of an organization's formal expectations and legal violations by organization members are referred to using the term "useful illegality" (see Luhmann 1964b, 304ff.).[70]

What are the differences between how binding rules are created in a legal system and in an organization?

---

68 For a fundamental analysis, see Stinchcombe 2001; also see Schauer 1991, 12, who refers to rule-making principles outside of the legal system, in institutions such as churches and associations. Unfortunately, in his standard work on the function of rules, Schauer does not systematically address the difference between positivization and formalization. For a treatment of the question in a textbook, see Twining and Miers 2010, 25–27.

69 Niklas Luhmann (2014, 197) uses the examples of "the law of the house of earlier high cultures" and the "corporation law" of the Middle Ages to point out that forms of "non-societal law" have emerged in all "differentiated" societies. However, he highlights "formal organization" as the characteristic specific of modern society.

70 The concept of "useful illegality" has been interpreted in conflicting ways. Some say that the very term "illegality" must refer to the legal system, while others argue that applying the concept of useful illegality to the legal system is not entirely unproblematic (see, e.g., Schröder 2019, 21). For an early formulation of the notion of useful illegality (though using different terms), see Busch 1933, 98ff.

The Differences between the Positivization of Legal Expectations and Formalization of Organizational Expectations

States and organizations fundamentally differ in one key aspect: namely, the mechanisms used to penalize deviations from expectations. States have a specific repertoire for this, including fines, imprisonment, and the death sentence. The behavioral norms stipulated by state laws are internalized by citizens so early on that there is no need for them to be familiar with the legal codes from which the behavioral norms stem. But in case of doubt, deviations from the behavioral expectations codified by the state can be punished on the basis of such legal codes.

Organizations do not have the same repertoire of penalties available to them. It would certainly cause consternation if an organization member's refusal to follow the instructions of the organization's security service resulted in a trial before an internal court and imprisonment in the organization's own jail located next to the warehouse. But it would also lead to considerable outrage if an organization not only withheld part of a member's salary due to a rule violation, but also seized the member's accounts and house for the damages caused without involving a court.

There are exceptions, however. Armies with conscription, companies with forced laborers, and construction crews with employees treated like slaves do not allow their members to leave the organization. Therefore, if necessary, they must enforce their behavioral expectations with mechanisms otherwise only used by states to force citizens to comply with the law. In general, organizations are not "ruled with pistols" but rather with "threatened dismissal" (Luhmann 2002a, 56). In coercive organizations, however, it is worth noting that pistols are kept at hand so they can be used to enforce expectations if necessary (Kühl 2012, 345ff.). But the exceptional nature of these coercive organizations is apparent in the fact that this type of organization has become increasingly delegitimized in modern society.[71]

---

71 Regarding the phenomenon of modern slave labor, see the thorough analysis by O'Connell Davidson 2015; also see Crane 2013.

The reason for this delegitimization is simple: Organizations have an instrument that is much more effective than explicit violence for enforcing expectations on their members. They allow members to leave the organization if they no longer want to meet the organization's expectations, and they give themselves the option of dismissing members if they fail to meet the expectations. This makes it possible to link membership to compliance with the organization's behavioral expectations (see Luhmann 2014, 197). "Only those who acknowledge the rules may join. Those who no longer want to follow them must leave" (Luhmann 2005a, 50). As long as someone wants to remain a member of an organization, they must act within the "framework of the system of rules" that they "accepted upon joining" (see Mayntz 1963, 106).

The effect of this is that organizations can generally count on a high level of compliance from their members.[72] Everything organizations need from their members—in terms of actions, attitudes, and self-presentation—are declared to be a condition of membership, thus enabling the organization to insist on such behavioral compliance. Furthermore, organizations can concretize or change their expectations even after a member has joined, and members can be forced to go along with these changes as well—at least as long as they want to remain members. This process is known as the formalization of expectations (Luhmann 2020, 431).

It is impossible to overestimate the associated potential to heighten the expectations placed on people. Expectations previously formulated on the state level through the positivization of laws, decrees, and directives are "activated again" by organizations, according to Niklas Luhmann (2014, 198). In this context, organizations can formulate behavioral expectations that states cannot demand of their members in many cases. For example, only in exceptional cases are states able to require their citizens to go to a specific place early each morning,

---

72 The degree to which expectations are enforceable obviously depends on whether the labor market is characterized by full employment or a high level of unemployment; regarding this, see the stimulus-contribution theory of March and Simon 1958.

perform the same actions at regular intervals, and spend hours enduring the insults of unpleasant peers. But organizations—at least the ones that pay their members—can fairly easily make these rather unusual behavioral expectations a condition of membership. By flagging up conditions for remaining in an organization, organizations—unlike states—can define and enforce "unnatural expectations [...] in the highest degree" (Luhmann 2014, 198).

What Laws and Regulations Mean for Organizations

Although organizations have many options for imposing their own detailed rules, the critical importance of state laws and regulations must not be underestimated. Organizations are founded when they are listed in a legally regulated register of associations or companies, or—in the case of public administrative bodies, police forces, and armies—by means of state laws and regulations. Their refinancing options are governed by laws, regardless of whether the organization receives income from product sales, tax collection or membership fees. Activities in companies and associations are precisely regulated by labor, health, and environmental laws, and the work of state organizations such as government departments, administrative bodies, police forces, and armies is defined down to the to smallest detail by laws and regulations. The dissolution of organizations through insolvency, by order of state officials or through the resolution of their members, is also legally regulated. In brief, "modern organizations are immersed in a sea of law"—whether they like it or not.[73]

State laws and regulations play a key role in the behavior of organization members. In most organizations, all decisions are (officially) expected to be made within the framework of state laws and regulations. It would certainly be exceptional for an organization to stipulate when

---

73 Quote from Edelman and Suchman 1997, 480. My description of the influence of the law is based on theirs. It is beyond the scope of this book to address the parallel differentiation of law as a functional system and organizations as a specific, membership-based system.

its members had to obey laws and when they could ignore them.[74] On the contrary, state guidelines are often carefully translated into organizational rules under the assumption that organization members would not be able to maintain an overview of the impact of fast-changing state laws and regulations on organizational decisions. Every month, stacks of new regulations are delivered to the legal departments of large organizations, where they are filed away and often translated into internal implementation guidelines.

Because the web of laws is so tightly woven, it is inevitable that organizations will sporadically violate laws and regulations. These occasional violations are not problematic in themselves. Criminological research has shown that minor infractions and offenses can even be committed by people who consider themselves law-abiding. Anyone who doubts this just needs to spend a week being carefully observed while driving or cycling. The point at which their many traffic infractions during the week would be considered a criminal offense often depends solely on whether one of these everyday transgressions results in a deadly accident or not. The situation is no different in organizations. Even organization members who are considered fairly conformist will commit numerous minor rule violations. The assertion that people in many professions are always "sailing close to the wind" merely shows that everyone is aware of these everyday transgressions.

The Difference between Organized and Organizational Criminality

In most cases, organizations take great care to ensure that the formal demands they make of their members are considered compliant with state laws and regulations. They would lose legitimacy if their formal

---

74 One example of such an exception is the varying sensitivity to compliance with legal norms in different countries. For example, some companies in developing countries take a more relaxed approach to the prevailing legal norms precisely because they believe these norms can only be enforced in exceptional situations anyway. This attitude is generally not expressed as an official maxim, however, but tends to creep in more informally.

requirements did not at least roughly correspond to the state's legal requirements—or could be passed off as legally compliant with the help of a good lawyer. There is an interesting exception to this, however. Criminal organizations such as terrorist groups, mafia-style associations, and youth gangs expect their members to violate state laws. This clearly illustrates the fundamental difference between organized and organizational criminality.[75]

In the case of organized criminality, the state's entitlement to establish a legal framework and penalize deviations from it is fundamentally not accepted (see Levi 1998). Crime syndicates, mafia-like associations and terrorist organizations would lose the basis of their "business" if they submitted to state laws. The violation of tax, criminal, and administrative laws is essentially part of the formal expectations these organizations place on their members (regarding this, see Dorn and Hoebel 2013, 90).[76] If a member of a band of thieves, mafia group or terrorist organization demanded compliance with the law, that member would probably be expelled from the organization. When criminal organizations are confronted with their own legal violations, they generally do not feign repentance but, instead, try to continue to exist as an organization despite the pressure of prosecution.

In the case of organizational criminality, by contrast, organizations formally accept the state's demand for compliance with the law, but they also informally expect their members to occasionally operate in the gray zone between legality and illegality, and to sometimes even violate laws in a controlled way (see Braithwaite 1984, 6; Baker and Faulkner 1993, 842). This type of organization follows state laws and regulations on the whole but occasionally displays an informally supported "criminal corporate attitude" (regarding this term, see Schünemann 1979, 22, and Schünemann 1999, 231). Unlike criminal organizations, these organizations do not move all of their work underground if they are

---

75 For a broad definition of criminal organizations encompassing political terrorist groups, organized street gangs, mercenaries acting illegally, and mafia-style organizations, see Albini 1971.

76 This is why it is a theoretical mistake to associate formality and legality, on the one hand, and informality and illegality, on the other. The relationship is more complex.

caught breaking the law; instead, after being convicted, they repent and promise to do better.[77]

Granted, the boundaries between organized criminality and organizational criminality are sometimes blurred. We need look no further than the army units in Mexico which always had a fairly casual relationship with the prevailing legal norms on account of their work against drug cartels, and which eventually moved entirely underground to become competing drug cartels themselves.[78] Or think of the mafia-style associations which take the capital they acquire through racketeering, drug dealing, and prostitution and invest it in legal fields of business such as real estate speculation, arms dealing, and waste management, thus mutating into socially accepted organizations.[79]

In general, however, such transitions between organizational and organized criminality are fairly rare.[80] This is partially because it is challenging for an organization that occasionally violates state laws and regulations to become a criminal organization. For example, it would be hard for an automotive company that was accused of violating environmental laws to avoid prosecution by moving its production plants underground. This mutation into a criminal organization would probably also lead to significant staff fluctuation because many employees would have had a different idea of what their job entailed when they joined the company as an assembly worker, sales specialist or marketing expert. The reverse situation is also fairly rare because law enforcement authorities generally do not readily accept the mutation of a criminal organization into a legalized one. Just as a thief can only mutate into an

---

77   Jens Bergmann (2016, 7) has written an informative overview (with reference to Croall 2009, Lynch et al. 2004, and Kölbel 2014) which points out that, unlike the research on organized criminality, hardly any progress has been made in the research on organizational criminality.

78   Regarding Los Zetas in Mexico, for example, see Fernández Menéndez and Ronquillo 2010; Grayson and Logan 2012. A closer conceptual analysis is required to determine whether Los Zetas represents a case of an organization with a distinct culture of organizational criminality being transformed into an organization with clearly organized criminality, or a case of a new criminal association being established by members who had deserted from an elite state military unit.

79   Regarding changes of form in the Mafia, see the early study by Catanzaro 1985; for a detailed analysis of the Sicilian Mafia, see Catanzaro 1992. The role of the Mafia in legal industries is analyzed by Gambetta and Reuter 2016.

80   However, see the attempt by Anthony Schneider (2004) to portray Tony Soprano from the Mafia TV series "The Sopranos" as a successful role model for managers.

honest citizen after serving a sentence, a criminal organization would have to atone and profess its commitment to lawfulness in order to be legalized—if this were even possible in the first place.[81]

Sociologists have clearly established that the activities of organizations that place great value in legal compliance barely differ from those of criminal organizations that systematically ignore laws (for example, see Tilly 1985). Purely in terms of the activity itself, the execution of a traitor by a terrorist organization is very similar to the execution of a prisoner condemned by a Chinese, US or Saudi Arabian court (regarding the similarity between violent organizations, see Kühl 2016, 135f.). The corporate pharmaceutical practice of getting patients "hooked" on drugs by aggressively prescribing opiate painkillers is no different from the strategy used by drug rings to acquire new long-term customers by offering them tasters (regarding these fluid boundaries, see McGreal 2018; Meier 2018). The international business of the Mafia is surprisingly similar to the practices of large companies (see Arlacchi 1986; Gambetta 1988; Gambetta 1993). The only difference—though it is a critical one—is whether the organization acknowledges the state's entitlement to impose universally binding laws.

How are legal violations handled when they are committed by organizations that actually strive to be more or less compliant with the law?[82]

2.2 Assigning Responsibility for Legal Violations

When laws are violated, responsibility can be assigned to a variety of actors. Blame can be placed on the organization members who bore operational responsibility for the violation, or on their

---

81 The case of FARC in Colombia is a recent example of a similar mutation with comparable difficulties on the organizational level (regarding this, see Guzman and Holá 2019, as well as Olasolo and Cantor 2019; five interesting interviews on the organization's transformation can be found in Davalos et al. 2018).

82 Regarding the difficulty of defining the "right guilty party," also see Fisse and Braithwaite 1993; Green 2004; Wells 2005.

immediate superiors who did not ensure legal compliance, or on the head of the organization. The organization as a whole can also be held accountable, or all organizations in a particular field might be implicated, and even lobby organizations can be blamed for working so successfully that they make their member organizations blind to potential criminal prosecution. The finger of blame can additionally be pointed at the state for having formulated the laws that were violated.

Modern society has experienced an "expansion of attribution" if not an outright "explosion of attribution" (Lübbe 1998, 36). Granted, the assignment of responsibility must be plausible to some degree if it is to receive social support. There would be little support for someone seeking to assign responsibility to a herd of elephants with limited legal capacity, to the unfavorable position of the stars, or to an error of judgment on the part of a god who could not be put on trial in any case. Responsibility can only be assigned to entities in modern society who have the status of actors with the capacity to act—particularly individuals, organizations, and states (regarding the neo-institutionalist construct of the actor, see in particular Meyer and Jepperson 2000; also see Hwang and Colyvas 2011).[83]

The Difficulty of Punishing Organizations

It seems evident that, in cases of useful illegality, the organization as a whole needs to be addressed first. The global trend in jurisprudence is not just to prosecute individual organization members, but to indict entire organizations (see Geis 2007a, 827). Even in the few states where offenses by organizations are treated as misdemeanors—equivalent to parking illegally, playing music too loudly, or begging in a pedestrian

---

83 Interestingly, responsibility is generally not assigned to the respective organizational units, as might be expected, unless they are differentiated as organizations with their own legal status. There appear to be only two options for punishment: either punishing the individual organization member or punishing the entire organization.

zone—serious thought is now being given to introducing some form of organizational criminal law.[84]

The policy taking hold worldwide is that organizations can be prosecuted for crimes committed by their members if it can be proven that they did not take the necessary measures to prevent or at least hinder these crimes. An organization can be culpable even without formally demanding that its members engage in criminal activity, like a terrorist or criminal organization would. Punishment can be meted out as long as it is proven that the organization did not take measures to prevent its members from breaking the law.[85]

This approach seems quite reasonable. If a company systematically greases palms for years to win contracts, if armies tolerate the torture of prisoners of war, if religious organizations use sexual abuse as a cost-effective means of motivating their male members—it is obvious to ask why only the implicated people should be held responsible for the activities within the organization, and whether it would not be better to hold the organization itself responsible for the actions of its members (see Brown 2000, 1317ff.).

In practice, an organization can be punished in this way because—unlike a group of friends, a protest movement or a large family—the organization is a clearly defined entity. Regulatory agencies, tax authorities, and the police know who to contact if they want to speak with a church, company or association as an organization. Churches,

---

84 In this case, organizational criminal law specifically means corporate criminal law, because the criminal prosecution of state organizations such as police forces, armies, and government administrations has proven difficult on the whole. Regarding the discussion of corporate liability, see the comprehensive analyses by, e.g., Gobert and Punch 2003; Wells 2005. Because I am interested in fundamental arguments here, I do not take the route of treating legal violations by companies as administrative offenses rather than as corporate criminal acts.

85 Regarding eight conditions for a compliance program, see Walsh and Pyrich 1994, 685f. In order to have a mitigating effect in case of doubt, a compliance program must (1) have been established for an appropriate length of time, (2) have been implemented by the top management, (3) also aim to prevent potential criminal behavior by organization members, (4) fit the culture of the organization, (5) express the organization's need for legal compliance, (6) be communicated to the organization members and (7) enforced as well as (8) regularly reviewed and revised. There is a wealth of literature on this subject; see, e.g., Stone 1980; Kraakman 1984; Pitt and Groskaufmanis 1989; Huff 1996; Laufer 1999; and Brown 2000. For a particularly comprehensive analysis, see Laufer 2006.

companies, and associations, in turn, know who to contact when they want to apply for permission to hold an event, request a tax refund or get help dismissing a difficult member as an organization.

This is because a process has been at work through which organizations have—over many centuries and sometimes in the face of fierce protest—developed into addressable entities.[86] The reason that organizations—unlike groups of friends, protest movements or large families—can be addressed through the positivized legal system in the first place is because they can define their conditions of membership via their formal structure and thus control and sanction the behavior of their members. This also creates a mechanism for enforcing expectations that is stable enough for the organization's environment to accept the organization as a contractual partner.

In the course of this process, it has become clear that organizations are not all that different from individuals in terms of their legal capacity. This similarity is expressed in the fact that organizations are referred to as "legal persons" who, from the perspective of the legal system, can be addressed in many of the same ways as "natural persons." In actor-centered sociology, organizations are also referred to as "corporative actors" who share a number of characteristics with "individual actors"—yet another indication of their similarity.[87]

There are obvious advantages to the "legal fiction" of treating organizations like people so that long-term cooperative relationships can be established. When a "natural person" is recruited to work in a school, hospital or public administrative body, their employment contract with the organization as a "legal person" will still hold even if the managers

---

86 For an interesting theoretical analysis, see Teubner 1987b, and especially Barkan 2013. For more details, see the best study of the formation of the idea of the "legal person" in the USA by Matys 2011. For a readable historical study of the development of companies as corporative actors in the USA and in connection with legal violations, see Nace 2003. For studies of the development of the idea of the legal person in France, see Saleilles 2003; in Spain, Gómez Tomillo 2015; in Germany, Rotter 1968 and Ott 1977. For an early general overview, see Hallis 1978.

87 This process has been described from very different theoretical perspectives. Regarding the actor status of organizations in neo-institutionalism, see Meyer 1992. Regarding the concept of the corporative actor in the actor-centered institutionalism approach, see Mayntz and Scharpf 1995. Finally, regarding the concept of the collective actor, see Coleman 1982.

who hired them retire. This model also functions between two "legal persons." When a service provider concludes a contract with a company, university or army, it knows that the contract will be observed even if the people who negotiated it no longer work for the organization in question.

The condition, however, is that these cooperative relationships must exist in a relatively functional legal system. Before entering a relationship not just with a specific natural person, but with a legal person, organization members must be confident that they can demand the payment of outstanding wages in court if necessary. And before agreeing to cooperate with an individual who has no personal ties of loyalty, an organization must be confident that it can legally enforce its demands.

The difficulty here is that while organizations can be fined and even dissolved as punishment, they cannot be sentenced to the radical penalty of imprisonment, like an individual could. There is no way to envision what kind of prison might be used to lock up an organization. "No soul to damn, no ass to kick"—this exclamation by Edward Thurlow, a former Lord Chancellor of England, describes the frustrating difficulty of penalizing organizations.[88]

Organizational Positions as Internal Mechanisms for Assigning Responsibility

Because it is hard to punish an organization, it has long been thought that only an organization's members can effectively be punished. Organizations are said to be nothing more than a "legal fiction" and "legal

---

88 His exact words were apparently slightly different from this modernized version: "No soul to damn, no body to kick." But there are doubts whether even this quote is exact. Other sources quote Edward Thurlow has having said: "Corporations have neither bodies to be punished, nor souls to be condemned; they therefore do as they like." Regarding the meaning of Edward Thurlow's statement in legal theory, see, e.g., Barrile 1993. Even though the statement is repeatedly used to prevent the establishment of some form of organizational criminal law (as criticized by Ortmann 2017, 249f.), this does not change the fact that, ever since the Lord Chancellor's comments, no method has been found of subjecting organizations to corporal punishment or imprisonment as legal persons.

fictions" cannot be punished.[89] It has been argued that organizations have neither their own intentions nor any sense of guilt and therefore cannot be touched by criminal law (Fischel and Sykes 1996, 320).[90] This argument contends that it is the members of an organization who should face criminal prosecution, not the organization itself.

With the exception of criminal or terrorist organizations whose members can be prosecuted on the basis of their membership alone, it would be hard to justify prosecuting all members of an organization for a legal violation. A Mexican assembly-line worker in an automotive plant would be surprised to be sent to prison because a few German engineers had come up with a creative but illegal device for defeating a car's emissions control system when the car was not in a test state. And a civilian employee in a US Army kitchen would be perplexed to face a court and have to personally answer for the torture of Iraqi prisoners by members of the military police.

This is why responsibility for legal violations in organizations is assigned to specific members. A second aspect of the formalization of expectations in organizations comes into play here, namely, the assignment of responsibility via a position defined in the organization's formal structure. A position formally determines which people must fulfill which tasks at which time, which rules they must observe when doing so, who they can take orders from and to whom they can give orders. As a result, every decision in an organization can be attributed to people, so there are always individuals available who can be held responsible for problems within the organization (see Luhmann 1964b, 177).

Responsibility can be formally assigned to a position both before and after a decision has been made. Based on their assignment to a posi-

---

89 In the field of sociology, the most prominent proponent of this position was Donald R. Cressey (1988) in his later years. Ultimately representing the sociological position of radical methodological individualism tempered by a certain pragmatism, Cressey demanded (1988, 34) that, for reasons of fairness, the "legal fiction" of the legal person should be maintained in jurisprudence. The first response to this came from Braithwaite and Fisse 1990. Also see the discussion by Geis 1995a.

90 Regarding this, see Wagner 2016, 124f. In terms of legal theory, this position is famously found in the *Vertretertheorie* or "representative theory" of Friedrich Carl von Savigny (1884), who further developed the idea of the "persona ficta." Regarding this, also see Kindler 2008, 24f.

tion, organization members know fairly quickly which tasks they have to complete, which rules they have to observe while doing so, whose orders they have to follow, and which orders they have to give to others. This pertains to the acceptance of responsibility, because decisions in organizations are always made under conditions of uncertainty. But positions also make it possible to identify individuals if something goes wrong in an organization, so they can be held personally responsible for mistakes. If an organization faces a problem on account of a legal violation, it can determine what position was responsible for it, how the position is formally programmed, who holds the position, and other position should have been monitoring it (see Luhmann 1964b, 178f.).[91]

However, for all of the effort to determine responsibility by means of positions, there is always a degree of uncertainty as to who can ultimately be held responsible for what. The division of labor in organizations means that attribution processes that function relatively well outside of organizations become much trickier inside them. Despite all attempts at formalization, the division of labor may not necessarily lead to an "organized lack of responsibility," but it often leads to an "organized diffusion of responsibility."

This explains why mutual accusations usually fly when legal violations in an organization become a public scandal. In searching for the responsible party, one department might point out that it had simply followed the procedures specified by another department and assumed that they had been checked for legal compliance, while the other department might claim that the original complicated procedure had indeed been legally compliant and only resulted in a legal violation when it was put into practice by a different department. Subordinates might say they had only followed the more or less explicit instructions of their superiors, while superiors might say in

---

91 Luhmann makes a conceptual distinction here between *Verantwortung* (responsibility), by which he means the "differentiation of decision-making jurisdiction according to exclusive competencies," and *Verantwortlichkeit* (accountability), meaning being "answerable for mistakes" (Luhmann 1964b, 178f.). Regarding the tension between responsibility and accountability, see the early discussion by Luhmann 2018b. Regarding the definition of responsibility as a contribution to the absorption of the uncertainty of decisions, also see Luhmann 2018b, 156, and Luhmann 2002b, 43.

return that they were not aware of the illegal actions of their organization members (regarding the assignment of guilt in organizations, see Laufer 2006, 130ff.).

The Interplay of Organizations and Their Members

When legal violations are revealed, it can be in the interest of both the organization and its members to mutually protect one another from punishment (regarding this risk strategy, see Laufer 1999, 1382ff.). One strategy is for organizations to promise to pay their members a high settlement fee if they leave the organization and to cover any court-imposed fines if they do not make incriminating statements against the organization (regarding the question of who should pay fines, see Coffee 1980, 456ff.). This can be a good deal for organization members if the organization does not provide any incriminating information about them to the law enforcement authorities and they receive a generous financial settlement at the same time (see Kraakman 1984, 858f.).[92]

This option offers organizations a relatively simple way to avoid criminal prosecution. It falls back on the overhasty personalization of responsibility when rules and laws are broken, and it takes advantage of the ability to exchange personnel in an organization. For this to be possible, the organization just needs to establish positions in legally sensitive areas that can be occupied by individuals who, in the event of a legal violation, can be swapped without causing major disruption in the organization, and it must set aside the financial reserves needed to compensate these sacrificial pawns. Developing extensive programs to prevent rule deviance and establishing compliance departments ultimately serves to shift responsibility, in a legally watertight way, to organization members who are easy to remove.[93]

---

92 Regarding the minimal retaliatory effect of criminal law aimed at individual organization members, see the early analysis by Busch 1933.

93 This function behind establishing compliance departments and compliance systems was first described by William S. Laufer: "The purchase of compliance for purposes of liability shifting and cost internalization results in a redefinition of this deviance. Acts that

In light of these options for personalizing responsibility, the current strategy for many law enforcement authorities—adopted with no thought for legal theory—is to prosecute both the organization and the responsible organization members, thus destroying the alliance between organizations under pressure from the law and organization members facing punishment.[94] Organization members are promised a reduced sentence if they provide material that incriminates the organization, and the organization is offered the prospect of reduced fines if it delivers up the organization members responsible for the decisions.[95]

Ultimately, these law enforcement authorities are playing through a more or less complex version of the prisoner's dilemma (see Rapoport and Chammah 1965). The accused—whether they are organization members in various positions or representatives of the entire organization—are communicatively separated from one another so they cannot coordinate their defense strategy. Then the prospect of a significant penalty reduction is held up if, by confessing to the offense, they deliver up not only themselves but also the other party. Since no one can be certain how the other party will react under pressure, the rational option is to help expose the offense that has been committed.

In this case, the law enforcement authorities are addressing both of the entities to whom responsibility can be assigned. They are taking advantage of the ability to address organizations as legal persons (which has been established through formal structures) so the organization as a whole can be held liable. Simultaneously, they are taking advantage of the ability to attribute responsibility to individual positions (also possible thanks to formal structures) so they can prosecute individual organization members. An organization's formal structure

---

were once held to be those of the firm, now remain those of individual employees. The evisceration of vicarious liability along with unbridled prosecutorial discretion in the intuitive evaluation of compliance effectiveness may be used to explain the steady increase in white-collar prosecution. Moral hazard theory reveals that certain compliance orientations have the counterintuitive effect of increasing white-collar deviance" (Laufer 1999, 1415f.).

94 Regarding this, see Gobert 2008, 62f. For more on this approach, see the early analysis by Lee 1928.

95 For a critique of this strategy from a free-market liberal perspective, see Hasnas 2006, 45–55.

diffuses responsibility—between organizations and their members, and between members themselves—and this diffusion is used as a lever for uncovering and punishing individual legal violations.

2.3 Sensitivities and Tolerance toward Legal Violations

The managers of many organizations tend to consider violations of state laws much more problematic and serious than violations of the organization's formal rules. Their view is that measures for enforcing rule compliance should focus on violations subject to criminal prosecution or fines because these not only carry special financial risks, they can also severely damage an organization's reputation.

Compliance officers thus focus not only on preventing classic legal violations such as corruption and cartel formation, but also, and above all, on environmental and export laws. Their attention has also increasingly turned to other rule violations that could potentially be prosecuted or fined, such as failing to prevent discrimination against individual organization members, employing people on the basis of false self-employment, and breaching health and safety regulations.

Does it make sense to announce different tolerance levels for violations of state laws and violations of an organization's formal rules? Is it reasonable to declare a zero-tolerance policy toward violations of state laws (like many organizations do) while offering the prospect of a certain degree of tolerance for deviations from the organization's formal rules?

Allowances for Tolerating Legal Violations

Some evidence suggests that it is easier for organizations to tolerate violations of the law than violations of their own formal regulations. Think of the threat or use of torture, which is prohibited in most countries but occasionally employed by the police nonetheless to coerce a kidnapper into revealing the location of a hostage, or of the manipulation of tachographs by haulage companies to illegally extend the driving times of their truckers, or of the prohibited bypassing of safety mechanisms with the help of wires so that production machines can continue to run even when they are defective (see Gray and Silbey 2014).

In the perception of the organization—or at least the people at the head of the organization—internal rules serve to make organization members perform more effectively and efficiently, while external legal norms are often felt to be unnecessarily rigid. Officially accepting these legal norms is considered essential to the perceived legitimacy of the organization. However, the organization's internal communication will imply that the norms are often unsuited to the organization's everyday activities.

This is why organizations often exhibit a high degree of tolerance for deviations from the formal structures designed to meet the expectations of their environment (according to Meyer and Rowan 1977, 341). Deviations and violations are thought of as reasonable protective reactions to unnecessarily rigid laws, badly formulated decrees, and administrative decisions that only complicate matters. These are, ultimately, considered to be "imposed illegalities" (according to Luhmann 1964b, 306) that must be accepted to a certain extent because organizations cannot change the legal framework themselves.

Lack of Containment Mechanisms for Legal Violations

However, organizations also have good reason to be especially sensitive to legal violations. While violations of an organization's formal rules can be handled without involving a third party, and the responsible managers can decide for themselves whether to punish the violation, tolerate it or even use it as an opportunity to change the relevant rule, this autonomy is largely lacking when it comes to violations of state laws.

Violations in the form of broken laws and ignored regulations are sensitive to being discovered. In principle, even the lowest-ranking member of an organization can report a legal violation to the law enforcement authorities and trigger a review process that the organization is unable to stop. Every customer and client—regardless of whether they are a product consumer, university student, medical patient or prisoner—can complain to the police or public prosecutor and kick off an investigation from outside the organization itself.[96]

When laws are broken in an organization, there is always a threat that external entities will be the ones to decide how the violation should be dealt with. If organization members try to bribe government employees to win big contracts for building warships, highways or airports, they run a considerable risk of facing prosecution from outside of the organization if their violation is discovered. One could plausibly argue that, when laws are broken, the violator is more or less at the mercy of the law enforcement authorities and civil courts, so organizations should take special precautions to prevent such legal violations.

Another exacerbating factor is that the public pays much more attention to legal violations than to violations of an organization's formal rules. While no one outside an organization can be expected to take an interest in breaches of an organization's formal order, such as a company smoking ban, violations of state laws immediately attract attention far beyond the organization itself (Luhmann 2014, 197).

2.4 Fluid Boundaries between Violations of Laws and Formal Structures

At first glance, it seems relatively reasonable to distinguish between violations of state laws and formal rules. One could argue that organization members can tell from the cover of the rulebook alone whether

---

96 The options available to organization members are discussed much more thoroughly in the literature than the options available to customers and clients; regarding the figure of the whistleblower, see, e.g., Dozier and Miceli 1985; Glazer 1989; Near and Miceli 1987; Fred 2001.

they are dealing with state laws or an organization's formal rules. If the document is a cross-organizational set of rules produced by a parliament or public authority, one can be fairly certain that it is a state law or regulation, while any reference to the member's own organization on the cover could be taken as an indication that the document is a formal guideline with limited scope.

At second glance, however, the distinction between violations of state laws and formal rules is much more complicated. The establishment of "shadow warehouses" to ensure that production can continue even if a logistics chain fails is, on the surface, just a violation of a company's internal inventory rules. But it can soon lead to legal violations if the existence of large illegal warehouses distort the accounts of a listed company. If a government borrower from a developing country gives a gold necklace to the representative of a development bank, he might initially only be violating the formal rules of his own organization, but this can very quickly turn into a legally relevant corruption case.

Ultimately, everything that happens in an organization can be viewed as something potentially relevant in a court of law. If a soldier dies during a training exercise, there is no way to prevent a criminal or civil court from investigating lapses in the military organization. If a student gets a bad grade on a test, no one can stop the student or their parents from having the grading process reviewed by an administrative court. If a bus driver causes an accident, the insurance company is free to try to hold the municipal transportation authority liable on account of "organizational errors." In principle, everything that does or does not happen in an organization can be construed as a decision after the fact and thus made legally relevant.

Difficulties in Distinguishing between Violations of State Laws and Formal Rules

These difficulties in distinguishing between state laws and organizational rules stem from the expansion of state laws to cover organizations. The very principle of modern organizations is based on the legal regulation of the status of organization members. Joining or leaving an organization, transferring within an organization, and changing organizational requirements can all give rise to opportunities for labor law disputes. After all, no one stops an organization or (more importantly) an individual member from checking whether the requirements formally demanded of them are legal or not.

An important role is played by the fact that many legal requirements are only actualized and specified for organizations through the creation of formal rules. Organizations therefore cannot assume that their members will know the details of all the state laws and regulations relevant to their activities. Considering that the legal norms for regulating financial markets grow by tens of thousands of pages every year, it is clear that banks and insurance companies must first somehow translate these into formal structural requirements for their employees so the employees do not violate them "by mistake" (for a concise analysis of this, see Haldane 2012). In brief, organizations are perpetually concerned with concretizing general legal requirements for their members so that, if need be, they can say they did everything they could to enforce state legislation with the organization.

This situation is further exacerbated by the fact that, in principle, every event in an organization can be turned into an opportunity for dispute in a criminal, administrative or civil court. Regulations governing the size of the gaskets required for new pipes may initially appear to be internal work rules, but if gas leaks from a pipe and leads to an explosion at a plant, the regulations immediately become relevant to criminal law (for a classic analysis, see Perrow 1984). City administrators routinely permit organizations to hold events, but if a mass panic takes place at a large gathering, this everyday activity immediately becomes relevant to both administrative and criminal law (regarding administrative disasters, see Seibel et al. 2017). Organizations are not protected against legal investigations into whether they bear any blame for disasters that happened because they failed to take formal precautions (for an general overview, see Kette 2014).

The Meaning of Law in Modern Society

The process by which the legal system can access organizations is not unusual. Ultimately, every conflict in a family, every encounter between the residents of a building, every argument on the street can become an occasion for legal intervention, and courts cannot avoid dealing with these incidents.[97] In social-scientific research, this process is referred to as juridification (for a general overview, see Teubner 1987a).

Parallels to this far-reaching access by the legal system can be found in the many expansion efforts of other subsets of society (see Kühl 2019b, 26ff.). The concept of the total economization of society sees the logic of the capitalist economy encompassing all aspects of life. The concept of the primacy of politics describes the possibility of every social relationship being subject to political regulation. The concept of scientification describes how a scientific expertocracy is increasingly striving to colonize all aspects of life. The complexity requirements of organizations arise largely from the fact that organizations are encompassed in parallel by opposing processes of juridification, economization, politicization, and scientification.

For organizations, the fact that juridification takes place parallel to economization, politicization, and scientification in modern society is not very comforting. In fact, it means that organizations must keep an eye not only on the economic, political, and scientific consequences of their decisions, but also on the legal ones. Ultimately, every organizational decision can become an opportunity for a dispute about the legality or illegality of the practices that result from it. The boundaries between the organization's formal expectations and the state's legal expectations are therefore much more fluid than they might appear at first glance.

---

97 Regarding the prohibition of the denial of justice in modern legal systems, see Luhmann 1990a, 467f.

3.
The Tricky Distinction between Useful and Non-useful Illegality

"[To live] without great Vices, is a vain / Eutopia seated in the Brain.
Fraud, Luxury, and Pride must live / Whilst we the Benefits receive."
18th-century philosopher Bernard Mandeville (1989, 76)
in his Fable of the Bees

Someone always benefits from the deviation from formal rules or state laws. Useful illegality and functional rule deviance have advantages for organizations. The activities of internet companies that avoid paying taxes by means that are, strictly speaking, prohibited but not prosecuted, or banks that prey on customers in ways that are half-legal at best, or terrorist groups that carry out bomb attacks may be detrimental to the state's citizens, the bank's customers or the victims of the attack, but the organizations themselves all reap immediate rewards. In many cases, however, even individual organization members can gain personal advantages from illegal behavior. Evading taxes, robbing a bank or carrying out a religiously motivated suicide bombing can give the tax evader, robber or bomber immediate advantages in the form of tax savings, monetary gain or the promise of virginal women in paradise.[98]

Organizations therefore watch very carefully to see who benefits from rule deviance and legal violations.[99] After all, it makes a critical difference to an organization whether tax evasion primarily benefits the whole organization or just an individual member, whether it is the bank's customers or the bank itself that is being ripped off, or whether the victims of an attack are an organization's opponents or

---

98 Regarding the complex but ultimately self-serving motives of suicide attackers, see Gambetta 2006.
99 Regarding this distinction, see, e.g., Michalowski 1985.

its own members. The former case involves rule deviance carried out by organization members for the sake of the organization—in other words, the actions of "honest crooks" who, by violating the organization's rules, are risking dismissal or even criminal prosecution if they have broken the law. The latter case involves rule deviance by means of which employees damage an organization for self-serving motives (see, e.g., Punch 1996, 2).[100]

While studies of rule deviance that revolve around the concept of white-collar criminality have taken a largely undifferentiated approach to exploring the question of who benefits from such deviance, scholars researching useful illegalities in organizations are looking increasingly closely at precisely who profits (for a prominent example, see Coleman 1987, 406; but also see, e.g., Palmer and Moore 2016, 205).[101] A distinction is made here between "corporate crimes," or legal violations that benefit the organization, and "occupational crimes," or rule deviance that only serves individual organization members (Clinard and Quinney 1973). In state administrative bodies, a distinction is made between "state-organized crimes," or illegalities useful to the state, and legal violations in which state officials exploit their position for personal gain (see Chambliss 1989; Friedrichs 2010). In police forces, rule deviance that serves to improve the job overall is distinguished from violations that serve the personal enrichment of individual police officers (for an overview, see Barker and Carter 1994).[102]

At first glance, one might assume that it would be easy to determine whether a rule violation involved an attempt to gain personal benefits at the expense of the organization, or whether the rule deviance was

---

100 For an early examination of this distinction, see Geis 1962.

101 See, e.g., Sutherland 1949, who largely ignores the difference. This issue can be found in later literature as well, however; see, e.g., Mars 2013, 48, who equates the rule deviance in aircraft manufacturing, which was functional (only) for the organization (as discussed in the study by Bensman und Gerver 1963) with illegalities that only benefit organization members.

102 In police research, rule deviance that is functional for the organization is primarily discussed with reference to the concept of "noble cause corruption"; see in particular Cooper 2012. A comprehensive analysis can be found in Caldero et al. 2018, and some very interesting comments on the topic can be found in Zum-Bruch 2019.

for the sake of the organization itself. When managers use banks to defraud depositors of their financial investments (see Calavita and Pontell 1993), or politicians financially gut a city with inflated purchase prices and fictitious invoices, it is difficult to see how the banks or cities would benefit from this (see, e.g., the case studies in Miller 1992). But when managers try to save banks by manipulating the balance sheets, or politicians try to get major construction projects finished on time by loosely interpreting the relevant building laws, one can initially assume that this rule deviance is supposed to be advantageous to the organization.

Looking more closely, however, it becomes clear that, in many cases of rule deviance, it is not easy to distinguish between rule violations that are useful for the organization as a whole and those that benefit the members alone. This is because rule deviance can often be beneficial to both the organization (or at least individual departments) and to individual members. We need look no further than the circumvention of seemingly overblown occupational safety measures, which can increase efficiency in an organization while also giving individual members a personally beneficial time buffer.

Instead of swiftly condemning rule deviance for personal gain, we must take a more nuanced view of the self-interest of individuals who deviate from the rules. For example, how should we judge bribery by the employees of a large electronics firm if the employees did not directly funnel off money, but received considerably higher bonuses from the organization for their sales successes? Or insider trading by banks, in which the bank profits at the expense of other investors, but the bank's traders make a profit as well? What should we think of the former chairman of an energy company who exploits his position as vice president of a country to make the administration's energy policy more "friendly" toward the corporation?[103] It is these gray zones between useful and non-useful illegalities that are interesting.

---

103 It is interesting to look at the policies of Dick Cheney, former chairman of Halliburton, in his role as US vice president; see Gellman 2009.

3.1 The Search for Personal Advantages: Embezzlement, Corruption and Refusal to Work

Organizations can quickly agree on which rule deviations are not useful to them—namely, the ones that employees commit in order to gain personal advantages in a prohibited way at the expense of the organization. Think of nurses stealing hospital gowns and using them to make shorts or cleaning rags at home (Dabney 1995, 320), or the tricks used by flight attendants to illicitly take food and drink from an aircraft by getting colleagues to certify their purchases and then ripping up the confirmation slips if no one checks them when they leave the airport, or the skill with which blackjack dealers in casinos give preference to players who tip generously, despite strict rules governing their interaction with customers and despite close video surveillance (Sallaz 2009).

Various Ways of Gaining Advantages from an Organizational Activity

Rule deviance for the personal gain of organization members is referred to in the literature as "crimes against bureaucracy" (Smigel and Ross 1970). Though organizations such as mafia-like associations, terrorist groups, marauding armies, and corrupt sports clubs can become perpetrators themselves, the emphasis is placed on the fact that many illegalities are committed by organization members at the expense of the organization.

An organization that has been deceived or robbed becomes the victim of illegality, but unlike a person who has been deceived or robbed, it often cannot count on the sympathy of the general public (Smigel and Ross 1970, 4f.). On the contrary, sympathy is often expressed instead for the people who manage to pull one over on a big, powerful organization and gain an advantage at its expense. We need look no further than literature dedicated to characters such as the Captain of Köpenick (Zuckmayer 2013), the Good Soldier Švejk (Hašek 1973) or the pretend Pan Am pilot, fake supervising doctor, and check forger Frank Abagnale (2000).[104]

People can gain an illegal advantage in various ways. One way is by embezzling material belonging to an organization. This can entail the prohibited use of telephones, copy machines or tools for private purposes, or the illegal sale of materials for the purpose of personal enrichment.[105] Such embezzlement can range from a waiter in a restaurant eating a bread roll intended for disposal, through the operation of a private side business using resources from the organization, all the way to the sale of entire weapons systems on the black market by members of an army (regarding the theft of materials in organizations, see, e.g., Tucker 1989).[106]

Another possibility involves using corrupt practices for personal enrichment. In this case, organization members use their activities at an organizational interface to gain a personal advantage. This could be corporate buyers who ensure kickbacks flow into their private account when they place an order, public administrators who demand private payments in return for speeding up applications for social welfare, construction permits or visas, or police officers who forgo prosecution in return for small or large favors. Unlike embezzlement, which can be carried out by an organization member working alone, corruption is *always* based on cooperation in the form of an immoral and, in many cases, prohibited exchange with someone outside of the organization (Neckel 1995).[107]

---

104 The sympathy for criminals who trick big organizations is even more pronounced in the film adaptation of Abagnale's autobiography—"Catch Me If You Can" starring Leonardo di Caprio—than in the book itself. It is interesting to note the difference between organization members who are driven to play tricks on an organization because they have suffered at its hands, and people who manage to simulate or even achieve membership in an organization by means of imposture.

105 Regarding the difference between use for private purposes and resale, see Henry and Mars 1978.

106 Hollinger and Clark (1982) distinguish this form of "property deviance," or the acquisition of "tangible assets," from "production deviance," or the violation of formal working norms for the preservation of one's own labor power.

107 Corruption among "public officials" such as administrative employees, police officers and teachers is particularly striking, of course, but I do not believe there is any reason to continue restricting the definition of corruption to the abuse of state positions of power for

Another variant involves easing the workload in an organization in a way that is formally prohibited. Usually when labor power is purchased, a formal framework is defined in which the employee can operate. This comprises rules governing the start and end of the working day, work breaks, handling personal business while on the job, and sick leave. But organization members can gain an illegal personal advantage by flouting these rules and coming to work late, leaving early, extending their breaks, using the workday for personal activities such as stock market speculation, communicating with friends online or taking drugs, or faking illness to get sick leave.[108]

Rule Deviance by Individuals, Groups or All Organization Members

Individuals working alone can gain illegal advantages at the expense of an organization. In the relevant literature, such people are referred to as hawks or vultures. Hawks are organization members who often self-evidently assume that their performance will be rewarded, even if the reward is barely legal. This attitude is frequently found among journalists, sales employees, and investment bankers (see Mars 1982, 40ff.; Mars 2013, 39–40). Vultures are individual organization members who cooperate with other members to enrich themselves at the organization's expense, but as soon as their "prey" has been brought down, they will try to take possession of it for themselves—at their colleagues' expense if necessary. They are often tradesmen, laborers or deliverymen who exploit the many opportunities to gain small or

personal gain (as is the case in, e.g., Senturia 1931 and Noonan 1984). In principle, every organization member at the interface to the organization has the opportunity to exploit their contact with the organization's environment for their own advantage. For an assessment of the legislation and jurisdiction connected to the expansion of this definition, see Green 2006, 195f.

108 Regarding the significance of this, see Clark and Hollinger 1983. This phenomenon is sometimes discussed with reference to the "withdrawal from work hypothesis," meaning physical or mental absence from a place of work on account of frustration (see, e.g., Bryant 1975).

large advantages at the organization's expense (see Mars 1982, 108ff.; Mars 2013, 41).

Groups of people will also often reach arrangements for enriching themselves from an organization. These are predator communities or enrichment cliques who work together to gain personal advantages at the expense of the organization. They are referred to as wolfpacks in the literature. Such groups often have informal leaders and a strong sense of internal solidarity, and their members cooperate closely to enrich themselves at the organization's expense. They can be teams of garbage collectors, unloading crews on docks or in warehouses, or police officers in a station who like to make arrests shortly before the end of the working day so they can generate financially lucrative overtime (see Mars 1982, 89ff.; Mars 2013, 40).[109]

But there are also organizations in which nearly all members engage in enrichment practices at the expense of the organization. In mining companies, for example, human resources departments will allow employees to take special leave by noting "sick leave without a sick note" in the shift schedule. In some organizations, the informal absence of employees is so firmly anchored in the organization's expectations that the presence of the entire staff poses a problem for the organization. Researchers refer to these as "organizations of corrupt individuals" (Pinto et al. 2008, 688).

Rule Deviance on Different Levels of an Organization

We know that rule deviance can be found in all functional areas and on all hierarchical levels of organizations. We find self-interested rule deviance in research and development, in purchasing and sales, in production, in human resources, and in quality management. And it has been well established that self-interested rule deviance occurs among top executives

---

109 Gerald Mars's classification is represented by four-field schema based on the work of Mary Douglas, with two dimensions: grid and group strength. It is beyond my scope to address the fatalistic "donkeys" who primarily damage organizations through frustration (see Mars 1982, 66ff.; Mars 2013, 41f.).

at the highest levels, among middle managers, among supervisors and team leaders on the lowest management levels, and among employees at the very bottom of the hierarchy (see Wardi and Weitz 2004, 4).

A surprisingly sharp distinction is made in the literature between self-interested illegalities committed by people who are "low down" or "high up" in an organization (regarding this, see Horning 1970). When the culprits are people on the lower levels of the hierarchy, their actions are referred to as "workplace delinquency," "workplace deviance," and "counterproductive work behavior" (see, e.g., Mangione and Quinn 1975). But when these people are on the upper levels of the hierarchy, the talk is of "upperworld crimes" (Morris 1934, 153), "suite crimes," and "white-collar criminality."[110]

The choice of terminology makes it clear just how heavily the organizational focus is shaped by a focus on class differences.[111] Terms such as "upperworld crime," "suite crime," and "white-collar crime" are meant to draw attention to the fact that legal violations are committed not only by members of the impoverished "lower classes" but also by members of the "upper classes." But their rule violations are not pursued in the same way, because people from the upper classes are in a position to evade labor law sanctions and criminal prosecution, and even if they are caught, they are treated more leniently by the courts (Sutherland 1983, 5–7).[112]

The organization is thus either a victim of its members, or it is used by its members to gain personal advantages in prohibited ways. Instead of employing guns or knives to commit their crimes, like street criminals, these criminals use the organization as a weapon (Wheeler and Rothman 1982, 1406; following Punch 1996, 214).

---

110 The reference to male clothing norms (which frequently have the character of a uniform) is not coincidental, because it was long assumed that it was primarily men who attained high societal positions in order to use these positions to engage in criminal activities.

111 Sutherland (1983, 7) defines white-collar crime as "a crime committed by a person of respectability and high social status in the course of his occupation."

112 The concept of white-collar crime has heavily shaped the discussion in the USA. But one fundamental problem with this concept is that it tied rule deviance to membership in a class, not an organization (see the early criticism by, e.g., Edelhertz 1970 or Lauderdale et al. 1978). Regarding the fundamental difference between a class-based, (implicitly) Marxist theory and a systems theory approach, see Kühl 2019c.

3.2 Illegal Solutions to the Motivation Problem

While organizations may exhibit a good deal of sympathy for individual deviations that benefit the organization as a whole, rule deviance for personal gain alone rarely generates any sympathy beyond the circle of employees who profit from it.[113] Members might occasionally exploit minor opportunities for personal gain in their own organization, but if their activities are discovered, the culprits are unlikely to receive social support. Instead, these incidents are chalked up to the everyday embezzlement, epidemic corruption, and systematic refusal to work that undermine performance morale (see Höffling 2002, 13).

But closer examination reveals that many organizations accept that their employees will gain small personal advantages in an illegal way. We need look no further than the tolerance for the prohibited private use of company telephones, cars or tools, the largely accepted use of company copy machines for private purposes, or the tolerated use of the internet during working hours to maintain Facebook friendships, get updates on the global political situation or optimize one's private stock portfolio.

If these personal advantages are actually prohibited, why are they tolerated? Could it sometimes be functional for an organization to allow its employees to gain personal advantages through embezzlement, theft, or withholding labor?

The Employee Motivation Problem

Most people do not join organizations such as companies, administrative bodies, police forces or armies because the aims of the organization seem particularly worthy of support or their activities are so attractive. Assembling refrigerators on a conveyor belt, selling insurance, processing asylum applications or performing drills in a barrack yard are not

---

113 For example, see the literature for practitioners that looks at theft by organization members, including the books of the same name by Bliss and Aoki 1993, and by New 1994.

activities that most people would find so satisfying that they would spend a good portion of their day doing them without any external incentive.[114]

Organizations therefore use a proven means of motivation to get their members to perform unattractive activities: money. The advantage of money is that it is a very flexible tool for producing motivation (Luhmann 1964b, 94ff.). Monetary payments can induce members to perform a variety of tasks, regardless of how attractive they are. People can even be motivated to perform tasks such as cleaning beaches polluted with oil, photocopying thick books, or processing building permits as long as the organization is willing to pay its members to do so.

But members do not need to be motivated by monetary payments for every single activity. A manager does not need to remunerate her assistants separately for every meeting they arrange, every slide presentation they prepare, or every letter they write. Instead, she can assume that the assistants' monthly salary covers all of these activities. An officer does not need to compensate his soldiers for every properly cleaned weapon, correctly made bed or successful forced march. Instead, he will assume that his orders will be followed as long as his soldiers have an interest in staying in the army. In organizational studies, this process is referred to as the generalization of membership motivation (Luhmann 1964b, 93ff.).

Granted, the zone of indifference toward organizational expectations that is generated by money cannot be expanded indefinitely. Most civil servants would not be prepared to use physical violence against clients, most employees in traditional production companies would refuse to work for a week without any breaks, and even soldiers are not willing to do absolutely everything demanded of them by the military leadership. But in most cases, the employees' zone of indifference is large enough for organizations to confront their members with a very wide range of demands.

---

114 For a fundamental analysis of the problem of alienation among organization members, see Blauner 1964.

This offers the organization a major advantage. Organizations purchase performance (the labor power of their members) for a lump sum so they do not have to record and remunerate every single activity. The organization simply assumes that its members will do what is expected of them within the framework of their wage or salary payments.

The Problem with Translating Motivation into Actual Performance

There is a problem with motivating organization members through monetary payments, however. Remuneration ensures that employees will be present and available in the organization at a particular time, but it does not enable the organization to control their behavior during this time. Unlike machines that have been purchased, the labor power purchased by an organization will not necessarily be smoothly incorporated into the labor process (see Braverman 1974, 57; Friedman 1977, 78; Berger 1999, 155).

Scholars have described this problem from various theoretical perspectives. Marxists say that the purchase of labor power by capitalists is not equivalent to the real use of labor power by capital (see Marx 2010a, 510f.). System theorists talk about the problem that membership motivation, or the motivation to join and remain in an organization, does not automatically lead to performance motivation, or the motivation to exhibit the performance expected by the organization (Luhmann 2017b, 204ff.). In addition, institutional economists note that the principle at the head of an organization has only a limited ability to ensure that the agents purchased with money actually work in the interests of the organization (Saam 2002, 28ff.).

Organizations therefore develop a high degree of creativity to get a handle on the problem of translating membership motivation into performance motivation. Employees working on an assembly line are given piece rate bonuses when they exhibit above-average performance.

Sales representatives are rewarded for selling an above-average number of products. And in the context of the performance-based allocation of funds, professors receive a small financial reward for every article they publish or third-party project funding they acquire. The thinking here is that employee labor power can be better harnessed if the employees do not only receive a flat payment but are also remunerated for precisely defined achievements.

But the limits of these formalized performance incentives soon become apparent. The criteria for receiving performance bonuses must be clearly defined in advance. The performance system must be generalized and objectivized so that all employees have access to these bonuses. And the approval of employee representation committees is often also required for these bonus payments. Performance incentive systems are therefore, by necessity, so static that they are, at best, suited to highly standardized labor processes such as working on a conveyor belt, selling products or—in the opinion of certain university management boards—writing academic articles.[115]

How can the disadvantages of such formalized performance incentive systems be avoided?

Subtle Reward Mechanisms

One option is to allow informal reward systems for special employee achievements. In a wide variety of organizations, informal reward mechanisms are not only tolerated by superiors, they are often actually encouraged. De jure, these mechanisms comprise forms of embezzlement, bribery, deception, and rape that are prosecutable

---

115 The limits are apparent even when it comes to payment for the publication of academic articles or the acquisition of external funding. In the management fantasies of certain university policymakers, academics work according to a simple causal model derived from assembly line work. The assumption here is that, if monetary bonuses are awarded for writing scholarly articles or acquiring external funding, academics will put extra effort into these areas. The negative effects of these motivation measures have been described in detail in the context of the concept of "crowding out" or motivation crowding; see Frey and Jegen 2001.

under labor and criminal law, but at the same time they are, de facto, frequently efficient informal gratification systems in organizations (Dalton 2013, 208).

One variant of such an informal reward system is the controlled tolerance of embezzlement and theft. We need look no further than some of the cleverly devised systems used in ports, hospitals, and department stores for declaring products damaged so that particularly deserving employees can acquire them cheaply or for free. Or the waiters in restaurants whose trickery at the cash register is viewed as part of their wages—and often those of their superiors as well. Or the newspaper editors who, for a long time, followed the rule that a "good story" should be rewarded with particularly generous expense coverage.[116]

Tolerating various forms of corruption is another version of subtle reward. This can include tolerance for accepting bribes, the expectation of expensive gifts, or tolerating the acceptance of sexual services. In many organizations, superiors will show a degree of tolerance for the acceptance of small amenities from customers or suppliers, and military commanders may tolerate sexual relations between their soldiers and local women, despite explicit prohibitions against this from the army high command, if they feel the soldiers have gone beyond what was required of them when they were asked to kill enemy soldiers—or indeed civilians (regarding the extreme case of the tolerance of sexual violence committed by German soldiers in the Soviet Union during World War II, see Mühlhäuser 2020).

Tolerating absences is yet another variant. There is an expectation among miners that they will work hard while underground—even going beyond what is formally required—but after three or four days of hard work, they can take an unplanned day off and get drunk together (see Gouldner 1954b). And companies that can no longer pay deserv-

---

116 In connection with this, see studies of the "knock-off" phenomenon in the hotel and catering industry by, e.g., Mars et al. 1979, 33–34. Mars and Nicod (1984, 8) calculate the "total rewards system" in the hotel and catering industry as the sum of "basic pay + subsidised lodging + subsidised or free food + tips + fiddles + 'knock-offs.'" Regarding informal remuneration in newspaper editorial offices, see the journalists' motto of "a good story deserves good expenses"; Mars 2013, 39.

ing employees due to company-wide guidelines will follow a strategy of giving these employees days off so the company does not lose them (Dalton 2013, 204).

3.3 The Allure of Informal Remuneration in Organizations

One might ask why such a reward structure is not simply formalized. It is clear that organization members particularly at the highest levels of an organization permit themselves a variety of legal privileges—not just high salaries, but also the use of company vehicles for private purposes, company-financed leisure opportunities for the whole family, access to sporting events, etc. Would it not be logical to formalize these diverse, informal reward mechanisms for all members?

Reasons for Informal Rewards

One reason for maintaining informal compensation is that formal compensation in the form of a promotion or higher salary is not always possible (Dalton 2013, 198). The pyramid structure of many organizations leads to limited opportunities to rise in the ranks. There are often just not enough positions available to promote high-performing members. At the same time, the options for raising the salaries of people on a particular level of the hierarchy are also limited. In these cases, informal forms of compensation are a way of ensuring that the high-performers do not leave the organization.

Another reason is that organization members must be motivated to carry out particularly unappealing activities (Dalton 2013, 198). Every organization struggles to find people to take on certain unpleasant jobs—such as anti-rust electroplating in the automotive supply industry, cleaning buses and trains, or removing child pornography from social networks for internet providers. In these cases, unofficial deals are often which allow employees to use tools for personal purposes, take home items left behind by customers, or use formally prohibited means of making their job easier as long as they complete the tasks to the satisfaction of the organization.

Sometimes it is not so much about minor illegal perks and workload reductions but about making work more exciting. When employees start to get bored at work, they can try to make their job more interesting by engaging in petty theft, attempting to gain advantages through their contact with customers, or cheating their way out of work. Doing something forbidden creates a little thrill at work which Lawrence R. Zeitlin (1971, 24) refers to as a kind of self-organized form of job enrichment that enables employees to find meaning in their work again.[117]

Last but not least, informal compensation is used when employees must be motivated to behave in an officially forbidden way. We need look no further than the executive boards that use creative financial instruments, such as the infamous "special purpose entities," to fudge their balance sheets and subsequently rake in additional millions as the managing directors of these entities—with the blessing of the auditor.[118] Or the members of the organizing committee for a soccer world cup who receive kickbacks in the hundreds of thousands of euros not just for legally awarding sponsorship, advertising, and financing contracts, but in particular for illegally purchasing the votes of soccer officials. Or the SS men, ordinary police, and Wehrmacht soldiers during the Nazi era who enriched themselves at the expense of their Jewish victims, which was officially forbidden under penalty of death but was actually within the gray zone of what was permitted and would be tolerated by their superiors because the killings they were assigned to carry out were considered a burden on the men.

---

117 Zeitlin's theory is based on studies of the motives behind employee theft in clothing stores. His considerations align closely with the concept of "making out on the shop floor" that was observed by Michael Burawoy (1979). Regarding problems with the question of motives, see Mills 1940; for a detailed overview, also see Gerth and Mills 1954.

118 Regarding the very well-researched case of special purpose entities at Enron, see Barreveld 2002; Fox 2004; Fusaro and Miller 2002; McLean and Elkind 2004; Salter 2008.

Such forms of useful illegality cannot be officially remunerated if for no other reason than it would shine a light on the illegal practices (Dalton 2013, 215).

Advantages of Informal Rewards

There are obviously advantages to informal rewards. Organizations are "exchange averse" in terms of their formal structure. Employees generally receive a flat wage and cannot expect to be additionally remunerated by their colleagues, superiors or subordinates for everything they do (see Luhmann 1964b, 288ff). An employee who is formally required to pass on information to a co-worker would cause consternation if they insisted that the provision of the information be treated as a personal favor.

But while organizations are formally "exchange averse," exchange plays a key role in enforcing informal expectations. However, this exchange is rarely direct in organizations. Straightforward deals along the lines of "if you let me smoke in my office, I'll stay longer today" tend to be the exception. Instead, there is an assumption that the informal accommodation of a co-worker, superior or subordinate will pay off later on (see Luhmann 2002b, 44). Employees carve out unofficial pathways with favors in the hope that others will do their part to maintain them. Tolerating embezzlement, corruption, and workload reduction is "a cheap way of buying good morale and personal relationships" (Martin 1962, 115).

Of course, this is risky for the party who puts in the preparatory effort because they can never be certain that their accommodations toward others will be reciprocated. If an employee is occasionally willing to stay at work longer than legally required to finish an important assignment, she can hope that her boss will look the other way if she shows up to work a bit late once in a while, but she can't be sure. If illegal donations to a political party come to light, the party secretary can take the fall and resign in the hope of eventually being rewarded with an appointment to an important government position, but it's not a sure thing. This preparatory effort, which offers no certainty of being recompensed, is based on an attitude celebrated in the management literature: trust (for a theoretical analysis, see the definitive work by Luhmann 2017b, 43ff.).

3.4 The Limits of Informal Reward Systems

The problem with informal rewards is that all employees would like to take advantage of them. In almost every organization, there is a tendency for employees to feel they are being treated more poorly than others. If employees notice that others are enjoying advantages by embezzling materials, accepting gifts, or conserving their labor power, their desire for comparable rewards will grow. This is why organizations try to regulate their informal reward systems.

Sensitivities

Generalizing the informal rewards for all employees is one form of regulation. Organizations are remarkably sensitive to ensuring that informal rewards do not remain the privilege of a few well-positioned employees, but instead benefit all high-performers. There are often mechanisms in organizations for sharing the informal rewards earned by employees in the field with employees working in the office. This often carefully balanced distribution of informal benefits guarantees that employees do not view the informal rewards as being unfair, so there are no unpleasant distribution conflicts or complaints.

Organizations are also highly sensitive to who bears the brunt of attempts to gain personal advantages (regarding this issue, see Robinson and Bennett 1995). Studies of rule deviance in restaurants, retail stores, and hospitals have shown that very precise distinctions are made between employees who enrich themselves at the expense of the organization, the customers or other employees (see, e.g., Martin 1962,

82f.; Mars 1973, 201; Hawkins 1984b, 48f.). The least acceptable option appears to be when employees enrich themselves at the expense of their co-workers—e.g., by cheating on the distribution of bonuses or tips, or by stealing the property of other employees (see Horning 1970). The greatest tolerance is shown for personal enrichment by means of taking an organization's property, using company tools for private purposes, or manipulating travel expenses. Enrichment at the expense of customers and clients—by issuing inflated invoices, using tricks when returning change, or stealing property—is not considered particularly legitimate, but it seems to be accepted if the employees feel their work has not been sufficiently appreciated.

Yet another method of regulation consists of informal agreements concerning the form of illegal rewards. In hotels and catering, for example, it is accepted that there will be fiddling when invoices and receipts are issued, but stealing from guests is considered taboo (Mars 1973, 202). If a dock work gang appropriates goods while unloading a ship, it is considered legitimate to pilfer items intended for sale, such as whisky, watches or radios, but stealing someone's personal baggage is considered illegitimate (Mars 1974, 224). All of these regulation processes ensure that employees do not take things too far.

The Role of Colleagues, Superiors, and Subordinates

Just as individual employees cannot specify their own official salaries, working hours, or job descriptions, they equally cannot specify their informal rewards, unofficial working hours, or actual work require-ments. Granted, there are differences between these factors. Formal remuneration and official working hours and job descriptions are reg-ulated by means of decisions, and they can be looked up in files and contested in court. Informal remuneration, unofficial working hours, and forms of workload reduction, by contrast, tend to develop over time, are not put on record, and cannot be enforced in court. But both cases involve the formation of expectations in which individual employees have no say.

An employee's immediate co-workers play an important role in the regulation of informal rewards. They make sure that advantages are obtained in accordance with generalized norms of fairness. But superiors also play a significant role in this regulation by using more or less subtle signs to indicate the limits of informal rewards. Even subordinates can play an important regulatory role, because their superiors know that the employees beneath them can observe and report any formally incorrect behavior on their part.

Mutual observation such as this generates sensitivity to ensuring that informal rewards remain tied to performance for the organization. This guarantees that the embezzlement of materials, acceptance of small favors from customers, or tolerance for formally prohibited forms of workload reduction benefit the employees who have distinguished themselves with their willingness to perform. After all, it makes a big difference for an organization whether police officers take some of the drug money seized from criminals in a raid as a reward for their engagement, or whether they allow themselves to be bribed with drug money from criminals so they do not carry out the raid in the first place.

Prevention or Tolerance

The risks of informal rewards must not be overlooked. Informal rewards can become part of the normal wage expectations of an organization's members (see Dalton 2013, 213). The organization thus risks losing sight of the fact that tolerating embezzlement, mild forms of corruption, or occasional absences from work are a means of motivating employees for special performance. As a result, employees might start taking advantage of informal rewards, prohibited bonus payments by partners, or occasional non-contractual absences from work independently of any special performance for the organization.

The mechanisms of informal rewards have all the usual drawbacks of illegal markets (see Schmidt and Garschagen 1978, 567f.). The "underground" nature of an informal reward system leads to a high degree of intransparency. The scope of the informal reward system cannot be systematically assessed or openly discussed. On account of this intransparency, there is a danger that the informal reward system will increasingly cause the organization to be seen as a self-service store.

It would therefore be logical for organizations to react to embezzlement, corruption, and the refusal to work by cracking down on informal reward systems and penalizing employees by means of warnings, dismissal, and criminal prosecution. In practice, however, organizations seem to respond very differently: they tolerate the attainment of personal advantages within a generally shared framework (see Henry 1978).

There may be a certain degree of organizational wisdom behind this tolerance, because it gives organizations the advantage of flexibility in their rewards system.[119] Since embezzlement, corruption and workload reduction are privileges that are not formally granted to employees in their employment contracts, superiors in particular can prevent others from availing themselves of these informal rewards at any time if their performance is no longer adequate. Furthermore, they can use the fact that their subordinates have claimed privileges as a kind of negative sanctioning by prosecuting these employees under labor or criminal law for embezzlement, corruption or refusal to perform.

---

119 Lawrence R. Zeitlin (1971, 26) suggests making the following calculation: "1. How much is employee theft actually costing us? 2. What increase in employee dissatisfaction could we expect if we controlled theft? 3. What increase in employee turnover could we expect? 4. What would it cost to build employee motivation up to a desirable level by conventional means of job enrichment or through higher salaries?"

4.

The Erosion of Formal Norms: Contact between Organizations with Contained Illegality and Organizations with Unbounded Illegality

> "The imperfection of our laws is compensated for
> by their non-observance."
> *Russian saying*[120]

It is relatively easy to create a rule. Any building superintendent can hang a sign saying ballgames are prohibited near the building. But rules only "come alive" when they are "put to use" or "when one must at least contend with the possibility that this will happen" (Luhmann 1964b, 308). If a rule is never cited, it will quickly be forgotten. If the prohibition against ballgames is never enforced, the sign announcing the rule will just become a future novelty item for an antiques dealer. The rule itself will erode.[121]

The efficacy of rules depends on whether someone cites them, how important this someone is, the situation in which this happens, and what the consequences are if this someone is ignored. Rule compliance is not guaranteed only by the people who make the rules. Others can also cite rules and thus increase the probability of compliance with them. A prohibition against ballgames outside a building will often be enforced not by the superintendent, who is usually indifferent to such issues, but rather by the tenants without children who use the intervention of the building superintendent as a threat to back up their complaints.

---

120 See Ledeneva 2011, 722.
121 Also see Möllers 2020, 167ff.

The first criterion for testing the effectiveness of a rule is whether a violation is painstakingly hidden or openly displayed. We know that, in conflict situations, soldiers and police will mistreat and even kill prisoners they consider to be the enemy.[122] But there is a critical difference between abuse and killings carried out openly and those that take place in secret. When a rule deviation is hidden, it actually expresses the acceptance of the rule by the deviator. Openly flouting rules, by contrast, calls the rules themselves into question (Luhmann 1964b, 311).

The second criterion for assessing effectiveness is how rule violators behave when their offense is revealed. Apologizing for a rule violation ultimately stabilizes the rule. If someone shows up late to an arranged meeting, deviates from prescribed procedures, or ignores official communication channels, offering an apology is an expression of their acceptance of the rule. The reason given for their rule deviance might be fictitious, and this fictitiousness might even be apparent to everyone. But the important thing is that their attempt to make an excuse for the deviation confirms the validity of the rule itself (Luhmann 2014, 46f.). Refusing to apologize for violating a rule ultimately delegitimizes the rule, as it expresses the notion that the violator sees no reason to accept the rule.

The third criterion relates to the question of how rule-breakers are dealt with after their violation has been revealed. If a rule is to be maintained, anyone who violates it must take into account that they will be "out on their own" in their deviance (Luhmann 2020, 444). Isolating rule-breakers helps ensure the effectiveness of the rule. A US president might have close ties to the CEO of an energy corporation, but the minute the mass media reports that the CEO manipulated his balance sheets, the president will try to keep his distance and thus contribute to stabilizing the violated law.[123] The president of an inter-

---

122 For analyses of this from various theoretical perspectives, see, e.g., Bourke 1999; Waller 2002; Collins 2008; Kühl 2016.

123 Regarding the close relationship between Enron and the administration of US president George W. Bush and the administration's sudden attempt to distance itself after Enron's bankruptcy, see, e.g., Nace 2003, 212.

national sports association might spend decades not just tolerating but even catering to corrupt board members, but he will distance himself if these officials are caught enriching themselves and he will then portray his own organization as a victim of corrupt individuals. But if a rule violation is discovered and it is not the rule-breakers who are socially isolated but the organization members who insist on following the rules, then the rule loses its effectiveness.

In brief, a rule violation in itself does not threaten the effectiveness of the rule. On the contrary, if a rule violation is concealed, excuses are made for it when it is discovered, and the rule-breakers are socially isolated, this ultimately supports the rule. Such an approach makes it clear that while you might have the "luxury" of breaking a rule or a law, you will also have to face consequences for doing so. Furthermore, public outrage and remorse on the part of the guilty strengthen the effectiveness of a violated norm, as noted by Émile Durkheim (1982, 97ff.). But if a norm is publicly violated, the violation is not penalized, and the violator is not socially isolated, it leads to an erosion of formal norms. As a result, no one will feel bound by them any longer.

What does this distinction mean for our understanding of rule deviance in organizations?

4.1 The Difference Between Epidemic and Contained Rule Deviance

If someone were to draw up a world map of organizations, it would show not only just how widespread they are worldwide, but also how organizations in different parts of the world seem to have developed in surprisingly similar ways at first glance (regarding the following, see Kühl 2015, 258). Looking at the command structures and rules of armies in the UK, Argentina, Mali, and Sri Lanka, it is remarkable how similar they are. There are government departments for science and technology in the USA and France, Taiwan and Pakistan, Nigeria and Chile (Jang 2000). Universities with very similar faculty structures exist in Berlin, Mexico City, Kabul, Jakarta, and Kinshasa (Ramirez and Riddle 1991). Schools in Germany, Japan, Brazil, and Ghana resemble each other in terms of their length of studies and their curricula much more than the different economic situations in these countries would lead one to expect (Meyer et al. 1992).

But if we look more closely at these organizations, it becomes apparent that many of them have only ceremonially adopted the bureaucratic standards of organizations as described by Max Weber (for example, see Rottenburg 1995, 19). Researchers realized early on that organizations in Asia, Africa, and Latin America do not function like copies of the organizations in North America, Europe, and Australia, which are glorified for their apparent modernity. A number of studies in different countries—including of public administration in the Philippines (see Heady 1957), Egypt (see Sharp 1957), and Thailand (see Riggs 1966)—revealed that organizations did not replace the structures of kinship networks or clan relations. Instead, activities in organizations were intertwined with existing kinship networks and clan relations, thus limiting formal opportunities to access the organization members.

What role do deviations from formal rules and state laws play in these organizations? How do these organizations differ from those in which rule deviance is only occasionally tolerated when useful for the organization?

Between Unbounded and Contained Informality

If formal rules or laws are openly violated in an organization and penalties are rarely imposed, it will be apparent to everyone that the organization does not take some of its rules very seriously. Since there are no stop mechanisms for legal violations or rule deviance in such organizations, they can become the site of epidemic deviations from their formal structure, which comes to be nothing more than a display side. These are organizations with unbounded or rampant illegality.[124]

There is a stark difference between these organizations and those in which it is assumed that formal rules will largely be upheld. Granted, even members of the latter type of organization will be allowed to violate the organization's formal expectations now and then. But these illegalities fill in the gaps left by the organization's formal structure. We could refer to this phenomenon as contained illegality because rather than invalidating the organization's formal structure, it actually contributes to its success.

Exchanging favors, providing assistance beyond what is formally permitted, and taking personal sensitivities into consideration are the order of the day in all organizations. But in organizations with unbounded illegality, the informal order exists not as a more or less pronounced supplement to the formal order, but largely as a substitute for it. In organizations with contained illegality, by contrast, deviations serve to reduce friction losses in an overly rigid formal structure while simultaneously being limited by this formal structure.[125]

The Litmus Test —
What Happens When Rules and Laws Are Broken?

The litmus test for distinguishing between organizations with contained and unbounded illegality is how they deal with rule deviance and legal violations that have been revealed. It is obvious that the

---

124 The relevant study here is by Holzer 2015, 48, who makes a fundamental distinction between "contained informality" and "unbounded informality." He further distinguishes between "conspiratorial informality" and "corrupt informality." Regarding the phenomenon of "unbounded informality," also see his earlier use of the term "wild informality" (Holzer 2007, 364). However, I am interested not so much in the broader phenomenon of informality, but rather its more specific manifestation in the form of illegality. It would be worth establishing a more precise theoretical definition of the relationship between "unbounded illegality" and "unbounded informality."

125 In the relevant literature, a distinction is made between "complementary" informal institutions, "conflicting" informal institutions, and "substitutive" informal orders; see Lauth 2000, 25; Helmke and Levitsky 2004, 728.

police in any country can creatively interpret or violate laws, administrative employees can ignore established guidelines when awarding contracts for services, and business associations can count on the support of willing politicians. The interesting question is how organizations—or state legal systems—respond when such rule violations are discovered. Is rule deviance considered normal, or is it a shocking violation of norms?

In organizations with contained illegality, the revelation of rule violations leads to sanctions and attempts to repair the system. The usual mechanisms of social isolation and visible punishment are put into play in order to uphold the norm (see Luhmann 1964b, 310f.). For example, the culprits might act as if they hadn't known about the rule and had thus violated it unintentionally. They might refer to exceptional circumstances behind the deviation to show that they would normally follow the rules, as the exception ultimately confirms (see Luhmann 1964b, 107). Everyone in these organizations is aware that members are constantly deviating from the official rules, but, if necessary, they can play their trump card by invoking the formal order.

In organizations with unbounded illegality, the revelation of rule violations has few, if any, consequences. It is clear to everyone that the organization is only outwardly pretending that its formal structures are generally binding. In everyday practice, it is unlikely that expectations can be enforced by referring to these formal structures. In these organizations, if a member, client, supplier, or partner assumes that they can invoke the organization's formal expectations if necessary, they will merely be laughed at.

We can test this by seeing how far one might get in such an organization if they assumed it was geared toward formal structures. Someone in Congo-Brazzaville would be considered highly naïve if they thought government ministries reached agreements with one other on the basis of cabinet guidelines developed with consultants. There would be astonishment if someone assumed that the procurement process in a Cuban hospital followed the state's regulations. These are Potemkin organizations which give the appearance of adhering to a formal structure, but in which formal rules can be ignored without consequences.[126]

It is important to remember, however, that even in organizations with unbounded illegality, there are sophisticated and well-developed expectation structures to which members must adhere. Comments such as "everyone does that here," "it's always been that way," or "nothing would get done otherwise" are all expressions of how strongly the expectation of rule-breaking has been institutionalized in these organizations. There are clear ideas of how arrangements should be made within the organization and how cross-organizational networks of trust should function. Unlike formal expectations, these expectations are not written down. Instead, organization members must painstakingly acquire knowledge of them through their own experience, observation, and explanation from others. Such expectations form a kind of informal superstructure in the organization which largely causes the formal structure to degenerate into a display side.

The Diffusion of Organizations with Erosive Formality

From an ethnocentric point of view, erosive organizations might primarily be thought of as companies, administrative bodies, hospitals, schools, armies, and police forces in African, Asian, and Latin American countries.[127] Admittedly, this association is not entirely incorrect.

---

126 Regarding the concept of "Potemkin" bureaucracy, see, e.g., Holzer 2015, 50. I would argue that the phrase "Potemkin organization" applies not to the "normal" management of an organization's display side, but rather to organizations in which the formal side and display side largely coincide. Also see the concept of "mock bureaucracy" developed by Gouldner 1954a, in which everyone assumes that rules are constantly being broken.

127 In economic research, this argument is often put forward with reference to the relationship between levels of corruption and per-capita income; for example, see Mauro 1995. Researchers who attributed a higher degree of corruption to individual countries soon came under fire for engaging in a kind of "cultural racism" through the absolutization of Western standards. See, e.g., the early critique by Gunnar Myrdal (1970, 230) of the self-censorship of corruption researchers as a result of "diplomacy in research." Regarding this problem, see Klitgaard 1988, 9f. Regarding the question of whether it makes sense at all to compile data about corruption on the level of nation-states, see Heywood 2014, 6f.

Anyone who has tried to navigate the road traffic in Cameroon, apply for a construction permit in the Philippines, or earn a university degree in Tajikistan knows that the responsible state administrative employees generally pay scant attention to the official rules and are not terribly swayed in their decisions when the existence of such rules is pointed out.[128]

Still, one should not assume that organizations exhibiting epidemic deviance from a formal structure are found only in Yaoundé, Manila or Dushanbe. Even in countries that rate fairly well in global corruption indexes, there are organizations with a relaxed attitude (to put it mildly) toward the formal order, where illegal practices are tolerated because the police and public prosecutors are very hesitant to pursue them. We need look no further than some of the international organizations based in Switzerland, some port companies in southern Italy, and some police forces in the USA.[129]

4.2 A Question of Loyalty: Organization Members in Role Conflicts

Membership motivations shift in organizations that have no functioning mechanisms for preventing rule violations. In organizations with contained illegality, the "deal" is that members will perform the services demanded by the organization in return for a wage. But there is a tacit understanding in organizations with unbounded illegality

---

128 However, even in countries rated as corrupt in lobbyist indexes, there are organizations that take the formal order seriously, companies who ensure their employees almost slavishly adhere to the rules, administrative bodies who follow central guidelines to guarantee the legality of their actions, and police forces that make sure their officers do what is formally expected of them, not least by paying them well and monitoring them closely.

129 On this last point, fans of fiction would do well to read *The Force*, a very informative crime novel by Don Winslow from 2017, in which the blurry line between controlled useful illegality and uncontrolled epidemic illegality is used as an arc of suspense in a story about a police unit in the USA. Regarding plausibility, see the book by Robert Mark (1977) on the work of the British police.

that members will exploit their position in the organization to gain personal advantages.

To distinguish organizations with unbounded illegality from those with contained illegality, one key question to ask is: to whom are the organization members loyal? Does the organization accept that its members will give contracts or jobs to their relatives or friends, even if they are not qualified? Or does the organization expect that obligations to family and friends will not come into play when contracts are awarded? If someone is arrested, will they be better off if they are a friend or relative of a police officer? Or does the organization systematically prevent preferential treatment on the basis of obligations to family or friends?

The Institutionalization of the Expectation of Deviance

Organizations with contained illegality expect their members to be loyal to the organization above all. To use Max Weber's term, these organizations are like a "steel-hard casing of bondage" that compels people to place the organization's demands above those of their family, at least for as long as they remain members. Their "lifeworld" is "colonized" by the organization's formal system in a way that forces them, as members of the organization, to systematically abstract themselves from other role relations. In organizations with unbounded illegality, by contrast, members are not primarily loyal to the organization, but rather to familial, collegial, or ethnic networks outside of the organization. If it comes down to it, these organization members are expected to put the demands of their family members, friends, and acquaintances before those of the organization.

Admittedly, in all organizations there will always be cases in which preferential treatment is given to someone on the basis of family ties, friendship or ethnic affiliation. The key point, however, is the way in which these organizations respond to such preferential treatment. Organizations with contained illegality systematically try to prevent the particularistic prioritization of family members and ensure that staffing and service decisions are made solely on the basis of their benefit for the organization. The only exception—in capitalist economic systems, anyway—are family-owned companies in which the capital owners can prioritize family members when it comes to staffing, even if this is very damaging to the company (see Scott 1969b, 320). In organizations with unbounded illegality, such containment mechanisms have only limited effect on particularistic preferential treatment.

Members of organizations with unbounded illegality are heavily subject to competing expectations. On their display side, at least, organizations with unbounded illegality try to maintain the impression that they are concerned primarily with providing services and not with being plundered by their own members. On the other side, however, expectations are placed on families, clans, and ethnic groups to exploit their organizational membership for their own benefit. As the employee of a public authority, police unit or transportation company with unbounded illegality, one cannot deflect the requests of one's own family, clan or ethnic group simply by referring to the separation of office and person—touted by Max Weber. In many parts of the world, it would cause great consternation if someone abstracted themselves from their membership of a clan, caste or ethnic group by referring to their membership in an organization. This consternation would be felt not just by members of their own clan, caste or ethnic group but also by the members of others.

A perspective has emerged in the literature that suggests people rationally calculate costs and benefits when they violate organizational rules or state laws (regarding corruption, see, e.g., Rose-Ackerman 1978; Klitgaard 1988; Shleifer and Vishny 1993).[130] This assumption may be plausible for organizations with contained illegality, in which the organization members do calculate benefits and costs when they steal from the organization, accept bribes or skip work without

---

130 This is often combined with a relatively simplistic belief that corruption can be reduced by changing the incentive structures in the relationship between principal and agent (see the concise overview in Jancsics 2014, 360). For a critique of this, see, e.g., Cartier-Bresson 1992; Cartier-Bresson 2000; Persson et al. 2013.

authorization. But it underestimates the fact that, in many regions, the expectations of one's own clan, caste or ethnic group can place so much pressure on an individual that it is almost impossible to perform a rational cost-benefit analysis. The behavioral expectations of families, clans, and ethnic groups are felt to be moral obligations that are deeply anchored in a regional culture and should obviously weigh much more heavily than the behavioral expectations of a seemingly anonymous organization. It is therefore self-evident that ties to one's family, clan or ethnic group offer long-term security, while loyalty to an organization tends to be viewed as precarious because it can be terminated at short notice. As a result of this, benefits and costs are never calculated in the first place when conflicts of loyalty arise (see Rottenburg 1996).

These culturally anchored expectation structures, which lie beyond the formal expectations of organizations, are described in different ways in various countries around the world (for a comprehensive overview, see Ledeneva 2018). In China they are referred to as *guanxi* (see Xin and Pearce 1996, and the detailed analysis by Guthrie et al. 2002), in Russia as *blat* (see Ledeneva 2008, and the detailed analysis by Ledeneva 1998), and in the Middle East as *wasta* (see Cunningham and Sarayrah 1993). In Cuba this is called *sociolismo* (see Díaz-Briquets and Pérez-López 2006), in Brazil it is *jeitinho* (see Motta and Alcadipani 1999), and in Georgia it is *natsnoboba* (see Aliyev and Honsel 2015). In Japan, these networks of personal connections, which are often based on families or clan structures, are known as *jinmyaku* (see Lincoln and Gerlach 2004), in Chile and other Latin American countries they are called *compadrazgo* (see Gomez Diaz and Rodriguez Ortiz 2005), and in Bulgaria they are *vruzki* (see Williams and Yang 2017). Granted, in some countries, external pressure to modernize has caused these expectation structures to devolve into informal supplements to the formal structure. In many countries, however, these principles are the dominant expectation structure, for which an organization's formal structure is nothing more than a façade.

The Organization as Booty

Organizations with unbounded illegality are primarily viewed as booty by their members (Holzer 2015, 51).[131] This shifts their motivation for membership. In brief, people do not go to work in organizations with unbounded illegality in order to live off their wages; they go to work to exploit the opportunities for personal enrichment offered by the organization.[132] In the words of Max Weber (1978, 235), we could call this a modern form of "prebendalism" in which members try to access the "benefices" of the organization.[133]

Members can try to profit from an organization in different ways (regarding the following, see Rottenburg 1994, 218). The simplest way involves using their membership to exchange the organization's services for other services. In return for granting admission to a demanding university, allocating subsidized housing, or ensuring preferential treatment in a hospital, an organization member might receive monetary payments, construction materials, jewelry, watches, or sexual favors, without this necessarily leading to a long-term cooperative relationship (for a detailed analysis, see Noonan 1984). These exchanges become more complex when, instead of involving immediate, specific payments, they develop into long-term, trust-based exchange relationships. An organization member might ensure that someone gets a specific job or receives preferential treatment in court, or that their child receives good grades, in the expectation that this other person will reciprocate when the opportunity arises. These exchange relationships become clientelistic when one of the parties has considerably more influence than the other. In this case, someone will be loyal to an influential person as long as this person uses their influence for the other's personal benefit (regarding clientelism in general, see Hutchcroft 1997; Stokes 2007;

---

131 As a reference for organizations, see the description of "booty capitalism" based on the banking system in the Philippines in Hutchcroft 1998, or of "booty socialism" using the example of the "bureau-preneurs" in China in Lu 2000. Regarding "booty" capitalism as a form of capitalism, see the analysis by Max Weber 2011.

132 Studies of socialist experiments in developing countries are interesting in this regard; see the critique of Cuban politics by Ángel Santiesteban (2017).

133 Regarding the application of this concept to Nigeria, see Joseph 2014.

Hilgers 2011; regarding Africa in particular, see Lemarchand 1972; Berman 1974; van de Walle 2009).

There are various ways for people to enrich themselves at the expense of an organization. One way is to systematically embezzle the organization's property. Organizational property is then viewed not as a tool for carrying out a job, but rather as an opportunity for personal enrichment (regarding kleptocracies in Africa, see Andreski 1979). Another way is personal enrichment through corruption. An individual can use their position at the interface to customers, clients, patients, students or prisoners to gain a personal advantage. Yet another method involves systematically refusing to work while simultaneously drawing benefits from the organization. In a number of countries, there are organizations whose members are registered with the intention of drawing money from the organization even though they never show up at work.[134] Organization members often face social pressure to make use of at least one of these possibilities for enrichment. If there is no opportunity to accept bribes or reduce the organization's materials, an individual must at least reduce their working time so that they can pursue other business.

At first glance, the principles for attaining personal advantages seem to resemble the mechanisms used to arrange informal rewards in organizations. Upon closer inspection, however, a fundamental difference becomes apparent. Organizations with contained illegality tolerate embezzlement, corruption, and the refusal to work as occasional, informal rewards for special performance on the part of them members. In organizations with unbounded illegality, by contrast, embezzlement, corruption, and the refusal to work bear no relation to the performance of their members.

In extreme cases, organizations that erode norms are merely shells in which the primary aim is for organization members to enrich themselves. Some administrative bodies in Central Africa exist only to guarantee that their personnel can work as little as possible while receiving a tax-financed salary. Some state-owned companies in Asia operate

---

134 For an interesting classification of corruption in developing countries, see Khan 2006.

only because it would amount to a political affront to rob the staff from a particular ethnic group of their access to sources of personal enrichment.[135] But these tend to be exceptions.

Most organizations with eroded formal norms do actually provide services. Ships are processed in Egyptian ports, the police in Chad occasionally solve crimes, and even the most corrupt international sports organizations usually manage to hold a world championship every four years. But these organization members must be motivated to perform by remuneration given to them personally. There are usually elaborate systems in place for ensuring that motivational payments made to individuals are shared with others by the recipients, thus ensuring that the respective services are provided.

The Importance of the Formal Order in Formality-Eroding Organizations

This does not mean that the formal order plays no role in these organizations, however. It is remarkable how extensive the formal rules are particularly in organizations viewed primarily as booty by their members. But formal orders are used in a fundamentally different way here than one would expect from a modern organization (regarding the following, see Kuchler 2014, 6ff.).

For example, the formal order can be a framework for organization members to receive bribes from outsiders to induce them to carry out a lawful activity. A registrar might refer to the formal order of a municipality and demand increasingly obscure documents from a couple intending to marry, until the couple finally places a twenty dollar bill on the table, thus submitting the "document" the registrar had been waiting for all along (regarding Kazakhstan, see Rigi

---

135 One example of this is the security staff at some African airports, where the scanning of luggage by non-functioning X-ray machines and superficial searches are no more than a justification for using various tricks to wrangle bribes out of the harried passengers. The actual security checks are then conducted at the plane itself by security personnel flown in by the international airlines.

2004, 111; regarding Ghana, see Price 1974, 117ff.). The head of a university's student registration office might mention strict admission requirements and then hint that, in exchange for a small favor, there could be a way to secure a coveted place at the university after all (regarding Indonesia, see Alatas 1980, 4). A police officer might say she will only investigate a break-in if the injured party makes a small donation to support her efforts. And organization members might declare that they will only follow lawful principles if they receive personal payments in the form of an "administrative" or "fast-track" fee (see Znoj 1994, 143).

In a more extreme version of this situation, the formal order of an organization can be used by its members to blackmail outsiders into paying bribes. In many countries, tradespeople may be accused of violating occupational safety, hygiene or tax regulations, and they can only fight such accusations by bribing the respective customs, tax, trade or public health officials (regarding Kazakhstan, see Rigi 2004, 111ff.). In quite a few countries, traffic regulations are not there to regulate traffic—as the name would imply—but to serve as a means of financing police officers. Barely legible road signs can be used by police to stop drivers in the hope that they will try to cut a lengthy discussion short by paying a bribe (regarding "road money" or *okpoho nda usung* in Nigeria, see Ekpo 1979, 171). Even an organization's internal formal rules will not be used to structure activities within the organization, but are instead used by superiors to punish subordinates who fail to pass on enough bribe money.

In an even more extreme scenario, rules for controlling and enforcing an organization's formal order can be used for the personal enrichment of the organization members. Anti-corruption standards, many of which are formulated in very similar ways, have been enacted worldwide (see Gutterman and Lohaus 2018; Hansen 2012; Jakobi 2013). But these anti-corruption rules are often used not only to enforce a formal order, but also to make people compliant within a system based on personal patronage. National anti-corruption authorities are important not only because they legitimize states in the eyes of the international community, but also because they are a key instrument of power to be wielded against political opponents (for an early analysis of the situation in Nigeria, see Ayeni 1987). In international sports associations riddled with corrupt officials, ethics commissions are not only a part of an association's display side, they are also used to get rid of disagreeable opponents who do not want to integrate themselves into the existing networks.

In brief, people in these situations cannot invoke the applicable laws if needed, much less rely on them. At the same time, it is always possible for influential players to occasionally use positivized state law or formal organizational rules to clear competitors from the field. In countries without a functioning legal system, illegal enrichment by influential oligarchs is tolerated as long as they support the ruling party. But the legal system will always be mobilized if an oligarch develops their own political ambitions. In other countries without an independent legal system, the federal prosecutor's office may tolerate the corruption of international organizations for decades, but it will occasionally help remove unpopular competitors by spreading certain information and initiating criminal proceedings against people from its own network.

The Improbability of the Formation of Organizations

From an ethnocentric point of view, it is easy to criticize organizations with unbounded illegality, in which members personally enrich themselves through corruption, embezzlement, and absenteeism. Organization members who are interested solely in their own advantages thwart the intentions of elected representatives of the people. Trust in the state order is systematically undermined because no one can count on the effectiveness of laws and regulations. The work ethic is systematically subverted when others see that organization members are personally enriching themselves without offering anything in return (for example, see Banfield 1975; Klitgaard 1988).[136]

---

136 Regarding the potential to observe corruption by establishing a functionally differentiated society, see Hiller 2005, 61ff.

But it is important to bear in mind how improbable it is to expect organization members not to give preferential treatment to their friends and relatives or use their membership to provide for their networks (for an early analysis of this, see Bayart 2009). Membership in a family, clan or tribe is based on relations between individuals, with all of their cares and concerns. Concrete knowledge of these other people and a willingness to rely on them enables the formation of relationships based on trust.

Membership in a company, administration or association initially reduces relationships to an exchange between role-bearers. The focus is no longer on personal trust but on appropriate behavior in a given role. In many societies, loyalty to one's family, clan, village, caste or ethnic group is therefore more important than following the formal criteria of an organization (regarding Myanmar, see Furnivall 1948, 170–178; for Asia in general, see Myrdal 1977, 166–176).

Granted, the stable combination of familial membership, social position, and financial opportunities has largely dissolved in the "whirlpool of modernization" (Luhmann 1995a, 21). Dynasties that assumed they would pass their income and social position down through generations are now generally only found in states such as North Korea, Kenya, and the USA. But even in these countries they have lost a good deal of legitimacy (regarding North Korea, see Martin 2004; regarding Kenya, see Tignor 1971; regarding the USA, see Scott 1969a).[137]

Nonetheless, in many regions, stable networks based on family or clan structures remain intact. The particularistic preference given to relatives, friends, or clan members initially appears to be a reversion to pre-modern relationship patterns, but these relationships provide more stability than the fragile membership in an organization.

These environmental conditions are hard to ignore. If someone wants to do business in Yemen or Somalia, they would do well not to

---

137 This does not lead to a reduction of social inequality in a society. Financial income and social position can increase the probability of acquiring a good college degree, but no direct claim can be made on good schools or good grades. Regions may still be shaped politically and economically by powerful family networks, but in most cases the state can intervene in certain areas, such as legislation, domestic security, or even transportation.

focus only on the official laws, but to also take the influence of various regional clans into account (see Lewis 2015). If someone wanted to influence politics in Kyrgyzstan, Tajikistan or Uzbekistan, they would probably have to engage intensively with the clan structures of the political elites (see Collins 2006). The payment of bribes, tolerance of embezzlement, and acceptance of unproductive but well-networked organization members are not sand in the wheels of business in these regions, they are the grease that keeps the wheels turning (regarding this, see Jackall 1988, 110).[138]

4.3 Points of Contact: Cooperation between Organizations with Contained and Unbounded Illegality

Organizations have very limited options when it comes to choosing the other organizations they want to form relationships with. It might theoretically be possible for a company to decide that it will only do business with other companies that share its organizational principles. But this would have economic disadvantages because the company would not be able to exploit the opportunities offered by a globalized economy. National police forces could restrict themselves to cooperating internationally only with foreign police forces that follow similar principles, and to working only within an international police organization with noble ethical values. But this would enable criminals to use the Interpol membership list to identify the countries where they would be least likely to be pursued. The International Olympic Committee could decide to admit only those organizations that meet the same universalistic—and almost inevitably "Western"—standards. But the

---

138 For an overview of the grease hypothesis versus the sand hypothesis, see Méon and Sekkat 2005; Méon and Weill 2010. Early proponents of the grease-the-wheels hypothesis in the development of states include Huntington 1971; Weiner 1962; Dwivedi 1967; Leff 1964; and Leys 1965. For a fundamental analysis of the function of the "political machine," see Merton 1957b. Early proponents of the sand hypothesis include McMullan 1961 and Myrdal 1970.

Olympic games would no longer be global in character, because athletes from only a few countries would be allowed to take part.

There is, therefore, not much of an argument to be made for organizations being all too picky about their partners' stance on formal rules or state laws. On the contrary, companies can use the "space between laws" to avoid paying taxes, ignore strict occupational safety guidelines, and circumvent environmental protection regulations (Michalowski and Kramer 1987).[139] Likewise, it can make sense for European national security organizations to cooperate with North African administrations that function in a different way, because these bodies have other options for curbing migration and fighting terrorism, for example.

Necessary Translations

The challenge for international sports committees, development organizations, and the branches of large Western companies is that they must cooperate with organizations they view as pre-modern while simultaneously maintaining the rigid standards they have set for themselves. For this cooperation to be possible, the members of these committees, organizations, and companies must at least partially defer to the practices of their business partners without demonstrably breaking their own rules and laws (see Rottenburg 2000, 143ff.).[140]

To use systems theory terminology, they must translate between their partners' organizational principles, which are based on personal trust, and their own principles of a constitutional state, which are based on system trust. The central feat here is to ensure that while decisions on one side are made under the influence of *compadrazgo, guanxi,* or *blat,* decisions on the other side can withstand rigid external review.[141]

---

139 Also see Stark 2019.

140 Quite a few development organizations are very adept at channeling tax money so that the use of these funds can withstand the scrutiny of auditors, but the money will still have at least some effect in developing countries.

141 Regarding the idea of translation between organizations, see Czarniawska and Joerges 1996; Sahlin-Andersson 1996; Rottenburg 1996.

This challenge must not be underestimated. How can a frigate belonging to a European army quickly pass through a canal in the Middle East when it is clear to everyone that—at least in peacetime—this is only possible with a bribe? How are national sports organizations supposed to win bids to host international competitions when it is clear that a significant number of the members of the selection committee will base their decision on personal advantages?

Beyond Simple Distinctions

Looking at the points of contact between these two "worlds of rules" might lead one to make a simple distinction: On the one side there are organizations whose representatives are interested primarily in personal advantages (often by necessity) and who exploit their position to gain benefits for themselves and their networks in ways that are sometimes illegal. On the other side there are organizations who must (also by necessity) adapt to their partners' expectations, but whose representatives do not seek personal enrichment and instead view participation in their partners' enrichment networks as a requirement of their membership obligations. Organizations made up of members who are very willing to engage in self-serving illegality thus come up against organizations whose members have an understanding of the concept of useful illegality (regarding their different observations and evaluations, see Hiller 2005, 65).

In some cases, an almost ideal-typical distinction can be made between organizations with members focused solely on personal advantages and those focused solely on rule deviance and legal violations that are functional for the organization (see Pohlmann et al. 2016). The remarkable thing about the systematic bribery by Western European and North American electronics firms to win contracts is that the bribes enabled Greek, Brazilian, and Kenyan decision-makers to personally enrich themselves, but detailed informal processes and approval by means of an informal principle of dual control ensured that the employees of the electronics firms were not involved in the illegal practices (arguments to this effect are put forward by, e.g., Sidhu 2009; Dombois 2009; Klinkhammer 2015).

Similar translations can be found to some extent in the successful attempts by Germany, South Africa, Russia, and Qatar to win the bid to host the soccer world cup. To make sure the prevailing mood was positive, various measures were taken which were correctly accounted for by the organizations of the bidding countries, but which could easily be interpreted as bribes paid to the officials making the decisions. The German bidding committee proposed hosting exhibition matches in Malta, Thailand, Tunisia, and Trinidad and Tobago—the home countries of the important voting delegates—and later claimed it was not responsible for the corrupt use of the proceeds from these matches. The Russian bidding committee did not directly bribe members of the FIFA executive committee. Instead, they awarded a lucrative advertising contract via a large state company shortly after the committee voted. And the bidding committee for Qatar avoided direct monetary payments to a member of the executive committee, but after the vote, the member's son was given a highly paid job in Qatar's national marketing agency. The principle is always the same: although there is a conspicuously short period of time between an organization member making a decision and receiving a financial reward, it is not possible to establish a direct causal link between the decision and the monetary payment.

Occupying forces and national development organizations in Afghanistan can purchase the occasional goodwill of local warlords by financing them. This financing may be indirect, in that the warlords are offered key ministerial positions with the understanding that they will use them as the basis for financing their ethnic networks, or it may be direct, in the form of a suitcase holding 100,000 dollars that is delivered each month to the private residence of the warlord in question. While funds are distributed by the head of the clan in ethnically structured networks (which can be considered rudimentary organizations at best due to their lack of formal structures), the organizations that provide the funds to placate the warlords must be able to properly account for these transactions.[142]

---

142 Regarding Afghanistan in particular, see Marquette 2011; Mujtaba 2013; Lauri 2013.

At first glance, we seem to be dealing with a simple distinction here. On the one hand, we have organizations with controlled illegality which use rule deviance and legal violations for the benefit of the organization. On the other hand, we have organizations which tend toward unbounded illegality, in which the organization members primarily enrich themselves. But the longer these organizations are in contact with one other, the blurrier the distinction becomes between organizations with contained useful illegality and those with unbounded illegality focused solely on personal advantages.

4.4 Organizations in the Gray Zone between Controlled and Uncontrolled Rule Deviance

Researchers to date have been concerned primarily with how organizations in so-called developing or emerging countries adapt "modern" standards so they can act as suitable points of contact for organizations shaped by these standards (for a detailed analysis, see Kühl 2015).[143] It has been noted that this frequently results in organizations that combine the principles of generalized membership expectations as followed by Western organizations with the constancy of the particularistic orientations of their members. These are referred to as "prismatic" organizations in which modern and traditional structures are fused as if in a prism (Riggs 1964, 20ff.).[144]

What is often overlooked here is that even organizations with contained illegality must be very adaptable when they come into contact with organizations whose formal structure is almost nothing more than a display side. The greater the expectation of achieving success through contact with this latter type of organization, the more the former type will adapt their internal procedures to these organizations.

---

143 Regarding the problematic terms "developing country" and "emerging country," see, e.g., Sachs 1990 or Escobar 1995; a good critical overview of the dominant concepts can be found in Sachs 1992.

144 Riggs himself speaks of "prismatic societies," but to be more precise, they are actually prismatic organizations. For a discussion of Riggs's concept, Chapman 1966.

Adaptations

When overly intensive contact with organizations with unbounded illegality in other countries leads organization members to lose their sense for the demands of the organization in their sending country, this is commonly referred to as "going native."[145] This has happened to aid workers who have spent so long in Chad that they no longer have any grasp of the accounting procedures of state development organizations; to sales representatives from multinational companies whose practices for winning contracts only loosely follow the official guidelines; and to the members of Western intelligence agencies who increasingly come to respect the interrogation methods of their partner organizations, which do not adhere very closely to human rights legislation.

The process of "going native" does not necessarily apply only to people; it can also affect the communication channels of organizational units. For example, we know of military units who spent months cut off from their regular chains of command while stuck on an island or in a jungle during combat, to the extent that their internal communication channels eventually eroded. A unit's traditional hierarchical command structure can grow increasingly irrelevant and be replaced by a form of interaction based more on equal rank, which functions on the level of individual personal relations.[146] But "going native" can also apply to the programs of these organizational units, and it can encompass their goals and instructions.

The Influence of Different Contextual Conditions

Western organizations working in certain regions can also be dramatically reshaped. There are stories from crisis-torn countries such as

---

145 To the best of my knowledge, the racist connotations of this term have not yet been systematically studied.

146 In their astute analysis of modern organizations, René Goscinny and Albert Uderzo repeatedly satirize this effect using the example of the Roman army; see, e.g., the character of the legionary Courtingdisastus, who is confronted with the practices of the troops posted in Corsica; Goscinny and Uderzo 1980, 28ff.

Afghanistan and Mali of how foreign armies and international development organizations bow to the corruption of regional clan chiefs and warlords placated by ministerial posts, and also of how deeply these practices come to permeate the organizations themselves. When members of these organizations try to prevent corruption—by refusing to approve funding for local officials to visit European resorts, for example—it leads not to the prevention of corruption but rather to the dismissal of the employees for their lack of cultural sensitivity. If the local employees of state aid organizations threaten their European colleagues with death for trying to prevent kickbacks, these employees do not need to fear dismissal as long as they are sufficiently connected to the respective Afghan or Malian networks.

This adaptation to local circumstances suggests that such developments are not confined to the liaisons in the respective countries, but that entire organizations increasingly adapt to the situation in the countries in which they operate. It is said that Afghanistan starts not in the Middle East, but rather in the headquarters of development organizations in the West. This refers to the fact that organizations in permanent contact with other organizations exhibiting unbounded illegality must almost inevitably align their own structures with them (see Kühl 2015).

But it is important not to exaggerate this seemingly plausible diagnosis. Western organizations have only limited tolerance for rule deviance. Development organizations may accept that aid workers posted in Africa for years will establish efficient patronage networks and lucrative sideline ventures across multiple countries, but they will prevent personal enrichment through embezzlement, corruption or absenteeism if it comes at the expense of their own organization. The bidding committee for the soccer world cup may accept that the "emperor of soccer" who is officially supporting the bid as a volunteer will profit from his advertising contracts with the committee, but it will balk if said "emperor" directly accepts bribes.

Organizations with unbounded illegality and organizations with contained illegality are subject to different forces. Organizations with unbounded illegality are often found in countries where it is considered normal for both members and non-members of the organization to openly break the law. Police forces that ignore state laws and torture their prisoners, or public administrations that only issue identity documents in return for bribes, or companies that buy the goodwill of politicians are not viewed as mafia-style or criminal organizations in these countries, but as ordinary police forces, administrations, and companies functioning in accordance with the standards of the respective state (regarding Russia, see Ledeneva 2001, 10).

Organizations with contained illegality, by contrast, operate under fundamentally different environmental conditions. In regions dominated by the concept of small families rather than extended ones, contact networks are often so loose that no one need worry about a distant cousin showing up at their doors to ask for help getting a job illegally or having an indictment thrown out (regarding this phenomenon, see Granovetter 2007). In these countries, unemployment is so low and the social welfare system is so stable that there is no existential need to call on relatives for help finding a job (however, for an overview of contact networks in countries such as Germany and Japan, see Ledeneva 2018). When an organization's central environmental condition is a functioning constitutional state, it not only means that illegal practices will be prosecuted by the police and punished in court, it also means that legal violations will usually become a media scandal.

For all that organizations must adapt to the working conditions of their partners in developing countries in Europe, Asia, Africa, and the Americas, they also must be aware of the conditions of a functioning constitutional state, a sensitive political system, and mass media outlets that are eager for scandals. As a result, while the members of these organizations may repeatedly observe incidents of unbounded illegality, the formal order of their own organization will win out in the end.

5.
The Emergence, Enforcement, and Regulation of Rule Deviance

*"Given the great rewards and low risks of detection,
why do so many business people adopt
the 'economically irrational' course of obeying the law?"*
Criminologist John Braithwaite (1985, 7)

Organization members might think they are on the safe side if they slavishly adhere to organizational rules and state laws. After all, their superiors should have no reason to reprimand or dismiss them for following the organization's formal rules. Furthermore, organization members who follow state laws to the letter provide no cause for criminal prosecution or civil action and can, therefore, take no blame. So the obvious question here is: Why do organization members ever take the risk of violating the rules or breaking the law?

The extent to which organization members weigh up the costs and benefits of deviating from formal rules and state laws is a matter of debate among organizational researchers. The proponents of one prominent line of thinking assume that organization members make rational decisions about violating rules and laws. They supposedly carefully consider the benefits they will gain from violating a rule and the risks they face for doing so. The advantages of ignoring state laws and formal rules are apparently systematically placed in relation to risk factors such as the authorities' willingness to prosecute, the probability of being discovered, and the potential penalties they face. This is used as the basis for making a rational decision.[147]

---

147 Researchers often do not systematically distinguish between the rationality and irrationality of individual organization members and the organization as a whole. I am focusing here on the question of whether rule deviance by organization members is rationally weighed up or not.

The assumption here is that rule- and law-breakers in organizations are often more rationally calculating than common criminals and norm-breakers outside of organizations (regarding the rationality of street criminals, see the analysis by Becker 1964). While spontaneous, emotionally driven crimes take place outside of organizations, legal violations inside of organizations are said to be almost always the actions of rational actors who weigh up the risks (according to Braithwaite and Geis 1982, 302f.; Paternoster and Simpson 2009, 196).[148] If organizations are viewed as the embodiment of rationality in modern society, one must assume that when a member decides to violate state laws or formal rules, this decision is dominated by rational criteria (for an overview and critique of this approach, see Coffee 1980, 419ff.; Friedrichs 2010, 227; Parker and Nielsen 2011, 10; Bergmann 2016, 8f.).

There is a good deal of convincing evidence that rule deviance is based on such rational calculations.[149] For example, we know that organization members factor in the low probability of being prosecuted when they decide to violate rules. This probability may be low for various reasons. For example, if an organization's regulations are complex, it might be very hard to prove that a rule was violated, so authorities will hesitate to pursue the matter; the violation may be trivial, making it difficult to mobilize social support for prosecuting it; or—as often happens in organizations—the rules might simply have been forgotten (Baysinger 1991, 354f.).[150] It can be sensible for organization members to take this low willingness to prosecute into account when they make their decisions.

This effect can be tested by conducting a little experiment involving the late-filing penalties charged by tax authorities—namely, by always

---

148 Specifically, Braithwaite and Geis (1982, 302) say: "Corporate crimes are almost never crimes of passion; they are not spontaneous or emotional, but calculated risks taken by rational actors."

149 Researchers are now looking into a variety of motivating factors for following or deviating from rules; see, e.g., Kagan et al. 2011; Parker and Nielsen 2011.

150 Regarding prosecution problems, see the arguments by Jacoby et al. 1977 concerning the difficulty of proving that foreign officials have been bribed. Regarding the controversy surrounding the importance of prosecuting petty offenses, see, e.g., Robinson und Darley 1995 or Green 1997.

appealing such penalties. If the fine is not above a certain amount, these appeals are generally accepted by most tax authorities. Appeals are accepted and fees are refunded based not on the goodwill of individual clerks, but on the guidelines of the tax authority (which are not made public, for understandable reasons), which stipulate that every appeal relating to a fine below a precisely defined amount should be accepted. It makes no difference whether the taxpayer says they filed late because they were using new accounting software, their grandparent got sick, they didn't feel like doing their taxes, or they struggle to meet deadlines on account of their early childhood socialization. Their appeal will be accepted in any event, because processing such cases costs much more than the additional revenue that would be brought in by enforcing these relatively minor late-filing penalties. Individuals can anticipate and exploit this decision-making behavior on the part of organizations. This is not fundamentally different from how organizations calculate their risks of discovery and prosecution with the help of lawyers and auditing firms.

Another approach to rule deviance based on rational calculation involves taking the potential consequences into account. Organization members sometimes take brief excursions into the realm of illegality knowing that the penalty will be manageable if the rule violation is discovered.[151] For example, it can be a rational decision for the heads of government departments to accept the fines imposed by administrative courts for legal violations. When it comes to environmental protection, for instance, government officials whose political parties have been in power for so long that they have developed a fairly relaxed attitude toward the concept of the constitutional state will sometimes refuse to implement court-ordered measures for adhering to legally established environmental standards. The fines imposed on the basis of complaints

---

151 Regarding the calculation of the "expected punishment costs" when organizations engage in criminal activity, see the early analysis by Coffee 1981, 389f. There is still a lack of research into the extent to which penalty fees are consciously taken into account. The destruction of the electric streetcar public transit system in Los Angeles by the monopoly made up of General Motors, Standard Oil and Firestone (see Mokhiber 1988) could be an interesting case study.

from environmental protection organizations are accepted because money is simply moving from the state's "left pocket" (the department of transportation) to its "right pocket" (the department of finance). Granted, openly ignoring laws in this way erodes the state's adherence to the rule of law in the medium term. But in the short term, this can be a rational decision for a government official in order to get around apparently inconvenient environmental protection requirements.[152]

The rational calculation of fines has been demonstrated in experimental studies of daycare centers, which show how parents take into account the penalty for picking up their children late. When multiple daycare centers introduced a fine equivalent to around three dollars if children were picked up more than ten minutes late, there was no reduction in the number of late pick-ups—instead, the number rose significantly. Parents had weighed up the disadvantages of a fine and the advantages of arriving late and, in many cases, they accepted the fine and picked up their children late anyway (Gneezy and Rustichini 2000). There is not much evidence to indicate that organization members would behave differently in such a situation.[153]

Another rational approach involves "outsourcing" the risk of rule deviance. It is always risky for organization members to deviate from the rules because the gray zone between legality and illegality can be interpreted in different ways at different times, and a violation that was originally unlikely to be pursued by public prosecutors or the police can suddenly become more risky on account of political changes or a media scandal. For this reason, the responsible individuals in companies, government ministries, administrative departments, and armies tend to outsource activities on the edge of legality to special providers. Sub-contracts may be given to tiny organizations that are not subject to

---

152 Such strategies are often seen particularly in developing countries in which the legal system is not yet entirely distinct from the political system. But they can also be found in industrialized countries in which political parties have been in power for decades. Regarding the question of whether criminal law should apply to the legal violations of low-level authorities, see Green 1993.

153 Considering the prominence of rational choice theory, it is not surprising that this experiment regularly crops up in popular scientific descriptions of behavioral economics; see, e.g., the description in Levitt and Dubner 2006 or Gneezy and List 2013.

the same rigid requirements and careful monitoring and can, therefore, move more confidently in the gray area between legality and illegality. A variety of evidence indicates that larger organizations use small ones as auxiliary structures in this way. Consortiums for major submarine projects might include small partners whose expertise lies not in bending or assembling steel parts, but rather in the use of creative methods for winning contracts. When large contracts are awarded in the airline industry, consulting contracts in the double- or even triple-digit millions are given to tiny organizations that are expected to support the business process. And during military operations, private mercenaries are sub-contracted because they have different ways of fighting the enemy than state armies, which are under closer public scrutiny. If rule violations are discovered, responsibility for them is initially passed off onto these small sub-contracted organizations.

From this perspective, the deviant behavior of organization members does not seem fundamentally different from the behavior of road users.[154] Publicly, they profess to follow the rules, but in everyday life they systematically use various methods of controlled rule violation. Drivers will slightly exceed the speed limit or park their car in a way that could barely be considered legal, cyclists will take advantage of the green light for pedestrians or cars depending on the situation, and all of them assume that they will not face prosecution in these legal gray zones. Road users often suspect the authorities have little desire to pursue many of these transgressions. It is useful for drivers to know which rules the police are particularly sensitive to, just as it is for cyclists to know where they can get away with running a red light or where they might be stopped. Road users also naturally take potential penalties into account when they consider the punishment they could face for driving slightly too fast, having slightly too much to drink, or running through a slightly red light.[155] The outsourcing of

---

154 Regarding the tendency to take established theories relating to street crime—such as rational choice theory, opportunity theory, and strain theory—and apply them to organizational crime, see Vaughan 1981; Shover and Bryant 1993; Shover and Hochstetler 2002; Bergmann 2016. This is also a prominent argument in Fisse and Braithwaite 1993.
155 Regarding the sociology of violating traffic rules, see the early analysis by Ross 1960.

rule violations also comes into play when a passenger suddenly mutates into the driver, because otherwise the actual driver would risk losing their license for speeding.

If it is true that rule deviance is based on rational calculations, the tools for preventing individual organization members from breaking rules and laws should be relatively simple. To identify rule-breakers, one would simply have to determine where it is particularly worth deviating from the rules and then monitor this area more carefully (regarding this kind of contingency theory for rule deviance, see Yeager 2007, 29; Croall 2009, xvi). Of course, monitoring and controlling authorities must always balance the costs of monitoring and punishment with the benefits of preventing rule deviance (regarding this calculation, see the fundamental analysis by Becker 1968; for its application to white-collar criminality, see Wheeler 1982).[156] If these calculations lead one to believe that more effort must go into preventing violations of rules and laws, the assumption is that the responsible individuals in the organization just have to increase the likelihood of violations being discovered. This is done by intensifying control and prosecution measures while simultaneously intensifying the penalties for breaking the rules to reduce the number of violations (regarding a similar perspective, see, e.g., McVisk 1978; Coleman 1985; Paternoster and Simpson 1993).[157]

But can this assumption of rationality explain why organization members are willing to participate in the emergence of rule deviance in organizations? How important are the rational calculations of organization members when it comes to learning deviant practices? What role does the weighing up of formal and informal penalties play in the participation in deviant practices?[158]

---

156 From a rational choice perspective, the aim is not to achieve a zero level in rule deviance and legal violations, but rather to ensure an optimal balance while taking into account the monitoring and punishment costs and the cost of the damages caused by rule deviance (see Palmer 2012, 59).

157 Regarding sanctioning on the basis of rational choice considerations, see, e.g., Garoupa 2000.

158 Research into rule deviance is currently dominated by two competing approaches. The first approach—as depicted here—explains rule deviance using rational cost-benefit calculations. The second culturalistic concept explains rule deviance using institutionalized behavioral patterns which organization members follow without giving any more careful

5.1 The Emergence of Regular Rule Deviance

Experimenting with rule deviance is a form of innovation management for an organization. Developing software that can determine when a car is in a test state and adjust its engine performance to achieve exemplary emissions values was undoubtedly an innovation for the automotive industry (Ewing 2017). Establishing special purpose vehicles to spruce up a company's financial situation was a significant innovation in the field of financial management (Salter 2008). In crises and wars, disasters and pandemics, approaches are hastily found that are often not in agreement with the prevailing state laws and organizational regulations (Weick 1988).[159]

These informal forms of innovation management are often overlooked by management studies fixated on formality. According to the classic concept of innovation management, when a problem is identified, organization members from all affected departments will come together and jointly consider how to solve it. As the official doctrine has it, various methods of innovation management should be applied here. Innovation programs referred to by fashionable terms such as "design thinking" are established, employees are pulled together in innovation circles, and innovation labs that are decoupled from the organization's core business are set up. The idea is that the solutions developed in these labs will be reviewed by the management and suitable solutions will be codified in a set of formal, legally compliant rules that become binding requirements for all employees.[160]

---

consideration to the costs and benefits (regarding the difference between these two approaches, see, e.g., Vaughan 1998 or Palmer 2008). This chapter follows in the footsteps of works that attempt to reconcile these two contradictory approaches by means of a process model (the most significant works are Brief et al. 2001; Ashforth and Anand 2003; Palmer 2008; Smith-Crowe and Warren 2014). This chapter picks up on deliberations from various process models but systematically expands them by applying an organizational sociology perspective. What sets it apart from established descriptions of the processes of creating, learning, producing, and enforcing rule-deviant practices—descriptions which are oriented on formal structures—is that it explores the role played by informal expectations.

159 Regarding the approach to formal and informal norms in crises, see, e.g., Bechky and Okhuysen 2011; M. Meyer and Simsa 2018; Kornberger, Leixnering, and R. E. Meyer 2019.

160 For an example of this classic approach to innovations, see Davenport et al. 2006; Tidd and Bessant 2014; Goffin et al. 2017.

In practice, however, innovations often arise in a different way. Organization members who are confronted with problems will start to experiment with potential solutions outside of the organization's formal structures without constantly thinking about whether these innovations are compatible with the organization's rules or not. This experimentation takes place as part of the members' everyday work and it does not necessarily have to be officially approved or granted a budget. If the experimentation produces a solution that is satisfactory to the affected employees, then it is implemented without immediately becoming a formal process.[161]

Many innovative solutions occupy the gray zone between rule compliance and rule deviance. It is an expression of the automotive industry's innovative power that it can massage vehicle consumption and emissions values to just within the limits of what is justifiable. Narrow tires with very good rolling characteristics are used to reduce rolling resistance, test vehicles have no special features and therefore weigh less, doors are masked to improve aerodynamics and lower fuel consumption, and test drives are conducted at optimal temperatures and in high gears because this makes the engine burn less fuel. From this perspective, using software that recognizes when a vehicle is being tested and regulates the engine to achieve optimum emissions values for the approval process is just another innovative means of making cars look environmentally friendly.[162]

In brief, when decentralized innovations are developed, the individuals responsible for them will think about how the solutions relate

---

161 Also see the critique by Donald Palmer (2008, 115, and 2012, 174) of the argument by Blake E. Ashforth and Vikas Anand (2003) that initiatives for rule deviance and legal violations are instigated from above and then passed down.

162 In many cases, practices that are only just permitted in one country may not be permitted in another. The tricks used by automotive companies to manipulate their emissions values occupy a legal gray zone in many countries. But when the knowledge of how to massage consumption and emissions values is transferred from one country to another (the keyword here is "knowledge management"), it is easy to overlook the fact that these practices violate laws. Individual employees may note that the worldwide diffusion of proven deceptive practices could mean the company is breaking laws in certain countries, but their warnings are often not heeded because the perspective of the company's executives is shaped by the legal situation in their home country.

to the existing formal rules and established laws, but their compliance with the rules is not systematically reviewed during their incremental development. Superiors will be informed of the solutions that have been found, or they might hear about the experimentation with new practices, but they will not be asked to make an official decision on formalizing these practices.[163]

Imitations of Innovations

Informally developed innovations are not spread by means of formal decisions made at the top of an organization, they stealthy diffuse through the organization. Organizations carefully observe whether an innovation that developed in the shadow of the organization's formal structure—be it a new software component or new way of working—proves successful. If the innovative solutions satisfy new demands placed on the organization, solve problems or simplify processes, then they are imitated. This is how rule deviance creeps into the everyday routine of an organization (Clinard und Yeager 1980, 43).

Imitation is the means by which formally innovative and often illegal solutions spread beyond the boundaries of the organization (see Cressey 1976; Baker and Faulkner 1993; Gabbioneta et al. 2013).[164] We see this in the discussion of innovative pharmaceutical marketing methods that are actually forbidden, in the diffusion of knowledge about the prohibited torture methods of intelligence services, and when allied or opposing armies copy established fighting methods that, strictly speaking, violate the laws of war.

Companies do not come together in working groups to talk about "proven industry-specific practices in the gray zone between legality

---

163 Regarding the distinction between isolated and systematic corruption, see Caiden and Caiden 1977, 304ff.; regarding the distinction between situational and structural corruption, see Höffling 2002, 78f.

164 Cressey (1976) compares industries with neighborhoods. Just as norms of rule deviance spread through neighborhoods via young people, norms of rule deviance with which employees must comply can spread through the defense, pharmaceutical and automotive industries, for example.

and illegality," intelligence agents at security conferences do not discuss the advantages and disadvantages of prohibited torture methods, and military representatives do not officially meet to decide on the best way to violate the Hague Convention on the customs of land war. Instead, innovative practices diffuse more tacitly. Staff changes lead companies to adopt the practices of other companies without carefully reviewing whether they are legal; intelligence services gradually adopt the established practices of their associates, which are legal in the respective countries; and armies in combat adopt the methods they observe among their allies or opponents without closely checking that they are compatible with their own rules of engagement.

This leads to the emergence of an institutionalized understanding of what is legal and what is illegal in organizational fields. As the early example of price-fixing in the electrical industry demonstrated (Geis 1995b), industry-specific norms are established which make deviation from the law appear so normal that such behavior is not even necessarily registered as being a violation by the employees of the involved companies. This understanding in the organizational field then influences the behavior of the members of individual organizations (Edelman and Talesh 2011).

Establishing Rule Deviance as an Organizational Cultural Expectation

Deviant informal rules become established in organizations through repetition. Rule deviance is increasingly "normalized" (regarding the concept of normalization, see Gioia 1992; Brief et al. 2001; Ashforth and Anand 2003), and the deviance comes to be viewed as an adapted practice that is efficient in the local situation—justified by the achievement of goals and legitimized through repetition (according to Snook 2002, 183). The deviance is then no longer the product of spontaneous actions by a few isolated people, it is part of the expectations held by the organization (Ermann and Lundman 1982, 91). This leads to the creation of unwritten laws or—to use management terminology—a kind of informal standard operating procedure (see the early analysis by Downs 1967, 62).

In sociology, this process is referred to as the gradual institutionalization of expectations (regarding organizations, see the incisive early study by Selznick 1948, 27). Institutionalization means that individuals can assume their own expectations will be supported by relevant third parties. These can be specific third parties such as co-workers, best friends, or one's own family, but they can also be anonymous third parties who can be counted on to support one's expectations if they find out about them (Luhmann 2014, 50f.).

5.2 Learning Rule Deviance

It is critical for organizations that new members familiarize themselves with what the organization expects from them. The most visible measures for this are ones that introduce new members to the organization's formal rules. New employees are given folders with information about key procedures and relevant points of contact, they attend on-boarding seminars about the organization's formal processes, and experienced employees are assigned to help them learn these formal processes. This planned conveyance of knowledge can be referred to as education (Luhmann 1987, 177).

However, these measures rooted in an organization's formal structure are not suitable for conveying knowledge of established useful illegalities. It would cause consternation if new members were given a folder of detailed information not only about an organization's formal procedures, but also about the rules and laws regularly broken in the organization. And it would be surprising if new employees attended an on-boarding seminar and were shown slides of the organization's official procedures that meet the relevant quality standards, and then slides of established practices of rule deviance.

For this reason, such information is conveyed to new employees in a different way. New employees might see their more experienced co-workers repeatedly deviating from official practice and subsequently adopt these deviations themselves, or experienced colleagues might take them aside and explain how to solve a problem more efficiently than by following the official rules.[165] Experienced police officers will take rookies aside, tell them to forget everything they learned in training, and gradually introduce them to the reality of police work (Caldero et al. 2018). When youth group leaders are trained, they are formally instructed to prevent their charges from smoking while on trips, but during training breaks they will be informally told when they can overlook smoking and when they should intervene (Schäfers 2018). This process of learning behavioral expectations can be referred to as socialization (Luhmann 1987, 176f.).[166]

Important informal rules are generally not written down for new-comers but are instead passed on verbally. In some cases, however, documents may circulate that tell newcomers how things "really work." In the pharmaceutical industry, strictly confidential reports on the production of medicines are quietly passed around so newcomers can quickly grasp how the manufacturing process stays just on this side of legality. And in the foreign aid scene, books are recommended on the sidelines of training programs that paint a realistic but not terribly flattering picture of the work of development banks (one particularly popular work is Rottenburg 2009).

This process of familiarizing organization members with deviant practices is usually part of the general socialization process, however (Brief et al. 2001, 487). It is fairly unusual for newcomers in an organization to be told explicitly that an established routine in a particular department actually violates a rule or breaks a law. Members are generally introduced to informal practices without detailed legal instruction.

---

165 There are connections here to works in the field of network theory on the diffusion of rule deviance in organizations; see Brass et al. 1998.

166 Researchers studying the socialization of newcomers in organizations are surprisingly blind to the distinction between formality and informality (for example, see the overview by Ellis et al. 2015). This leads directly to the "differential association" approach of Edwin Sutherland, who shows that the motives, techniques, and attitudes toward deviant behavior are learned in socially condensed interactions. See the first explicit thoughts on this in the third edition of Sutherland's *Principles of Criminology* (Sutherland 1939) and the revised approach in the fourth edition (Sutherland 1947). For an overview, see Matsueda 1988.

Newcomers are often only gradually exposed to the practices that deviate from an organization's formal structure (see Palmer 2012, 162). This usually starts with the voicing of expectations that newcomers may think are unusual but do not have negative consequences. After they have agreed to engage in such practices once, however, there is often no reason not to commit another rule deviation that is more serious in scope and consequence (for a social psychological description of this "foot-in-the-door technique," see Freedman and Fraser 1966).[167]

Newcomers in particular make decisions of only limited rationality. They are overwhelmed by the demands of the organization, so they base their behavior on that of their colleagues. Copying, emulation, and imitation are the approaches that work best for someone who has just joined an organization.

Controlling the Socialization Process

Despite this, organizations quite often develop very specific approaches for introducing employees to illegal practices in a controlled way. Organization members learn not only how to deviate from internal rules or state laws, but also when to do so (Sutherland 1983, 245). Organizations therefore use informal controls not primarily to prevent rule deviance (as argued by, e.g., Braithwaite 1989, 144f.; Simpson 2002, 106f.), but to manage their accepted level of rule deviance.

In fact, many organizations have programs for socializing new employees that are sophisticated but have never been systematically developed and that exist in the shadow of the formal on-boarding processes handled by training and human resources departments.[168] In armies, new recruits are taught the formal safety guidelines for

---

167 The feeling that newcomers have a choice in following or deviating from a rule plays an important role in their gradual familiarization with deviant practices. Socialization in deviant practices is especially effective when newcomers work under the "illusion" that they have decided for themselves to deviate from the rules (Anand et al. 2005, 15).

168 This process has been particularly thoroughly researched with regard to socialization in illegal enrichment practices; see Mars and Nicod 1984, 117ff.

the use of weapons by their trainers and superiors, but they are also informally instructed in the possibilities and limits of bypassing these formal guidelines. And in aircraft factories, new employees are gradually instructed in the use of the strictly prohibited tool known as a tap while simultaneously told about the restrictions on using it.[169]

Unofficial Distinctions

Researchers noted very early on that newcomers in organizations develop a certain pride in their increasingly professional handling of rule deviance. Organization members receive recognition when they know how to "game the system" to achieve the specified objectives. This recognition often consists not of material rewards, but rather of an improvement in status among the member's relevant colleagues (see Ashforth and Anand 2003, 13).

Sometimes status improvements are symbolized by unofficial distinctions. In an aircraft factory, being allowed to have your own tap—even though this is officially forbidden—is a more important distinction for an employee than a certificate from HR for having successfully completed a welding course. When soldiers have served in Afghanistan, Iraq, the Central African Republic, or Mali, their superiors may allow them to wear the scarf known as a shemagh, even though this is officially only permitted on missions in desert regions. In the USA, France, and Germany, these scarves are viewed as an unofficial distinction for having completed an overseas mission and are more important to the soldiers than official decorations for bravery.

These unofficial distinctions are attractive to organization members not only because they are the product of informal subcultures, but also because they play with deviations from informal structures. Émile Durkheim was one of the first to suggest that distance from generally shared norms can create a strong sense of identity (March

---

169 Using the example of the tap, Bensman and Gerver (1963) very clearly demonstrate how employees are gradually inducted into an illegal practice.

2010, 87f.). This applies to small groups of punks, avant-gardists, and revolutionaries whose identity stems from their position as social outsiders (Becker 1963, 8f.), as well as to cliques in organizations that base their identity on their difference from the "higher-ups" (Luhmann 1964b, 331f.).

Informal distinctions are awarded not to organization members who have pulled one over on the organization for their own advantage, but to members who have managed to achieve the specified objectives despite (apparently) being permanently hobbled by the organization's formal rules. This gives rise to a unique form of professional identity.

5.3 Forming Cooperative Relationships for Useful Illegality

Traditional management theories with a focus on formal structures assume that organization members are willing to cooperate with one another.[170] This view is reasonable at first glance. Organizations use the principle of the formalization of expectations to create cooperative relationships within the organization. When people join an organization, they commit to meeting the cooperative expectations placed on them, regardless of whether they have a "good relationship" with their cooperative partners or not. If they fail to meet these formal expectations, they risk losing their membership in the organization.

However, a closer look reveals that the cooperative expectations specified by an organization's formal structure are often not sufficient because they lack situational elasticity. If organization members restrict themselves to communicating only via formally specified channels, they will generally not be able to coordinate their activities enough to meet the requirements of the organization. In addition to ensuring a basic willingness to cooperate by means of their formal structure, organiza-

---

170 The most prominent proponents of this traditional focus on formal structures include Fayol 1949; Taylor 1967; Gutenberg 1958.

tions weave a much finer network of cooperative expectations through informal structures. Collegiality and comradeship are the terms used to describe these informal cooperative expectations.

Exchange in Organizations

Expectations of collegiality and comradeship are based largely on mechanisms of exchange between organization members. The rule that applies here is: "You do something nice to me and I will do something nice to you" (Boulding 1963, 424). If you cover up the necessary little tricks I use when tendering for contracts, you can count on me to help you ensure that auditors cannot raise any objections to the contracts.[171]

The formation of exchange mechanisms in organizations is remarkable inasmuch as organizations are "exchange averse" on account of their formal structure. Employees cannot expect to receive additional rewards or remuneration from their colleagues, superiors or subordinates for everything they do (see Luhmann 1964b, 288ff). A personal assistant who expects their boss to reward them with chocolates and flowers, special paid leave, or extended breaks every time they type a letter will have trouble staying in the organization in the medium term. In their informal structure, however, organizations are extremely "exchange friendly" (see Luhmann 1964b, 339).

Informal exchange processes often take place between employees on the same level of hierarchy. Production managers in a factory will expect maintenance personnel to drop all other obligations and fix a broken machine if there are "hot" jobs holding up the work. In return, the maintenance technicians can count on the production officers to help conceal any maintenance errors from management (Dalton 2013, 34). But informal exchange processes also take place between employees

---

171 Regarding exchange theory, see the definitive study by Blau 1964, but also Emerson 1976. The study by Umphress and Bingham (2011, 624) rightly points out that, contrary to the assumptions of Kamdar et al. 2006 and Tekleab et al. 2005, for example, exchange theory suggests that exchange practices can encourage rule-deviant behavior rather than compliant behavior.

on different hierarchical levels. On long-haul flights, for instance, the leaden monotony of a journey controlled by autopilot may cause both pilots to nod off. Flight attendants are informally expected to tactfully wake the pilots by knocking or clearing their throat, indicating that this officially serious violation of the rules does not need to become an issue. In return, flight attendants can count on the pilots to refrain from immediately making a scene if they show up late for a briefing (regarding the role of flight attendants in general, see Scott 2003).[172]

The perpetuation and expansion of such personal relationships can lead to the formation of loyalty networks, cliques, "old boys' networks," and promotion alliances in which organization members commit themselves to each other over long periods of time. When these networks form between people on the same hierarchical level, they are seen as close collegial or comradely relationships (regarding police forces, for example, see Stoddard 1968). But when the networks in administrations, companies, hospitals or political parties are dominated by a single person, they can be said to follow the "Don Corleone principle," in reference to *The Godfather* (Puzo 1969). Just as a Mafia boss ensures the loyalty of his underlings by doing "good deeds" for them, superiors make concessions to their employees so they can count on their loyalty at a later date (Bosetzky 2019, 29ff.).[173] The social mechanism upon which such relationships are based is trust.

The Meaning of Trust

Management theory is dominated by a glorified and almost naïve image of trust. Management books monotonously promote the transformation of "mistrust organizations" into "trust organizations" with catch-

---

172 We can see what happens when these exchange processes do not work well enough by looking at examples of flights missing their destinations because the pilots were apparently asleep. The record seems to be held by pilots from Northwest Airlines, who overshot their destination by 240 kilometers and were out of radio contact for 78 minutes; see Pelczar 2019, 27.

173 Also see the reference to "godfatherism" in studies of rule deviance by, e.g., Needleman and Needleman 1979, 518.

phrases such as "trust leads," "trust wins," and "success through trust." The greater the perceived uncertainties in an organization, the more important it is to use trust-building measures to coordinate cooperation between the organization's members. The thinking here is that the winning formula for a "good marriage" or a "good friendship" (personal trust) must also be the winning formula for a "good organization."

But glorifying trust in this way overlooks what an achievement it is to no longer have to depend on personal trust in modern society. Shopping is much easier if you can count on being able to buy products for money in a supermarket without having to be acquainted with the cashier. And there are certain advantages to being able to call the police even if you don't know exactly which police officer will show up. The performance of modern organizations is based largely on the abstraction of personal trust. Organization members can rely on the fact that their employment contracts will be valid, that they will be paid a salary and can sue for it if necessary, and that departments will supply information when asked to do so because the formal rules demand it, regardless of whether or not someone has a personal relationship with the responsible employees (see Luhmann 2020, 445). Systemic trust is the complicated-sounding term used to refer to this abstraction of personal trust (for a detailed analysis, see Luhmann 2017b).

Nonetheless, management consultants—who are clearly enthusiastic about trust—do have a point. Without personal trust as the informal "grease" that lubricates formal structures, organizations could not exist. That said, management consultants depict informal coordination mechanisms in a strangely "glorified" way. When it comes to the effectiveness of personal trust, they think primarily of informal expectations that can productively supplement or even replace formal ones. A number of organizational cultural expectations are certainly compatible with the formal rules of organizations. Organizations have diverse cultural expectations that cannot be enforced by referring to their conditions of membership, but that also do not violate their formal rules (see Luhmann 1964b, 283ff.). Think of the maintenance technicians at Xerox who exchange knowledge not via formalized knowledge platforms, but rather at get-togethers outside of work when they swap "war stories" over a drink or two about dealing with particularly difficult customers or stubborn copy machines (see Orr 1996, 125–143), or the costumed employees at Disneyland who are compelled by the cultural expectations of the "smile factory" to exceed the organization's formal expectations (van Maanen 1991).

But what the management literature quietly overlooks is that many organizational cultural expectations based on personal trust do not fit seamlessly into the control gaps in an organization's formal structure. Instead, they actually constitute violations of the organization's formal structure or of state laws. It is easy for the executive board of an automotive company to demand that emissions be controlled in compliance with environmental laws, that fuel consumption does not increase, that the required apparatus does not take up too much space, and that customers are not forced to visit the workshops more often than necessary. But when concrete plans are drawn up, it will quickly become clear that these objectives are fundamentally contradictory, and the employees will be expected to prioritize some goals over others. This often results in a deviation from legal requirements in order to achieve other goals. So when managers and consultants push the notion that trust is a key form of control, they should know that they are touting the very mechanism critical to the practice of useful illegality.

5.4 Enforcing Informal Expectations

Organizations have a simple mechanism for enforcing their formal expectations: they make the fulfillment of these expectations a condition of membership in the organization. In rare cases, organization members may need to be given explicit instructions or a written warning to remind them of this obligation. But in the vast majority of cases, organization members need no prompting to meet an organization's formal expectations. This explains the high degree of conformity found in organizations as compared to small families, groups of friends, or protest movements.

The challenging aspect of enforcing informal expectations is that they cannot be linked to an organization's conditions of membership. Since an organization cannot officially announce that working time directives may occasionally be ignored if a job is particularly important, employees also cannot be officially punished for going home at the end of the official workday. This is why organizations rely on informal and often implicitly communicated enforcement mechanisms (Pinto et al. 2008, 692).

Ultimately, every organization member withdraws into their formal role and thus overrides the informal expectations. After all, no one can stop a member from following an organization's formal rules, even if the organization itself has informally expected those rules to be ignored for years (Ortmann 2003, 104). Members can only be tacitly reproached for withdrawing into their formal role, they cannot be openly accused of falling down on the job (see Luhmann 2020, 442).

Nonetheless, organization members think very carefully about whether or not to ignore the informal demand that they violate formal structures. The question is not just whether they are officially in the right, but whether they can expect social support from anyone else in the event of a conflict. Just like in the legal system, members must anticipate not only how the formal question will be decided in the organization, but also and especially how their environment will respond to their formal attempt at clarification (Luhmann 2015, 238). They may well be formally in the right by refusing to break the rules, but their initiative may also socially isolate them.[174]

There is always a threat lurking in the background that the refusal to participate in rule deviance will result in negative sanctions imposed by force. This negative sanctioning is a mirror image to the positive sanctioning of an informal order (see Kuchler 2014, 3). While the exchange mechanism is based on the promise that if "you do something nice to me [...] I will do something nice to you," negative sanctions are

---

174 Regarding this dual thematization threshold in the legal system, see the thorough analysis by Luhmann 2015, 238f. The relevant factor is that in organizations (unlike in the legal system), legal questions and power questions are not separated on the level of interaction systems.

based on a threat, namely, "you do something nice to me or I will do something nasty to you" (Boulding 1963, 426).

The methods for enforcing compliance with informal expectations are considered more consequential by organization members than the formally limited powers available to their superiors. The mechanisms by which soldiers are persuaded to follow informal norms are often more brutal than an army unit's official penalties. The mechanisms for withholding critical information from "uptight" co-workers in offices have sometimes caused employees to lose what should have been a job for life. Employees have even been driven to commit suicide not because of the formal expectations placed on them, but on account of the informal pressure from their co-workers, superiors, and sometimes subordinates.

Informal sanctioning takes place particularly between organization members on the same level of hierarchy. This is especially significant to organization members because they depend on the support of their colleagues for many aspects of their work. But informal sanctions can also be used by superiors against their subordinates to enforce informal expectations. If "underlings" invoke their formal rights too insistently, their superiors might engage in bullying from above and withhold the important resources they need to do their job. However, informal sanctions can be imposed from below as well. If managers evade "sousveillance" by the organization members below them, their employees will stop covering up mistakes made by their "uncooperative boss" and let him dig his own grave.

Only in extreme cases do informal sanctions involve shutting out colleagues altogether. Organization members must give up all hope of being able to "get anywhere" with a colleague before triggering a kind of informal dismissal procedure from below that ultimately leads to the organization's formal separation from the member in question. In most cases, however, informal norms can be enforced by occasionally blocking the flow of information, sometimes ignoring important work meetings, or giving someone a stern talking to in order to turn the organization member back into a "good colleague."

Drawing on Formal Resources

To enforce informal expectations, organizations can also draw on the resources provided by the organization's formal structure (see Kühl 2013, 124ff.). For example, the directors of vocational schools are in a weak hierarchical position which makes it hard for them to impose their expectations on instructors. They usually do not have the power to force instructors out of the school, and their ability to influence a teacher's career is also fairly limited. One way of inducing stubborn instructors to conform is by assigning them unpopular subjects, such as having to teach English or history to students taking "Introduction to Plumbing" or "Intermediate Hairdressing." If the instructors don't get the message, they can find themselves stuck with an ever-changing timetable of classes until they either fall in line or ask to be transferred to a different school.

From this perspective, it can be functional for organization members to be utterly overwhelmed by formal expectations, as is common in some organizations. The constant violation of formal expectations gives superiors opportunities to impose sanctions that can be exchanged for good behavior on the part of their subordinates. Research has shown that soldiers in particular are caught in a "norm trap." Through a multitude of formalized regulations covering forms of address and deportment, uniform care and personal grooming, and the cleanliness of quarters and equipment, soldiers are placed in a state of being "continually open to criticism" (Treiber 1973, 51). Superiors can tolerate the violation of formal expectations as a way of ensuring the goodwill of their subordinates, and this goodwill can then be used to compel subordinates to behave in ways not covered by the organization's formal structure. But subordinates, too, can benefit from a heavily formalized organization. Elaborate rules, specific instructions, bureaucratic regulations, and precisely defined working hours are not just restrictions for employees, they are also bargaining chips to be used with superiors if they need to deviate from the rules (see Gouldner 1954a).

Beyond the Complaint

Sanctioning practices such as these are often referred to somewhat plaintively as bullying. The measures are denounced as "psychological terror at work," "workplace harassment," and "inhumane behavior between co-workers." The individuals involved are certainly justified in lamenting the perceived "sadism" of their boss, "brutality" of their co-workers, or "cruelty" of their subordinates. But from the perspective of organizational research, it is important to systematically determine who benefits from this bullying.

In many cases, no doubt, bullying serves only to satisfy the personal desires of individual organization members. For example, the sexual harassment of female employees at a Japanese automotive company serves the personal satisfaction of their male managers. The enforcement of the organization's informal requirements plays a relatively minor role here (see Ashforth and Anand 2003, 4).

But in some cases, informal sanctions are used to help enforce the informal norms that are essential to an organization. In this situation, organization members must decide whether to comply with either the formal regulations or the informal norms. Even if organization members do not generally conduct a systematic cost/benefit analysis to determine whether they are more like to receive social support by behaving in a formally correct or informally expected way, the trade-off between the threat of formal sanctions for deviating from the rules and the threat of informal sanctions for strict rule conformity is not an irrelevant aspect to consider.

5.5 Opening and Closing Windows of Rational Calculation

It would be naïve to assume that rule deviance can always be traced back to the calculations of organization members acting in a rational way. It is often not at all clear how eager the authorities would be to prosecute such deviance, what punishment the organization member might face, and whether it would be possible to minimize the risk by outsourcing responsibility (Vaughan 1998, 29ff.). State laws and formal rules are so complex that organization members frequently do not know if they are deviating from them or not (Palmer 2012, 64). On account of the division of labor in organizations, members may suspect that they are violating a rule, but they will often not be aware of the scope of their rule deviance (Stone 1975, 51f.). Decisions in organizations are generally made on the basis of limited information which is influenced by the myths, dogmas, and fictions nurtured by the organization, and they are, in any case, often compromises based on the lowest common denominator (March 2010, 55ff.).[175]

Nonetheless, decision windows will frequently open up, giving organization members an opportunity to carefully consider whether they will deviate from a rule or not (arguments along these lines can be found in, e.g., Luhmann 1985, 119; Box 1998, 41ff.; Palmer 2012, 43f.).[176] In these cases, the fact of deviance leads organization members—even in organizations that otherwise adhere to routines—to assess the benefit of violating a rule compared to the risk of being discovered and the severity of the potential punishment (see Paternoster and Simpson 1993, 37ff.). The institutionalized formal expectations that demand compliance with the rules are inevitably conflated here with the informal expectations that call for violating these rules (see, e.g., Warren 2003, 624). Organization members are expected to adhere to their organization's decided decision premises—i.e., the formal rules—but they are also expected to follow the undecided decision premises that frequently entail violating these rules. In these cases, employees must choose between the formal and informal expectations—and the pressure to be efficient and innovative in an organization is often so strong that, for rational reasons, employees will choose to break the

---

175 There is now an extensive body of literature that goes beyond rational choice theory to explain rule deviance (for an overview, see, e.g., Vaughan 1998; Palmer 2008).

176 This approach, based on rational choice theory, raises the question of why so many organization members actually do follow the rules considering the low risk of any deviance being discovered (see, e.g., Braithwaite 1985, 7).

organization's rules or even state laws.[177]

When organization members have to justify their decision to deviate from the rules, they employ a variety of neutralization techniques (for a general analysis, see Sykes and Matza 1957; also see Kaptein und van Helvoort 2019). They will say the rules that were violated were poorly formulated and totally inappropriate, but also vague and contradictory. They will emphasize the benefits of the rule deviance for the organization—and perhaps for society as a whole—and contrast this with the manageable risks. And if the rule deviance is discovered, they will contend that there were no real victims, so the cost/benefit calculation worked out in the end (for examples of this argument being applied to rule deviance, see, e.g., Box 1998, 54–57; Piquero et al. 2005, 163f.; Umphress and Bingham 2011, 625–626).

However, it is rare for decision-making situations to arise in which the advantages and disadvantages of rule deviance are carefully weighed up and systematically contrasted with other alternatives.[178] As informal organizational practices become more established, the organization's original open-ended decision-making situations are increasingly "defined out of existence." For newcomers in an organization, the informal expectations will seem so self-evident that they will never even consider calculating the risks and maximizing the benefits (for an analysis from the perspective of obedience research, see Hamilton and Sanders 1992; Hamilton and Sanders 1999). The individuals involved are so entwined in informal exchange relationships that it does not even cross their mind to refuse to participate in deviant practices (see in particular Umphress et al. 2010). Through repetition, rule deviance

---

177 Managers will more or less explicitly demand that a job be completed punctually even if an employee has to work from home to do so; the HR department will expect employees to strictly adhere to the formally established working hours; the quality management department will demand that work be carried out strictly in accordance with specifications to avoid endangering customer quality certifications; and co-workers will push for the use of proven shortcuts to reach productivity objectives.

178 The aim of these deliberations is to move away from the simple contrast between rule-breakers acting in either a rational or irrational way. For this type of differentiation, see Pohlmann et al. 2016, who argue that the recipients of bribes are driven by rational calculations while the bribers tend to be driven by their organization's institutionalized expectations in a way that is beyond rational calculation.

increasingly becomes a matter of course. Organization members assume that this deviance began for a good reason and that this reason does not need to be reviewed (see Ashforth and Anand 2003, 8).[179] The decision windows in which members systematically weigh up the advantages and disadvantages of rule deviance and conformity are gradually closed by established informal practices.[180]

---

179 Organizations become fast and efficient when their members do not continually question their established routines. What is often overlooked here is that this applies both to routines that are compatible with the formal structures and those that run counter to them.

180 The institutionalization of rule deviance to the point that it becomes unrecognizable as such has consequences for legal theory, because the *mens rea* principle states that a rule violation may only be punished if the rule-breakers were aware of the nature of the rule violation or at least could have been aware.

6.
Book of Rules Not Breach of Rules: Reacting to the Disclosure of Useful Illegality

"No system of social norms could be subjected to perfect
behavioral transparency without being utterly disgraced."
*Sociologist Heinrich Popitz (1968, 10) on
the preventive effect of non-knowledge*

Most norm breaches, rule deviations, and legal violations are never discovered, and this is probably a good thing.[181] If every violation of an established norm were revealed, according to sociologist Heinrich Popitz (1968, 4), communities would degenerate into societies of judges, police, and prison guards. And organizations, one might add, would mutate into collections of monitors, controllers, and sanctioners.[182]

This is why organizations are very sensitive to the norm breaches, rule deviations, and legal violations that need to be addressed and those that do not. Police officers have a good sense of when they should deal with broken laws and when they can let them go (Lundman 1979). Occupational safety inspectors will forgo punishing many violations and instead try to improve the situation through a combination of persuasion and latent threat (Carson 1970). Environmental protection

---

181 See Greve et al. 2010, 85. It is impossible to empirically determine just how widespread undiscovered rule deviance actually is. Unreported cases cannot be counted precisely because they are unreported.

182 Günther Ortmann (2003, 33) paraphrases Popitz's theory when he refers to a "society of judges, police and prison guards." Popitz (1968, 4) was drawing on a thought experiment by the British essayist William Makepeace Thackeray, who challenged his readers to imagine what would happen if every single person who committed a misdeed was found out and had to be punished. Popitz found the reference to Thackeray's essay "On Being Found Out" in Robert Merton 1957a, 345.

agencies will not intervene every time a company generates pollution, but will instead only step in when the legal violations are so obvious that ignoring them would call the legitimacy of agency into question (Hawkins 1984a).[183]

However, organizations always encounter problems when, for one reason or another, people outside the organization become aware of norm breaches, rule deviance or legal violations.[184] Sometimes individuals will uncover illegal practices by using their opportunity to bring a complaint to court. The legal system in some countries offers organization members financial incentives to report unlawful practices to the authorities.[185] In the pharmaceutical industry in particular, this has resulted in employees reporting illegal marketing practices and subsequently profiting from the fines paid by the company to the state (see Greve et al. 2010, 79).[186] Sometimes disasters turn rule deviance into a public scandal. When 3,000 people died in Bhopal, India, after a toxic gas leak at a Union Carbide plant (see Shrivastava 1987), when the space shuttle Challenger exploded and killed all of the astronauts on board (see Heimann 1993), when the US Air Force shot down its own helicopters in the Iraq war (see Snook 2002), and when the Exxon Valdez tanker spilled 40 million liters of oil off the coast of Alaska, public attention was almost inevitably drawn to the rule deviance that occurred in advance of those catastrophes (see Williams and Treadaway 1992).[187]

But sometimes rule violations come to light by chance. For example, a lawyer casually mentioned in the course of a labor dispute that purchasing the services of prostitutes was a proven method of motivating the network marketing employees of an insurance company.

---

183 Also see the interesting case study by Hawkins (2001) on the British Health and Safety Executive.
184 These problems are not only theoretically possible, they have been empirically demonstrated. For example, Sullivan et al. 2007 point to the reputational damage suffered by an organization in a network of companies after a scandal came to light.
185 Regarding these *qui tam* laws, see, e.g., Caminker 1989 and Broderick 2007.
186 Sometimes lobbies also use legal proceedings to drawn attention to rule violations; regarding the field of environmental policy, see Hoffman 1999.
187 Even science is not immune to scandal and often tends to condemn everyday practices it would normally ignore. For an example, see Ashforth and Anand 2003, 1ff.

In an age in which the public was already bemoaning the excesses of finance capital, the mass media picked up the story and the insurance company was unable to block its publication. Likewise, it was somewhat by chance that scientists realized the vehicle emissions values achieved on a rolling road by a German automotive company in no way corresponded to the values achieved on an actual road—a revelation that supported the strategy deployed against the company by an environmental protection agency.

Even though it is rare for rule violations to be discovered, once they have been made public, a self-reinforcing effect takes over (for a pertinent analysis, see Ortmann 2003, 268–271). The mass media—with its hunger for scandals, conflicts, and crises—will pick up the story and amplify it. Complaints will be submitted to state prosecutors, and while they will not necessarily result in convictions, they will draw further attention to the case. And finally, politicians will feel compelled to comment on the scandal, thus generating further press coverage.

This increased attention often leads to the discovery of other transgressions by the organization which probably would have gone unnoticed otherwise. Journalists will carefully research the organization in question and try to uncover further violations. Searches and questioning conducted by public prosecutors will turn up other legal violations as a kind of "bycatch" which intensify the organization's legitimacy problems. Politicians will set up investigative committees which not only perpetuate interest in the case but also bring additional details to light.

In this supercharged atmosphere, the lines between legal infringements, breaches of internal organizational rules, and violations of general public standards of acceptability are often blurred. Once an automotive company has been pilloried for illegally manipulating its emissions values, there is little opportunity for it to defend itself against the outrage generated by the additional revelation of emissions experiments on animals and humans, even if these experiments violated neither state laws nor the company's internal guidelines. Once the public has become aware of an organization's legal violations, all of the organization's transgressions, illegal and legal alike, come to be viewed as signs of the organization's lack of scruples.

How do organizations react to the scandals generated by their rule deviance? What consequences do these reactions have in the respective organizations?

6.1 Searching for the Transparent, Thoroughly Formalized Organization

When organizations come under pressure for having deviated from the rules, they start making a concerted effort to improve their external presentation.[188] Companies like Shell will use the fierce criticism of their plan to sink a drilling platform as an opportunity to engage in dialog with NGOs for good publicity (see Holzer 2010). Financial institutions like Deutsche Bank—which long tried to block critical reports in the media—will, when faced with fines in the billions for illegal financial transactions in the USA, find themselves forced to facilitate interviews between their top managers and journalists considered critical of them (see Laabs 2018). And when mercenary companies face reputational damage for the murder of civilians by their own personnel, they will change their name in a desperate attempt to manage the fallout—think of Blackwater, which became Xe Services and then Academia few years later (see Scahill 2011).

Organizations will invest significant resources to spruce up their display side. Marketing departments will take out full-page ads in which the senior management apologizes for its mistakes and promises to do better. Press offices will hire crisis communication specialists who recycle the usual sound bites, in which the organization assures the public that it is "doing everything it can to get to the bottom of the matter" and "cooperating fully with the authorities," and HR depart-

---

188 Regarding the problem of reputational damage in particular, see Karpoff and Lott 1993; Deephouse and Carter 2005; Power et al. 2009.

ments will launch extensive "error management" projects intended to prevent future rule deviance and thus future scandals.

Granted, even measures intended primarily to improve an organization's display side will affect the organization itself (see Edelman 1992). Full-page ads in daily newspapers in which company representatives make apologies temporarily limit the options available to organization leaders. Hiring crisis communication specialists will influence how rule deviance can be discussed within the organization. But these measures have a relatively weak effect on the organization's core processes.[189]

What is worse for an organization is that attempts to regain legitimacy through superficial improvements can backfire. Expensive ad campaigns touting compliance with social welfare standards and unusually long sustainability reports can quite plausibly be taken as indicators that an organization is struggling to comply with social welfare standards and environmental protection directives. Organizations that adopt a code of ethics and publicly trumpet its existence will almost inevitably be suspected of having a disproportionately high probability of deceitful behavior. And organizations that aggressively tout their transparency after a scandal may give the public a reason to believe that their actual measures for enforcing compliance leave something to be desired.[190]

Starting Points for Changing a Formal Structure

Once a rule deviation has become the subject of a media scandal, it is not enough for an organization to simply promise to do better. Updating the organization's values on the display side is considered insufficient, and cosmetic changes to the organization's façade are viewed as

---

189 Regarding different forms of compliance measures, see Krawiec 2003; Parker and Nielsen 2009. For a critique of "cosmetic compliance," see Laufer 1999, 1407.

190 For an extensive analysis, see Brunsson 2003; regarding the plausibility of this assumption, see Mathews 1988. This is an old insight, however. Even Jonathan Swift, author of *Gulliver's Travels*, noted back in the early 17th century that merchants who swindled and cheated on a daily basis liked to present themselves as especially honest individuals; see Geis 2009, 62.

an indication that the organization does not actually want to change anything. Organizations must therefore make visible changes to their formal structure to signal that they are seriously committed to remedying the legal breaches and rule violations. A "break" is demanded from the consolidated organization, meaning that it must admit to the mistakes of the past but also clearly show that many things will be different from now on thanks to changes in its formal structure.

An organization's first response is to modify its communication channels so that rule compliance is given more significance. Public scandals surrounding legal violations are always growth opportunities for an organization's compliance, controlling and auditing departments. In the wake of scandals, these departments hire more staff and their managers move up the organization's hierarchy. Procedures are carefully established for communicating rules in the hope that this will ensure processes remain lawful in the future. By doing this, the organization signals that its leaders are earnest when they say they want to guarantee compliance with state laws and internal rules.

The second response is for the organization to refine its programs in a way that makes scandals more unlikely. The goal is to formalize the relevant expectations in the organization, thus making their fulfillment an enforceable and controllable condition of membership. To this end, the entire organization is planned around specific goals—following the "management by objectives" approach— and the accepted means for achieving these goals are precisely defined. At the same time, instructions in the form of mandatory "if-then" regulations are specified in detail, and formerly vague rules for hiring, procurement, and accounting are refined to cover a variety of potential cases.

The third response to a scandal is a change in personnel. When it comes to filling newly vacant positions at the top of an organization—a measure often required to regain legitimacy—the organization makes sure to hire only non-incriminated people (see Bonazzi 1983). Administrative authorities whose senior personnel are usually recruited from their own ranks look to external people instead, the assumption being that they will not have been touched by the scandal. Government departments whose leadership consisted almost solely of men will hire more women to signal that they are open to cultural change. Companies that come under pressure due to unscrupulous employees who were socialized in business schools will instead hire lawyers who are expected to be more law-abiding than business administrators. In many cases, increasing an organization's legitimacy is a more important aspect of this hiring process than finding new people whose skills actually fit with the organization. The ideal employee is the *homo complicius* who will make every effort to stay within the framework of the specified formal structure.

The Implicit Machine Model of the Organization

These reactions cause many organizations to fall back on a purposive-rational understanding of themselves. In light of the scandalous rule deviance, the entire organization is supposed to be geared toward the objectives stipulated from above, and following the rules is viewed as the basic, key requirement. Both the goals and the if-then programs of individual departments must be consistently oriented toward these objectives to prevent individual departments from becoming independent. When positions are filled with qualified personnel, the individuals who are hired should be capable of meeting the specified objectives and implementing the if-then programs without violating laws. Everything that happens in the organization should serve to achieve the goals specified from above in a formally correct way.

This purposive-rational ideal is propagated in conjunction with the prose of participations now found in most companies, hospitals, universities, and schools, as well as many armies, police forces, and administrations. The notion here is that a rule-compliant organization can only be established when managers "set goals together with the employees," give employees the "opportunity to share their opinion," and then "demonstrate active interest in how the employees achieve the agreed goals." Managers are expected to be "proactive" in communicating to their employees that rule deviance never benefits the organization. Employees are told that the organization expects "proactive communication about problems" and "active error management." Managers should "take the concerns and fears of employees seriously," find solutions to problems "jointly," and also occasionally "accept the unfeasible" (a characteristic view of this can be found in Müthel 2017, 35).

The idea behind this is that organizations can get a handle on the problem of deviance from state laws and internal rules if they take care to ensure that there are no discrepancies between the principles touted externally and everyday practice within the organization. According to this ideology, it is necessary to make the formal structure as transparent as possible to all of the organization members as well as to outsiders. The thinking here is that, ultimately, transparency is the best "disinfectant" for preventing the emergence of more "rotten apples" (regarding this image, see Etzioni 2010; regarding transparency in general, see Power 1997; Hood 2001; Heald 2006; Ringel 2017).[191]

Refining the formal structure is supposed to minimize risks for the organization by clearly defining which part of the organization is responsible for which decision or non-decision. Instead of counting on organization members to develop a sense of how far they can deviate from the formal rules without endangering the existence of their unit or even the organization as a whole, the organization aims to develop formal rules for every imaginable eventuality. In the event that these detailed specifications are not applicable to a particularly unique situation, the organization will establish as many formal rules on deviance as possible, or at least define communication channels through which decisions can be secured (regarding the growing importance of risk management, see Hood et al. 2001; Kalthoff 2005; Power 2005; Power 2007; Ringel 2017).

This understanding of organizations is based on an idealized image of the organization as a perfectly functioning machine (see Kühl 2013, p.89). Very few US presidents are likely to believe that their administration will start functioning like a "fine-tuned machine" within a

---

191 The idea of the transparency of political organizations such as political parties, parliaments, and administrations has increasingly crept into the discourse on economic organizations. Regarding Jeremy Bentham's early deliberations on transparency in politics, see in particular Hood 2001, 864f.

few days of taking office, but the hope remains that by consistently formalizing all processes, they can gradually move closer to this ideal image. Following this thinking, the job of social engineers is to install the mechanisms, set them in motion, and continually adjust them. They are supposed to ensure that the organization is composed of precisely defined individual parts—like a machine—and that each part serves a specific function within the machine and all the gears mesh (see Ward 1964, 37ff.).

By changing their structure, organizations signal that they are undergoing an "exercise of cleansing." The message broadcast in times of crisis is that the dirty organization is subjecting itself to the "purifying power" of a structural change process geared strictly toward the values of law-abidance, integrity, and transparency (see Garsten and Lindh de Montoya 2008, 89). The motto after a scandal, according to Sven Kette, is "from now on we do everything by the book." Every attempt must be made to drag informal processes into "the light of formality" and thus resolve the "difference between formality and informality" in "favor of formality" (Kette 2018a, 5).

6.2 The Undesired Side Effects of a Policy of Consistent Rule Compliance

The ideal image of a purposive-rational, thoroughly formalized, and consistently transparent organization seems convincing at first glance. In any case, it would cause consternation if managers announced that it was irrelevant to them whether members focused on the goals of the organization, thus allowing them to decide for themselves whether they would comply with the formal requirements or not. Managers would also have to explain themselves if they argued for an inconsistent and opaque form of organization in which they were regularly surprised by situations.

It is the apparent plausibility of this ideal of the purposive-rational, thoroughly formalized and transparent organization that prompts so many organizations to gear their self-perception toward it. Traditional consultants will confirm their assumption that they could get closer to this ideal if they only allowed their organization to be consistently rationalized, and management studies based on organizational optimization help maintain this image as well.

Representatives of a purposive-rational understanding of organizations hope that establishing precise, detailed rules will improve both the quality and efficiency of an organization. According to Max Weber, it is the "precision, speed, unambiguity, knowledge of the files," and "strict subordination" that make a "fully developed bureaucratic apparatus" not only more precise, but also cheaper than other mechanisms for completing complex tasks (Weber 1976, 973f.).

In reality, however, the efficiency promised by a purposive-rational organization is often illusory. Thoroughly formalizing an organization does not bring it closer to the purposive-rational ideal—on the contrary, it leads to ever greater deviance. This can be seen in three undesirable side effects that arise when organizations turn to increased formalization after a scandal.[192]

Bureaucratization Effects in Formal Organizations

After a scandal, organizations introduce new formal rules without fundamentally overhauling their existing ones. Even when formal structural rules are revised, Sebastian Barnutz and Sven Kette have noted that regulations are almost never thinned out, they are just defined more precisely. More and more rule specifications, trigger conditions, and exceptions are defined to create "clarity." The end effect of this is that the organization's formal structure gradually "grows inward" (Kette and Barnutz 2019, 59).

This inward growth of an organization's formal structure is brought into sharp relief when we look at nuclear power plans, aircraft carriers,

---

192 The most important empirical study on this problem, to which all works in this field refer either explicitly or implicitly, is by Anechiarico and Jacobs 1996. It is impossible to overestimate how significant this study is to the discussion.

and space programs. The thinking here is that a constant high level of attentiveness is required in these organizations because even tiny lapses can lead to disasters (see Roberts 1989; Roberts and Rousseau 1989; Rochlin 1996; Tolk et al. 2013). In these organizations, so the argument goes, the aim is not to view a low accident rate as a given, but rather to keep alive the knowledge of (near) accidents from the past. Incidents are supposed to be used as opportunities to permanently refine and improve the organization's formal rules. This very precise formal specification of if-then programs, rules of conduct in exceptional situations, and alert systems for close calls obviously makes sense for nuclear power plants, battleships, and rockets because an accumulation of minor errors and lapses can have major effects. But it is doubtful whether it makes sense to promote the expansion and densification of formal structural rules under the heading of the "high-reliability organization" as a recipe for success for all types of organizations (see in particular Weick und Sutcliffe 2007).[193]

Organizational studies have shown that making formal rules more detailed and assigning clear responsibilities—activities that go hand-in-hand with far-reaching mandatory record-keeping regulations—significantly aggravates the usual pathologies of bureaucratized organizations (see the overview in Ringel 2017, 81ff.). In police forces, increased documentation requirements and intensified monitoring by superiors causes police officers to focus on "paper wars" (see the studies by Anechiarico and Jacobs 1994; Chan 1999). In universities, the effort to prevent cronyism in professorial and presidential appointments by issuing more detailed rules and creating as much transparency as possible leads to an increase in documentation that can also be viewed by the public (see the study by McLaughlin 1985).

These effects of the refinement of formal rules are particularly apparent in organizations shaken by scandals. The organizations initially suffer from the fines imposed by courts, the departure of the executives

---

193 By contrast, Perrow (1984) points out that accidents are normal. The hype surrounding the "high-reliability organization" has since encompassed nearly every type of organization. It is therefore only a matter of time before associations, political parties, and NGOs start to take an interest in this principle.

held responsible for the legal violations, and the public loss of reputation. These effects gradually taper off as the court proceedings come to
an end, new executives are broken in, and the media turns its attention
to other things (not least, scandals in other organizations). But then
the effects of the refined formal rules and increased monitoring become
increasingly apparent. The organization loses flexibility and the ability
to make decisions quickly, and the delegitimization of all forms of
rule deviance and violation leads to "non-useful legality" (succinctly
described by Kette 2018b) and even to the threat of "failure according
to regulations" (Kette and Barnutz 2019, 41).

Displacement of Goals:
Better to Follow Rules Than Achieve Results

The idea behind the classic purposive-rational understanding of organizations is simple: The leadership sets a general goal for the organization
and then defines the formal rules that all members must observe to
achieve this primary goal. The formal rules are considered a suitable
means of achieving the organization's end objective. But this purposive-rational ideal has nothing to do with the reality of organizations.
Organizations have competing goals, and the means used to achieve
them can be justified by referring to any one of them. Means can also
take on a life of their own and increasingly become independent of the
ends they were actually intended to achieve.

This independence of means is brought into sharp relief when we
look at organizational restructuring in the wake of a crisis triggered by
the exposure of rule deviance. When an organization is forced to profess
its dedication to rule conformity, complying with the rules becomes
more important than achieving goals. Focusing on rule-abidance can be
costly for an organization, not because of the costs of running departments for compliance, controlling, and auditing, or for hiring external
auditors, lawyers, and consultants, but because attention shifts away
from the issues central to the survival of the organization (as pointed
out by Klitgaard 1988, 25ff.).

This effect can be seen in government administrative departments which continually tighten their formal procurement rules in an attempt to combat corruption. Contracts must be precisely defined before being awarded; depending on their volume, they must be advertised nationally or internationally; and all information surrounding the procurement must be accessible at all times. Since defeated competitors can always appeal against a violation of the procurement rules, they focus ever more intensively on adhering to the rules—as a result of which, the intended goal of the procurement is lost (see Lennerfors 2007). In police departments, the introduction of strict monitoring shifts the focus from "catching criminals" to complying with the carefully monitored rules (see the case study by Anechiarico and Jacobs 1996, 180). In universities, the orientation on detailed formal rules for appointing professors and presidents makes compliance with the rules more important than finding the most suitable candidates (see McLaughlin 1985). James Q. Wilson (1989, 69) noted that strictly following laws and rules eventually becomes more important than achieving the original goals.

In organizational research, this undesired shift in attention is referred to as the "displacement of goals" (Merton 1940, 563). In political parties, winning votes in an election and achieving a majority ceases to be a means of implementing a political program; it instead becomes an end in itself, and the party adapts its programs to this goal. In schools, grades cease to be a means of giving pupils a way to gauge their learning progress and instead become the reason pupils study in the first place. And in public administration, rule compliance is given higher priority than serving the needs of the citizens for whom the rules were introduced. The means that were originally formulated to achieve a goal gradually become a goal in themselves.

This kind of goal displacement does not necessarily have to be a problem. In some manufacturing companies that sought to digitize their production for greater efficacy, the digitization itself became so important that they stopped generating revenue with their original products and instead started helping other companies with their digitization projects. For some state aid organizations, following formal procedures for allocating aid funding was originally a means of improving the situation in developing countries, but over time, their expert understanding of the increasingly refined and controlled procedures has become their core competency. This shift can be functional for development organizations because it means their survival no longer depends primarily on efficiently combatting water shortages, malnourishment, child mortality, and energy scarcity, but rather on their ability to funnel large amounts of money through auditors in developing countries without formal complaint. And it is not out of the question that a government administration could survive even if it lost sight of goals such as reintegrating the long-term unemployed, reducing traffic fatalities or winning wars, as long as its processes were perfectly in tune with the laws. But such cases tend to be the exception.

In most cases, when following the rules becomes more important than achieving an organization's primary goals, it has devastating consequences for the organization. The entire organization then focuses solely on following the increasingly specific rules and loses sight of why these rules were created in the first place (see Anonymous 2003, 2141). This effect is apparent not least in the demotivation of the organization's members (see Anechiarico and Jacobs 1996, 62). Granted, some people may view rule compliance as the actual purpose of their membership in an organization, or sometimes even of their life (see Whyte 1956). But many people feel the purpose of their membership in an organization is to achieve the organization's goals— and these are the people most likely to be demotivated by an overemphasis on rule conformity.

Displacement of Power Relations

The idea of purposive-rational management assumes that the different parts of an organization mesh together like the gears of a machine. Following this thinking, if an organization's leadership simply pursued its goal in accordance with clearly described tasks, then different departments would be able to cooperate largely without conflict. It would then be the task of assurance departments such as human resources, quality, and compliance to support the operative departments central to the organization's core processes (see Thompson 1967). But the reality in organizations is far removed from the purposive-rational ideal. In fact, departments always develop their own local rationalities (see Cyert and March 1963). It seems to be almost a law of nature in the division of labor in organizations for a department to consider the goals imposed from above to be more important than the goals of others. This inevitably results in conflicts between departments as they struggle to achieve their goals at the cost of others.

We find an almost ideal-typical example of this in the position of departments for compliance, controlling, and auditing. These departments describe themselves—along with the external auditors, lawyers, and quality consultants who assist them—as service providers for everyone else. But this self-description conceals the opposing interests of the departments responsible for rule compliance and all other departments in an organization. Compliance, controlling, and auditing departments often have the attitude that only they can prevent epidemic rule deviance and legal violations. Other departments may describe compliance officers, controllers, and auditors as people who observe the gunshots and explosions of a battle from a safe distance, emerging only after the smoke has cleared so they can shoot the survivors (Jackall 1988, 29).

If the hierarchical position of compliance, controlling, and auditing departments improves in the wake of a scandal, this inevitably results in a displacement of power—from the operative departments responsible for the "actual work" to the departments responsible for monitoring. One study on the introduction of far-reaching compliance measures in a public administration showed how the newly established monitoring departments tried to sign off on all relevant decisions made by other departments (Anechiarico and Jacobs 1996, 63–66). And in universities, increasingly complex reforms have given legal departments more and more power, enabling them to invoke actual or invented legal norms to intervene in the curricula designed by the faculties (Kühl 2014, 64ff.).

The displacement of power to rule compliance departments is intensified by the fact that superiors can no longer be certain whether, in the event of a conflict, employees will contact these control departments instead of trying to resolve the issue more informally on their own. Company employees can use hotlines to contact a centralized complaints office to report rule violations by their superiors, soldiers can involve a military ombudsman if they witness violations of military law, and administrative employees are encouraged to report violations anonymously.[194] This can not only erode personal trust between superiors and their subordinates, it can also undermine the authority of superiors in general. Bosses can never be sure whether critical decisions might be taken by their employees as an opportunity to contact a central complaints authority.[195]

Confusion can also arise regarding which office is responsible for central strategic decisions—the responsible operative units of the organization, or the departments responsible for monitoring? Particularly after scandals, there are good reasons to argue for centralizing decision-making at the head of the organization and shifting power to departments responsible for compliance. Ultimately, however, this also shifts the right to issue instructions to parts of the organization that are not qualified to make informed decisions. Formal competence is then held by departments whose technical competence is fairly low with regard to the issues at hand.[196]

6.3 Concealing Rule Deviance More Skillfully

Working to rule is an obvious way for organization members to react to stricter regulations and intensified controls. The rules imposed from above might not suit the current situation, they might have problematic side effects, or they could even endanger the existence of the organization, but as long as organization members rigidly adhere to the formal

---

194 Regarding these types of institutionalized whistleblowing, see, e.g., Miethe and Rothschild 1994; Perry 1998; Maria 2008. A good overview can be found in Vandekerckhove 2006.
195 See the interesting case study on whistleblowing in the Soviet Union by Lampert 1985.
196 Anechiarico and Jacobs (1996, 177) refer to this as "inadequate authority."

order, they cannot be accused of wrongdoing.

But in many situations, working to rule is not an option for organization members. Often when rules are refined and controls intensified, an organization will also expect greater customer satisfaction, higher efficiency, and more innovation—not understanding that these demands can contradict one another in practice. Employees who identify strongly with an organization often cannot reconcile their self-perception with the realization that all-too-rigid regulations are preventing the achievement of goals.[197]

The Irony of Tightened Rules

Since organizations cannot survive without rule deviance, the consistent implementation of programs for specifying rules in more detail and intensifying controls forces organization members to expend more effort hiding their rule deviance. This increased effort is required because, first, rule deviance itself becomes more necessary due to the increasingly detailed regulations and, second, it is vital that this deviance not be discovered by the senior management or monitoring departments. We can refer to this as the irony of tightened rules.[198]

Automotive companies not only issue very precise quality specifications to their suppliers when procuring dashboards, steering wheels, and axles, they also heavily influence production processes by means of certification procedures. These interventions have become so rigid that suppliers must now routinize the deviations necessitated by last-minute production adjustments and turn them into a second, unofficial con-

---

197 Regarding the willingness to break rules on the part of employees who identify closely with an organization, see Dukerich et al. 1998, 253; Umphress and Bingham 2011, 625; and Chen et al. 2016, 1082. No systematic distinction is made here between goal identification and organizational identification.

198 In a similar vein, Marx (1981, 222ff.) speaks of the "ironies of social control." He develops his argument with reference to the relationship between police officers and criminals, but I believe it can also be applied to the effects of tighter controls on rule deviance in organizations. Marcel Schütz, Richard Beckmann and Heinke Röbken (2018, 20) call this a compliance paradox: the flood of norms triggered by compliance authorities leads to the increased corrosion of these norms.

trol system—parallel to their ongoing efforts at standardization and formalization (Kühl 2020, 71ff.). Municipal administrative employees will resort to using public telephone booths and private phones to carry out their official business to avoid strict monitoring. They do so not to hide illegal practices for personal enrichment, but to be able to carry out their everyday work without being pestered by guardians of the formal order (Anechiarico and Jacobs 1996, 89ff.). Intensified auditing initiatives in colleges have resulted in information being "filtered" on various levels of the hierarchy. Even on the faculty level, information is spruced up before being passed on to the head of the organization, which then presents the information in a way that reflects well on the university. The effect of this is that processes within the university become more opaque because the faculties set up a "screen" between themselves and the head of the organization (Neyland 2007, 510ff.).

Transparency measures place pressure on organizations and result in the formation of distinct cultures of verbal agreement. Instead of writing short messages, employees will discuss relevant points in person because it lowers the probability of leaving behind traces in the files. This face-to-face communication does not involve PowerPoint presentations or written minutes, because such files could be found later on (see the case studies by, e.g., Roberts 2006; Ringel 2018). What emerges instead is a "sofa culture" in which decisions are made not in formal, logged meetings but in informal, non-documented circles.[199]

According to Fran Osrecki (2015, 355), strict regimes for enforcing rule compliance can make organizations much more transparent and opaque at the same time.[200] In organizations subject to transparency measures, everything is accessible through the organization's formal structure. Processes are visible to everyone, documents can be retrieved, and instructions are written down in memos. A "box-ticking culture"

---

199 "Sofa culture" is a term coined in connection with the Iraq War by Lord Butler of Brockwell, who complained that, under Tony Blair, decisions were made not via the official channels but in small groups on a sofa. The term does not appear in the Butler report itself. See Butler Committee 2004; but also see, e.g., Roberts 2006, 113 and Riley 2009, 197.

200 Also see the empirically impressive study by Bernstein 2012. For a similar argument from the perspective of principal-agent theory, see Prat 2005.

thus emerges in which organization members must permanently confirm that they have been made aware of information, they have followed a procedure, or they have carried out an activity (see O'Neill 2010).[201] But this is accompanied by increasingly opaque information and documentation processes in the organization's informal structure. Wastelands of files are deliberately produced to make it impossible to find sensitive information, superficial PowerPoint presentations are filed away as records of meetings to prevent precise documentation, and sensitive comments are written on sticky notes because they can be removed before a file is archived (regarding these strategies, see Hood 2007, 204).

The Bureaucratic Vicious Circle

Particularly when organizations have been sensitized to rule violations following scandals, they will try to drain any remaining swamps of deviance. The discovery of a deviation will then normally lead to the introduction of more regulations, which in turn increase the likelihood of new forms of deviance. This then results in tighter, more specific rules which force organization members to find innovative ways to deviate from them if they want to do their job properly.

In organizational research, this process of spelling out formal rules in ever greater detail is referred to as a bureaucratic vicious circle (Crozier 2010, 187ff.).[202] Instead of reacting to rule violations, inconsistencies, and irritations by eliminating or questioning the rules, organizations supplement, differentiate, and expand the rules, thus amplifying the need to deviate from them. Since decision-making programs can, in principle, be divided arbitrarily into sub-programs and sub-sub-programs, organizations can "arbitrarily grow inward" without any improvement in how tasks are completed (Luhmann 1988, 289).

---

201 Regarding this "box-ticking culture" in organizations, also see McGivern and Ferlie 2007, as well as Larner and Mason 2014. Regarding complaints about the "kindergarten level" of these tests and the training that precedes them, see Bergmann 2015, 353.

202 Regarding the sociology of vicious circles in general, see Masuch 1985.

We see this when offices issue guidelines on "using the 'To,' 'Cc' and 'Bcc' fields in emails" after a scandal. This purpose of these guidelines is to enable managers to fall back on the argument that they had not read any "toxic emails" with critical information because they were only cc'd in on them (see, e.g., Lepper 2018). But the introduction of new guidelines always leads to confusion and deviation which necessitates even more detailed specifications. In the end, the rules become so complex that employees have no idea how to send formally correct emails.

The bureaucratization of universities, which was kicked off by university reforms, can also be traced back to this vicious circle. In order to coordinate study and exam regulations—which can change almost yearly for a single course of study—universities need to continually issue new rules, which then produce new and unwanted side effects. The creation of more rules leads to a proliferation of local adaptations so that students can complete their studies within an acceptable time frame. The head of the organization and their subordinate legal departments then respond to these local procedures using the only means available to them: issuing new rules (see Kühl 2014, 67ff.).

The state-owned companies of the Eastern Bloc were prime examples of the effects of over-formalization. State planning authorities defined the amount and quality of the products a company had to produce, as well as the vendor parts the company should receive to do so. This led to the emergence of an intensive "underlife" based on exchange relationships in these socialist planned economies. The only way for the directors of companies in the Soviet Union, East Germany and Yugoslavia to succeed was by using a number of officially forbidden practices when coordinating with other companies. The state responded to these deviations not by reducing the number of rules, but by tightening the regulations and monitoring them more closely (Berliner 1952, 353–365; for a detailed analysis, see Berliner 1957; Nove 1961; Dobb 1970).

Instead of increasing the reliability of expectations through ever more formalized organizational structures, the bureaucratic vicious circle results in a considerable increase in the uncertainty of expectations (see Kette 2018a). Established and thus predictable interdependencies between formal and informal expectations are replaced by growing discrepancies between these expectations.

6.4 The Destruction of Informal Knowledge Management

In many organizations, members make no attempt to hide their creative deviance, because they count on their superiors to look the other way if they break rules in a way that is functional for the organization (Laufer 1999, 1403). Military commanders have a good sense of when they should excuse themselves from a discussion among their officers to take an urgent phone call so the officers can speak openly about practices on the border of legality. Managers in transportation companies know exactly what direction to look in when a careless mechanic stumbles out of a room used for illegal purposes during a sightseeing tour (Kühl 2007a, 285). Legal theorists refer to this as "willful blindness," which means deliberately overlooking violations of formal rules or state laws in organizations (see Wilson 1979).

These practices between superiors and subordinates become established over long periods of time. Subordinates develop a sense for the information their superiors will not officially want to hear and forgo telling them about it via formal channels. But if subordinates are naïve enough to draw attention to a useful illegality in an organization, their superiors will respond with an "I didn't hear that" or "I don't want to know anything about it" as a way of indicating that such information should not be passed on, because otherwise the superior would have to intervene.

The advantage of this formal protection practice is that superiors informally know what is happening in an organization without being forced to take action, and it is hard to hold them accountable later on because they were never formally told about the matter. This enables them to estimate the risks of deviant practices in various areas and judge whether different deviances could accumulate in a way that might lead to disaster.

Intensified rule-compliance measures destroy this proven form of informal knowledge management.[203] Knowledge of rule violations is no longer willingly shared with superiors in the affected parts of the organization and instead only circulates among small cliques of trusted co-workers on the same hierarchical level. Organizations with strict rules are no longer in the know when it comes to their everyday practices and are therefore increasingly surprised by rule-breaking and legal violations.

When knowledge of legal violations and rule deviance is held only by small, protected circles of employees, the probability increases that the potential advantages of such deviance—in the form of increased flexibility or efficiency—will no longer benefit the company, but only the employees breaking the rules. Illegal software innovations will no longer adapt products to overly strict environmental regulations, they will just make the employees' work easier. Bribes will no longer promote sales for a company, they will only personally enrich the marketing staff. And brothel visits will no longer be a way of motivating sales representatives, they will merely be a pleasant windfall effect financed by the company. The pressure to keep rule deviance a secret in small groups turns what would be a useful illegality for the organization into a non-useful illegality.

---

203 Regarding the concept of the perverse side effects of a policy based on transparency, see in particular Hood 2007.

7.
The Moralization of the Organization: On the Production of Hypocrisy

"Virtue is just a lack of opportunity"
Attributed to the poet Wilhelm Busch

Looking at organizations that have come under public fire for rule deviance, one thing is apparent: Before the scandal was exposed, many of these companies had established supposedly exemplary systems for ensuring legal compliance (see Chen und Soltes 2008, 116f.). Siemens was viewed as a global pioneer in compliance management when it was revealed that the company had systematically used bribes to win contracts. After all, Siemens had played a direct role in Germany's endorsement of the OECD Anti-Bribery Convention and had itself been a member of the Global Compact dedicated to fighting corruption (Dombois 2009, 131). Similarly, before Volkswagen's manipulation of emissions tests came to light, the company's systems for ensuring rule compliance were thought to be exemplary. The general view was that, in the wake of a bribery scandal in the early 2000s, Volkswagen had set up a system for preventing violations of labor, antitrust, and environmental laws that was far superior to other automotive companies (Bauschke 2014, 174).[204] These cases teach us that even the most

---

204 According to the Dow Jones Sustainability World Index, Volkswagen was considered the most sustainable company in the automobile industry, not least on account of having its own sustainability office, a corporate sustainability steering committee, and a sustainability board. It was counted among the "top 10 ethical car brands," and the Calvert Sustainability Research Department referred to it as an exceptional company in the industry thanks to its environmental, social, and governance standards (regarding this and other praise heaped on the company prior to the emissions scandal, see Rhodes 2016, 1502–1505). There are endless examples of the "moral failure" of organizations with model systems for rule compliance. For instance, before the revelation that the managers of the energy company Enron were using financial manipulation for personal gain, Enron's systems for preventing personal enrichment in such financial transactions were considered exemplary; see Anonymous 2003, 2129f.

sophisticated system for controlling rule compliance cannot prevent an organization from plunging into an existentially threatening crisis of legitimacy on account of rule violations.[205]

This is a key factor driving more and more organizations to embrace the management of moral integrity as a new wonder drug against legal violations and rule deviance (for an overview, see Paine 2006; George 2010; Wieland 2010).[206] Organizations hope that by managing integrity, the organization as a whole will act in a moral way. The demand for social responsibility on the part of organizations boils down to taking the concept of the "honest businessman"—in which moral values are anchored to an individual actor—and expanding it to encompass organizations, which are conceived of as collective actors. If decisions can be attributed to organizations as collective actors like they can be attributed to individual actors, then organizations have a responsibility to ensure that their decisions are made on a moral foundation.[207] Companies and associations, as well as hospitals, armies, universities, and schools are—so the argument goes—nothing other than "composite moral individuals" whose actions must be judged against moral values.[208]

The ramifications of this pursuit of integrity for the moral orientation of individual organization members are clear. The upshot is that organization members are not only expected to follow the formal rules, they must also systematically base their actions on values such as integrity, human dignity, tolerance, and justice (for early arguments

---

205 The effect of compliance programs has been relatively under-researched, in part due to methodological problems. However, see Treviño et al. 1999 for a fairly skeptical view. It is not terribly surprising that surveys of senior corporate executives and compliance officers imply there is a positive correlation between compliance management and preventing legal violations (see, e.g., Parker and Nielsen 2009).

206 Regarding the connection between integrity and morality, see Becker 1998, 158–160. However, the discussion of organizations and morals is much older. Regarding this discussion after World War II, see, e.g., Barnard 1958 and Golembiewski 1965.

207 Regarding the vast body of literature on corporate social responsibility, which generally offers little in the way of theoretical innovation, see, e.g., Carroll 1999; Fukukawa et al. 2007; McWilliams and Siegel 2001. An overview can be found in Idowu et al. 2013, for example.

208 The concept of the *persona moralis composita* comes from Samuel Pufendorf (1703); regarding this, see Aichele 2008, 8f. A similar position is adopted by Peter French (1984), who attributes the status of a moral person to "conglomerate collectivities" such as companies, but not to "aggregate collectivities" such as mobs or masses.

along these lines, see, e.g., Badaracco and Ellsworth 1989; Srivastva 1988; Paine 1994). Blindly following rules should not be the basis of action in organizations; what is important is developing a "specific value-oriented attitude" that goes far beyond the rules set by the organization (Schöttl and Ranisch 2016). Organization members are supposed to adhere to central moral values out of an "understanding of what is right," not because violating these values would entail painful sanctions (Grüninger et al. 2015, 7).

This pursuit of morality is expressed through the adoption of moral guidelines (regarding the hopes associated with this, see, e.g., Ferrell and Gardiner 1991; Weaver et al. 1999), referred to as a code of ethics, code of conduct, corporate credo, or values statement. Precisely what these guidelines are meant to represent oscillates between rather generalized value formulations and very concrete behavioral programs. But for all of their underlying differences, they are usual official documents that set binding moral standards for all organization members (see Schwartz 2001, 248).[209]

This process is supported by "moral entrepreneurs" who sell "morals" to organizations. In their seminars, checklists, and certifications, behaviors such as the controlled violation of laws and creative interpretation of rules are visibly branded as being deviant and morally reprehensible. The purpose of this is not just to morally assert rules that are generally shared, but to set new moral rules by making reference to noble goals (regarding the concept of the moral entrepreneur, see Becker 1963, 147–163).[210]

Moral entrepreneurs are legitimized by scholars who attempt to substantiate the moral principles promoted in organizations by means of a complex ethical reflexive theory.[211] An entire academic sub-discipline has coalesced around concepts such as organizational ethics, economic ethics,

---

209 Regarding the diffusion of these guidelines in companies in particular, see Ziegleder 2007.
210 Howard S. Becker developed the concept of the "moral entrepreneur" in his analysis of how deviant behaviors are labeled in society. This concept has yet to be specified any further as regards how moral codes are defined and enforced in organizations. The literature on this topic deals primarily with organizations that influence political processes in their role as moral entrepreneurs.
211 For good examples of this, see Duska 2007 and Abend 2014. An overview of the relevant texts in this field can be found in Calabretta et al. 2011. The fact that even scholars participate in this moralization of organizations was criticized early on, especially in the US. For example, see the critique by Shapiro 1983, 307. Regarding ethics as a reflexive theory of morality, see Luhmann 1995b, 236; in general, see Luhmann 2008a.

and business ethics, one which aims to theoretically underpin the moral principles introduced in organizations and support their implementation in practice.[212] Along with political ethics, scientific ethics, medical ethics, religious ethics, and sports ethics—fields which act as service providers for the organizations in the respective sub-sections of society—there is now a domain of economic ethics for the world of business.

Moral guidelines confront employees with an almost endless list of exemplary behaviors they are expected to emulate. Employees are supposed to act "in accordance with their own values" and permanently strive for a "fair balance" between what helps them personally and what benefits others. The supposed key here is "authenticity," or the agreement between the "values one holds and the actions one takes." The important aspect in acting with integrity is "moral fortitude in the face of resistance," meaning that, in conflicts, one should strive for the result that "best realizes the values held." Employees must develop the "strength of character" to stand up for what is "right and just" even in difficult situations and even when one must pay a high price for this behavior.[213] The entire organization is thus gripped by a "suasionism" that compels organization members to mutually lecture one other on correct moral behavior.[214]

Since mindsets and attitudes cannot be imposed from above, the popularity of the topic of integrity has led to a boom in cultural programs in organizations.[215] Many managers and consultants believe

---

212 This demonstrates what has generally emerged as a division of labor between ethics and morality in the modern age. At the end of the 18th century, ethics established itself as a scholarly discipline which "dealt with the justification of moral judgments while simultaneously advocating practically for justifiable behavior" (Luhmann 2008e, 196f.).

213 For a detailed analysis, see Palanski and Yammarino 2007, who define morality according to five characteristics: the wholeness of a person's thoughts, feelings and actions; authenticity as a person; morality in the form of focusing on the benefits not only to oneself but to others; consistency of words and deeds; and steadfastness in the face of opposition. Organizational researchers also think morality is a great thing and thus search intensively for the morality of organizations, as can be seen in Clegg et al. 2007, 107ff.

214 Niklas Luhmann (2008e, 196) refers to "suasionism" as an "illness" that is "benign in principle and not at all life-threatening, but occasionally quite painful for those afflicted by it." It can be detected in "peculiar twitching and the intensity and insistency with which the afflicted person acts and tries to infect others."

215 Influential works contributing to this discussion include Jones et al. 2007 and Maon et al. 2010. These are a specific type of cultural program that are rolled out at regular intervals in organizations; see Kühl 2019a.

they can shape an organization's culture using measures that create a "sense of purpose" and help employees understand the "values" of their organization. Integrity training programs are launched to establish a "do-it-right climate" which emphasizes values such as "honesty and fair play" (Paine 1994, 111ff.). Workshops on error culture encourage managers to "show exemplary leadership behavior," encourage others to take "joy in responsibility," "demonstrate confidence," and "promote trust-oriented error management." A rotating cast of morally exemplary "sub-culture representatives" are supposed to help promote integrity. "Interdisciplinary learning groups" are assembled as a "human resources development measure" to anchor the touted moral values in the organization's culture. Employees in large organizations are taken on "culture journeys" by "chief integrity evangelists" which are supposed to help them learn from small organizations how to overcome the "dark triad" of "authoritarian leadership," "aggressive goals," and a "hire-and-fire culture." Cultural mission statements are issued requiring all employees to be "sincere" with one another, deal with each other in a "straightforward and dependable" way, treat others as "equals," and feel a "friendly bond" with others. In brief, many managers and consultants think that promoting moral integrity through a variety of organizational cultural programs is the solution to their perceived problem, namely, that the classic measures for rule compliance do not work.

7.1 The Difference Between Legality and Morality

The promotion of integrity in organizations has led to an odd conflation of legality and morality.[216] Violations of internal organizational rules or state laws are now considered not just illegal but also amoral (see, e.g., Anand et al. 2005, 9). Following this logic, all decisions that

---

216 This can also be found in academic literature on the subject, in which violations of the law and of standards of justice are lumped together as examples of morally objectionable behavior; see, e.g., Jones 1991; Donaldson and Dunfee 1994; Palmer 2008; Umphress and Bingham 2011; Palmer et al. 2016; Hirsch et al. 2018.

cause physical or financial damage to an organization's own customers, employees, other organizations, state institutions, or the general public are considered "organizational crimes"—regardless of whether or not a law has actually been broken (see, e.g., Frank and Lynch 1992, 17). From the perspective of "moral formalists," all organization members who violate state laws after rationally weighing up the risks and benefits are not just calculators who tolerate illegality, they are "amoral calculators" (Kagan and Scholz 1984).[217]

The Relationship Between Morality and Legality

At first glance, this link between morality and legality seems rather reasonable. If laws were too far removed from generally accepted moral values, it would be hard to enforce them. The police, public prosecutors, and courts would have to constantly work to assert the law against a generally shared idea of morality. The state would have to increasingly employ its monopoly on the use of force to impose laws on its citizens.[218] Legal philosophers who are moral legalists, therefore, argue that all state legislation must be steeped in morality. The thinking here is that all jurisdiction is necessarily tied to a moral judgment.[219]

---

217 This conflation is more or less explicit in the literature. For example, see the findings from a workshop on definition problems concerning the term "white-collar criminality": "Illegal or unethical acts that violate fiduciary responsibility or public trust, committed by an individual or organization, usually during the course of legitimate occupational activity, by persons of high or respectable status for personal or organizational gain" (in Helmkamp et al. 1996, 351). Such conflation can also be found in comments to the effect that only organizations in which no laws are violated can be considered consistently ethical (see Greve et al. 2010).

218 Or laws would merely be a legal façade to which no one felt bound because their socially shared moral values would be fundamentally different from the laws of the state. Such processes can be seen clearly in countries where legislation has been introduced—often under pressure from the international community—that contradicts the traditional moral ideas of the society. These processes become particularly virulent when they relate to differences on issues of gender equality or sexual orientation.

219 I feel the term "moral legalists" is more fitting than the usual "legal moralists." Regarding legal moralism in legal theory, see in particular the dispute between Hart 1968 and Devlin 2009; a good overview can be found in Kahan 1997. Legal moralists assume that the punishment of legal violations is justified if the rule deviance involves a violation of key rules founded in generally accepted moral values (also see Green 2006, 21f.).

In this context—and this is often overlooked—not only do legislation and jurisdiction follow on from general social moral values, the laws come to shape the moral values of society.[220] We see this in how the producers of permitted drugs are judged differently than those of forbidden drugs. The moral condemnation of heroin producers or cocaine dealers feels imperative to many observers because these drugs are legally prohibited—but cigarette manufacturers and alcohol sellers do not seem to be morally objectionable in the same way, because these narcotics are not forbidden in most countries. Consequently, politicians usually do not allow the operators of large cocaine labs or dealer networks to set up booths at their party conferences, they do not issue lobbyist passes to them, and they do not publicize meetings with them on their websites. Meanwhile, lobbyists for cigarette and alcohol companies are popular and well-paying advertising partners at party conferences, they have no problem gaining access to parliaments or the US Congress, and politicians will meet with them in public.[221]

But upon closer inspection, the relationship between morality and legality is much more complex (see Heimer 2010).[222] This is apparent in the fact that many legal decisions could be considered morally objectionable by critics. We see this in the morally charged criticism of addictive products such as cigarettes, alcohol, and painkillers; in the aggressive promotion of salt/fat/sugar mixtures as food; and in the export of machine guns and tanks to states in which critics of the regime are sometimes tortured to death in prison. These practices remain within the bounds of what is legally allowed in most states, but this certainly does not make them immune to moral criticism. On the contrary, precisely because a behavior is considered compatible

---

220 Regarding this point, also see Walker 1980.
221 The opioid crisis in the USA is just one example of how differently legal and illegal "drug dealers" are treated; see McGreal 2018; Meier 2018. For a very similar debate, see the popular-science analysis of the approach to amphetamines by Graham 1972 and the more detailed work on this topic by Rasmussen 2008. For an early critique of the double standards in drug policy, see Duster 1970.
222 Regarding the separation of morals and law in the context of the modernization process starting in the 18th century, see Hart 1968 or Mitchell 1978.

with the law, it can be particularly fiercely criticized so it is eventually legally prohibited.[223]

However, even obviously illegal behavior can be viewed as highly moral (see Hasnas 2006, 59f.). Assassinating a head of state, refusing to follow military orders, or sailing a ship into national territorial waters without permission are punishable crimes in most states, but they can also be held up as morally exemplary actions. We need look no further than the attempts to assassinate Hitler in Nazi Germany, the incidents of insubordination in Cambodia under Pol Pot, or the ships working for private rescue missions who drop refugees in Italy. The risk of legal prosecution for the individuals in each of these cases contributes significantly to their positive moral assessment. As Georg Wilhelm Friedrich Hegel might say, it is sometimes the moral honor of great figures to make themselves legally guilty.

Granted, some states have managed to tie morality closely to legality. The closest connection can be found in states that consistently try to place generally binding legal concepts on a moral foundation. We need look no further than countries with strong evangelical movements that attempt to heavily regulate family law, states under the control of Islamists who strive to establish generally binding sharia law, or socialist states with Marxist-Leninist notions of a proper way of life. What all these states have in common is that do not try to legitimize their legal orders by making fairly generalized references to largely accepted values, they actually aim to prescribe concrete behaviors by referring to a morality that is binding for everyone.[224] However, states with such a close coupling of morality and legality can easily be accused of totalitarianism, because when morality is enforced as a state program that stands above the legal system, it can easily turn into tyranny (see Arendt 1958).[225]

---

223 Passas and Goodwin 2004 summarize this in the title of their book: *It's Legal but It Ain't Right*.

224 It is important to note that the moralization of society—and thus of law—has always been criticized from within as well. For example, see the criticism of the moralism of socialism by Alexander Bogdanov 1984, 25.

225 In keeping with this, see the comment by Niklas Luhmann (2014, 171) that the "differentiation between law and morality becomes the condition of freedom."

There are clearly advantages to the generally loose connections between morality and legality in modern society. Legislation and jurisdiction cannot completely ignore morally charged debates, but conflicts are reduced because every single decision does not need to be additionally weighed up from a moral perspective. A breach of state law therefore does not necessarily entail a violation of social moral values, and not every violation of social moral values necessarily represents a breach of state law.[226]

The Different Clarities of Legality and Morality

One reason for the loose coupling of morality and legality is that the concepts differ in their specificity. For all of the gray zones that exist, it is still relatively easy to determine whether something is legal or illegal. Behavioral expectations can only be legally standardized if there are precise specifications regarding what can be expected and what cannot (Luhmann 2008c, 127). Granted, it is not possible to formulate legal behavioral expectations in a way that is perfectly clear. But courts ultimately give us a complex process for creating clarity that spans multiple authorities. Someone may believe a judgment is morally wrong, but they will still be legally obligated to adhere to it.

While it is fundamentally possible to determine the legality or illegality of a behavior, the possibilities are much more limited for making clear distinctions between morality and immorality (Luhmann 2014, 167). People will generally quickly agree that morality is important to society, but they can then fiercely debate the definition of morally correct behavior. In view of the claim that morality is the cement holding society together, it is remarkable how people can have such different notions of what is good and what is bad (Luhmann 2004, 107).

---

226 This was also the criticism of the broad definition of white-collar criminality developed by Sutherland (1940), who did not clearly distinguish between legalistic and moral considerations (see, e.g., the early critique by Tappan 1947, 96ff.). Contrary to the broad concept of white-collar criminality, which encompasses moral violations as well, Tappan argues for strictly limiting the definition to legal violations by organizations that have been confirmed in court. Regarding this debate, see, e.g., Friedrichs 2010, 251 and Reurink 2016, 388f.

In modern society, behaviors considered moral or immoral are always judged from the viewpoint of the respective observer and the emergent spirit of the age (see Cooper 1981 for a general overview; regarding organizations, see Manning and Anteby 2016). Even if states were to respond to moral criticism by forbidding the distribution and consumption of previously legalized drugs, the sale of fattening processed foods, or the export of weapons to regimes that practice torture, it would still not resolve the difference between legality and morality. On the contrary, some observers would undoubtedly get worked up over their freedom being restricted by elites dreaming of an eco-dictatorship, and they would demand an end to the "prohibitionism" with a great deal of moral fervor.

Intensified Discrepancy in Organizations

The discrepancy between legality and morality is considerably intensified in organizations. While state laws generally provide a fairly rough framework of legally binding behavioral expectations, these expectations are significantly enhanced in the form of formal behavioral expectations in organizations (Luhmann 2014, 198).[227] Organizations can formally specify where their members must be at what time, what they must do once they are there, and what clothing they must wear while doing so. By formulating their conditions of membership, organizations specify behavioral expectations for individuals who would find such demands unreasonable outside of the organization.

The highly specific formalization of organizations contrasts even more radically with subjectively tinged moral values than does the relatively generalized legislation of the state. Granted, one could argue that the moral directives in organizations are often just abstract guidelines that cannot be used to derive concrete instructions for action. The thinking behind this argument is that moral guidelines formulate abstract demands—such as respecting the organization's requirements,

---

227 Some state laws are also specified more precisely, such as tax legislation and road traffic regulations.

cooperating with co-workers, or appreciating customers, clients or patients—but they do not outline specific behavioral expectations.

Advocates of the moralization of organizations overlook the key effect of the moral integrity they demand. In an organization gripped by morality campaigns, every single behavior can be viewed from a moral standpoint. Showing up late to a meeting can be interpreted as a lack of respect; refusing to carry out a formally prescribed activity can be interpreted as uncooperativeness; and inattention to one's clothing can be interpreted as a lack of regard for customers, clients or patients. In principle, organization members could never be certain that their behavior was not being morally judged by someone else.[228]

7.2 Morals as an Expression of Esteem and Disdain for People

At first glance, committing oneself to the values touted in moral communication seems to be a relatively reasonable approach.[229] It would be surprising if a company's managing directors openly advocated a "corrupt corporate policy," demanded that their employees take an "immoral stance," and promoted "value-free leadership." The appeal of values is that they have "high chances for consensus" because people can quickly

---

228 In principle, there are no limits to moralization in organizations. In the temporal dimension, there is hardly any way to demand a moral time-out. Precisely because moral communication encompasses the person as a whole, time-limited activities in an organizational role are not accepted as an excuse. It would contradict all notions of moral integrity to say that someone had only acted immorally from 9:00 to 5:00 but had behaved in a morally impeccable way the rest of the time. In the factual dimension, every issue can be judged in terms of esteem or disdain for other people. Every advantage supposedly gained at the expense of others can be presented as an expression of moral perfidy. Every thoughtless comment can be interpreted as an expression of a lack of respect. Every lie told to protect someone else—or the entire organization—can be viewed as an indication of a lack of integrity. In the social dimension, it is almost impossible to escape the moralization of others. If the rules governing "good behavior" are supposed to be the same for everyone, it means that no one is safe from the moral judgment of others (regarding the universality of morality, see Besio 2018, 32).

229 Regarding the emergence of the idea of social responsibility in companies in the USA in the early 20th century, see Marens 2013.

and abstractly agree that human rights, environmental protection, justice, peace, and liberty are worth striving for (Luhmann 2014, 69f.).[230]

The need for consensus is apparent in the way values are strung together in official announcements and public conferences. Without encountering opposition, management consultants can advise organizations to demonstrate "exemplary leadership behavior," "a sense of community," and "constructive leadership." Again without encountering opposition, the heads of organizations can pledge to "eliminate destructive leadership behavior," encourage "self-critical examination of one's own leadership behavior," and "bring a stop to ineffective and inefficient measures." And at no risk to themselves, organization members can speak up at public events and call for their organization to "demonstrate confidence," "take joy in responsibility," and "strengthen personal initiative."[231] In brief, "one assumes that there is a consensus regarding values" (Luhmann 2008b, 241).[232]

The use of abstract value formulations ultimately paints a harmonious picture of an organization, one which assumes that the norms by which organizations measure themselves can be easily combined with the predominant social norms.[233] On an abstract level, everyone can agree that civic behavior on the part of organizations should involve maintaining and promoting general social values such as nature conservancy, humane working conditions, gender equality, and the preservation of individual freedom.[234]

---

230 As Bandura (1999, 206) puts it: "Almost everyone is virtuous at the abstract level."

231 These quotes are taken from an event on error culture held by a European army and attended by nearly the entire general staff. It was interesting that this feedback—in the form of value formulations from the workshops and summaries from the plenary discussions—consisted of slides produced prior to the event.

232 To put it another way: "It is striking that the communication is not about values. Rather, the validity of values is assumed" (Luhmann 1996a, 65).

233 This is clearly expressed by, e.g., Carroll 1991. Also see the error commonly made in the literature, which largely equates deviations from organizational norms with deviations from social norms. See, e.g., the definition of "organizational misbehavior" as "any intentional action by members of organizations that violates core organizational and/or societal norms" (Vardi and Wiener 1996, 151).

234 Regarding the concept of "organizational citizenship behavior" see van Dyne et al. 1994. Deviations from general social hypernorms thus appear to be deviations from organizational expectations as well. Regarding the concept of hypernorms—ultimately just another term for values—see Donaldson and Dunfee 1994.

But precisely because everyone can agree so quickly on abstract values, such values are very indeterminate points of reference for decisions. They leave it largely unclear as to which decision must be give preference over another (Luhmann 2014, 69; Luhmann 2012, 205f.; also see Groddeck 2011, 73). How should one react when the freedom to drive around in cars results in the premature deaths of thousands of people living near highways inhaling nitrogen oxides and particulate pollution? In conflict situations, should people support a war and tolerate arms exports to crisis regions in an effort to enforce human rights? When it comes to making concrete decisions, being guided by values—as opposed to programs—leads to a number of very practical contradictions.

What effects emerge when these generally accepted and harmonious-sounding values are charged with certain moral demands?

The Concretion Suggestion of Morality

Moral arguments make use of generally accepted values, but they also suggest that the proclaimed values should lead to very specific actions.[235] When the critics of private vehicles with combustion engines demand stricter environmental protections, they are drawing on a value largely shared by drivers. The issue becomes moralized, however, if they subsequently insist that people should refrain from using private vehicles at all. By proclaiming general values and then demanding a specific morality, moral campaigners postulate a concretization of values that many people will not find convincing. As a result of this

---

235 The importance of shared values in moral communication can be demonstrated with a simple experiment. Individuals will quickly face social isolation if they fail to draw on generally shared values when communicating their own ideas of morality. This would be immediately apparent if someone in the Taliban-controlled parts of Afghanistan, in Shia-dominated Iran, or in the evangelic communities of the southern United States enthusiastically argued for the right to sexual self-determination. It would be equally apparent if Taliban supporters, radical Iranian Shiites, or evangelical Americans claimed that homosexuality was a sin during a panel discussion in Sweden, in a liberal religious congregation in the Netherlands, or at a university in the northeastern United States. For an analysis of somewhat more innocuous topics, such as keeping dogs as pets and doing the laundry, see Chaudhary 2006.

suggested concretization, moralization can lead to fierce debates even if (almost) everyone actually agrees on the values from which the moral guiding principles have been derived.

The proclamation of moral values is an expression of esteem or disdain toward others (regarding the communication of esteem in general, see Luhmann 1995b, 235; Luhmann 1990b, 18; Luhmann 2012, 239; Luhmann 2008c, 102ff.). By taking a moral stance, individuals can present themselves as "worthy of esteem" or test the reaction of others to see who "deserves esteem." Moralization can also be used to "trap others in the net of the conditions for esteem in order to carry them off in it" or leave them stuck in a sea of moral demands (according to Luhmann 1995b, 156).

Esteem is a way of honoring others for behaving in the way that one believes is right. Appreciation is the currency awarded to those whose words and deeds are in accord with one's own moral values (Luhmann 1995b, 235). Recognition is given to people who are consistent in their thoughts, feelings, and actions and whose actual behavior aligns with their proclaimed values, even in the face of resistance (Palanski and Yammarino 2007).

When moral demands are made of others, the appeal to a common good may conceal personal interests (Luhmann 2013, 277ff.). The people making the appeal may present themselves as representatives of "the big picture," the "previously disregarded," or even "future generations" (see Luhmann 2017a, xxxi). This (inevitably communicative) abstraction from the interests of the person making the moral argument is what gives moral demands their power when appeals are made to others. It is difficult for someone to communicatively evade a moral demand without being suspected of selfish motives (Besio 2013, 316).

Moralization as Personalization

The demand for integrity management based on widely shared morals personalizes the issue of rule violations in organizations to an unprecedented degree. When laws are violated, this is then attributed to a "lack of morals," "lack of backbone," or "moral backwardness" on the part of the people blamed for breaking the rules.

Observers may acknowledge that people in organizations always act in their roles as organization members, but even in these roles, they are expected to oppose any demands considered immoral. Calculated violations of the law and creative rule deviance are thus interpreted not as necessarily flexible actions in the context of informal role expectations, but as a contemptible weaknesses of a person's character.

Furthermore, moralization leads to the implication that an individual's behavior in their role as an organization member is a reflection of their personal integrity as a whole. Anyone who breaks the law in their role as an organization member will thus be suspected of not taking rules seriously in any of their other roles. If someone tortures others in their role as an organization member, the fact that they might be a caring mother or loving father outside of the organization will not make up for it.[236] Morally objectionable behavior "contaminates" individuals not as organization members, but as people in their entirety (Fuchs 2010, 18).

But what is the concrete effect of moralization in organizations?

7.3 Morally Charged Cultural Programs as an Incitement to Hypocrisy

The fact that values fail to offer any concrete points of reference for decisions is not, in itself, a problem for organizations. Once an organization member has cast off the idealism of the newcomer, they quickly learn to accept that the noble values extolled externally by the organization have very little to do with the actual decision-making within it. In light of the popular value of "authenticity," it may sound reasonable for senior executives to demand that organization

---

236 Holocaust researchers have spent decades investigating this issue; for just one example, see the concept of doubling developed by Robert Jay Lifton 1986.

members say what they think and do what they say. But at the same time, it is clear to everyone that the relationship between what is thought, what is said and what is done is fairly loose in organizations (see Brunsson 1989).

Problems always arise when an organization increases the moral pressure on its members—for instance, after a scandal involving broken rules or laws. This is because demanding that organization members gear themselves toward integrity does not mean they will behave in a more moral way. Morality is not like a trivial machine where you can insert the demand for a morally guided approach on one side and have moral behavior emerge from the other.

Various empirical studies have raised serious doubts about whether codes of ethics, moral codes, and guiding principles actually lead to fundamental behavioral changes in organizations (see, e.g., the early analysis by Cressey and Moore 1983 or Weaver 1984).[237] Hardly any organization member could name a situation in which they were able to change a behavior by invoking a code of ethics (Schwartz 2001, 247). Organization members report that such codes do little to help them fend off demands for deviant behavior (Badaracco and Webb 1995, 10). Organization members regularly take ethical aspects into account when making decisions, but these decisions are not influenced by the organization's ethical guidelines—in fact, they sometimes contradict them (Cleek and Leonard 1998, 628f.).[238]

The main effect of integrity campaigns is that employees portray their behavior differently in workshops and at conferences. They quickly realize that, because the organization has been morally charged by the management, they can no longer present their actions as being merely compliant, efficient and innovative, they must also be morally exemplary. Everyone knows there is an "immoral world" in the organi-

---

237 However, see the much more optimistic analyses by, e.g., Bowman 1981 and Benson 1989.
238 There is a great deal of empirical evidence to back this up. For example, see the organizational studies of banks which show that account managers are taught in ethics workshops not to "rip off" customers purchasing financial products—particularly widows and orphans—but are then expected to demonstrate precisely this type of behavior in order to meet ambitious sales goals.

zation, but integrity campaigns compel them to publicly act as though they lived in a "moral world." Campaigns meant to promote integrity produce precisely what they actually want to prevent: hypocrisy.[239]

Hypocrisy Instead of Conflict:
The Effects of Moral Communication in Organizations

It may initially come as a surprise to find that moral campaigns lead to hypocrisy. After all, empirical research has shown that the foremost result of morally charged communication is conflict (see Luhmann 2012, 244). Morally charged encounters lead to "over-engagement by the participants" which often results in conflicts that can barely be contained (Luhmann 1990b, 26). "When one believes they are morally on the right side," according to Niklas Luhmann (2008d, 349), "there is little reason to attempt to reach an understanding. Then the only aim can be to help the good cause achieve victory, even using ever more severe means."

This potential for conflict relating to morals is why many family get-togethers are governed by the rule that religious and political topics will not be discussed. The "pseudoethical dogmatism" in such conflicts leads people to cast themselves in a morally "good" light while others appear morally "bad"—a description that the others often will not readily accept. There is, therefore, a great danger that the personal esteem or disdain expressed in these situations will lead to unlimited conflict. This is because "open moralizing" is always a more or less risky "invitation to conflict" (Luhmann 2008c, 112).

A few organizations face serious conflicts because the topics they deal with are charged with questions of esteem and disdain. We need look no further than self-governing enterprises, grassroots religious organizations, and political parties. Because their members identify so closely with the goals of the organization, all economic, religious, and political topics are viewed through the lens of their members' lifestyle.

---

239 See Coffee 1977, 1099ff. who argues that moral reactions to rule deviance are often not just inefficient but actually counterproductive.

The moral conflicts that result from this can be so serious that organizations will frequently split apart because of them. Through moralization, the material conflicts found in every organization become identity conflicts in which everything is on the line for the members. Because their members are largely on an equal footing with each other, these organizations have no efficient mechanism for stopping the escalation of conflicts charged with questions of esteem or disdain.[240]

In most organizations with a basic hierarchical structure, however, moralization leads not to conflict but to hypocrisy. The reason for this is the considerable formal power symmetry in these organizations. If the head of an organization, as defined by its formal hierarchy, announces that all organization members must now adhere to society's current mainstream values, it is usually not advisable for members to take this as an opportunity to express their personal disdain toward people higher than them in the hierarchy for having violated moral standards (also see Jackall 1988, 6). Morally charged comments about behavior in the organization tend to be made in the members' backstage area, while the officially proclaimed values are followed on the front stage.

The hypocrisy demanded by programs for value-centered organizational leadership and integrity-oriented management is functional for organizations. Organizational research has shown that no organization can survive without a certain degree of hypocrisy (Brunsson 1989, 194ff.; also see Brunsson 1986; Brunsson 1993). Every company, administration, hospital, political party, and non-governmental organization is forced to present a spruced-up version of itself to its environment (see Kühl 2013, 138ff.). Hypocrisy—as harsh as it may sound to practitioners—is simply the established term in the field of organizational studies for the sprucing-up of an organization's display side.

At the same time, hypocrisy is a long-term investment in the morality nurtured in organizations (March 1978, 604).[241] Organizations are

---

240 Moralization in organizations such as these has been relatively well researched; see, e.g., the classic study by Freeman 1972 on the tyranny of structurelessness. For an overview, see Parker et al. 2013 and Meyers 2013.

241 Specifically: "Hypocrisy is a long-run investment in morality made at some cost (the chance that, in fact, action might otherwise adjust to morals)" (March 1978, 604).

The Moralization of the Organization **183**

aware that they would be ruined if their members consistently followed the moral standards they proclaimed. Through hypocrisy, moral standards are maintained as part of the organization's display side, but a high degree of deviation from these standards is tolerated within the organization. Hypocrisy therefore supports the proclaimed morality because, for all that they may deviate from it, organization members are forced to pledge themselves to it.[242]

But there are good reasons to leave it to specialists to carry out this organizational sprucing-up, which is needed to produce legitimacy. It is a key component of the job descriptions of managing directors, marketing experts, and press officers to construct a convincing façade for the organization, maintain it, and repair it if necessary. But if the head of an organization demands vocal professions of moral integrity from every employee, this blocks the necessary debates within the organization. Integrity then becomes an abstract formula everyone must profess if they want to have a career in the organization.

The Emergence of Censorship Mechanisms

Moralization in organizations leads to censorship effects. In their opening remarks at events on integrity or error culture, organization heads like to announce that "everything can be laid out on the table." They explain that their "doors are always open" to employees who witness rule violations or law-breaking in the organization. They also claim that "everything can be discussed openly." But organization members would be naïve to heed this call for openness. Everyone knows that organizational events focusing on morality, integrity, and error culture always have both an official and an unofficial agenda. Officially, the organization is signaling that it expects straight talk and frank discussion of the reasons for rule violations. Unofficially, however, there are very precise

---

242 The thinking behind this is echoed in the famous maxim by perhaps the best-known moralist of the early modern era, François de La Rochefoucauld: "L'hypocrisie est un hommage que le vice rend à la vertu."—"Hypocrisy is a tribute vice pays to virtue."

norms governing what may and may not be said, and employees unfamiliar with them would cause a great deal of consternation.

At corporate quality management workshops, everyone knows that the management wants to hear one success story after another, and that anyone who openly discusses potentially prosecutable procurement "tricks" or the illegal use of company premises will face pressure, not only from their colleagues but also (and especially) from the company's executives. At events focusing on error culture in the military, it is clear to everyone that façades of formality will be presented to the senior leadership, and if a regimental commander openly points out the existence of fundamental problems, the other attendees will joke during the coffee break that military intelligence had probably already come for her.

Three effects usually come into play at events on integrity and morality. The first effect is the retreat to general value formulations. Values that can be easily professed by anyone are bandied about in every organization: collegiality, integrity, creativity, trust, and openness. If someone does not want to remain totally silent at an event on error culture, moral management or organizational integrity, they can always just celebrate the values generally cultivated by the organization. Observers can easily get the impression that they are participating in something like a religious service, in which one participant after another publicly professes their commitment to the organization's current list of values.

The second effect is the celebration of rule compliance. The monotonous repetition of this refrain suggests that organizations can function on the basis of formal principles geared toward noble moral values. If rule deviance is addressed at all, then it is only discussed in terms of how it must be prevented in the future. Everyone is aware that it is necessary to surreptitiously skirt around official channels, ignore organizational programs, and modify goals without consulting with the hierarchy—but at these events, they pretend that these everyday forms of rule-breaking are not really necessary for the organization.

The third effect is the retreat to innocuous topics. If pressure builds at an event for everyone to "put their cards on the table," then harmless topics will be addressed. Instead of mentioning tricks for manipulating procurement processes, using prohibited tools, or regularly exceeding established working hours as examples relevant to error culture, participants will discuss risk-free topics such as vaccinations that have yet to be carried out, untidy social spaces, or broken disinfection facilities in the showers. We see the same distraction techniques in documents submitted to auditors and tax authorities, which draw attention to minor inconsistencies in order to distract from more serious irregularities.

This avoidance of critical topics in an interaction is referred to by scholars as a taboo or, more precisely, a "latency of communication." In the terminology of systems theory, it entails a "lack of specific themes to enable and steer communication" (Luhmann 1995b, 335). Nearly everyone is aware of the sensitive topics, but this situation can only be addressed with great difficulty, if at all. It is an "open secret" that problematic topics must not be spoken of. Particularly at events focusing on morality and integrity, one often gets the impression that there is a rather loud "conspiracy of silence" at play (Luhmann 1964b, 281).[243]

There are undoubtedly good reasons for the formation of these chatty circles of silence in morally charged organizations. Informal censorship mechanisms are "structurally functional" for an organization (see Luhmann 1995b, 336) because formal interactions would otherwise be overloaded with too much critical information. The plausible assumption here is that this kind of information is almost impossible to address in formal interaction formats such as training events, workshops and conferences.

7.4 Accepting the Functionality of Rule Deviance

Formal attempts to introduce "open communication" in organizations—under the heading of "moral integrity"—quite often lead to morally charged informal counter-reactions. While formal cultural

---

243 Regarding the police, see, e.g., the older research by Westley 1956; for more recent works, also see Skolnick 2002 and Rothwell and Baldwin 2007.

programs make allowances for organization members to profess their commitment to the official moral code at workshops and conferences, similar behavior outside of these settings is frequently morally condemned. The members who engage in such behavior are referred to as "boot-lickers," "brown-nosers" or "toadies" who "kiss up" to their superiors with demonstrative professions of morality while simultaneously violating their proclaimed moral principles and punching down or even to the side.[244]

The only way of addressing rule deviance in organizations in a formal context is to consistently remove morality from the equation. Instead of tying everyday rule deviance to issues of personal esteem or disdain by proclaiming moral codes, de-moralization—and the associated de-personalization—allows rule deviance to be traced back more systematically to informal behavioral expectations in organizations.

De-personalizing rule deviance makes it possible to create at least a few communicative niches in which specific rule deviations can be discussed. In these safe spaces, employees can talk about the functionalities and dysfunctionalities of rule deviance without the respective violations immediately being tied to personal shortcomings on account of on morally charged communication from above.

However, this process of de-moralization is complicated by the fact that the pressure to establish moral communication in organizations has increased significantly. The heads of organizations can be prosecuted under civil or criminal law not only if they violate their formal supervisory duties, but also if they allow their organization to develop a culture of rule deviance. The arguments have grown louder for holding organization heads responsible not just for gaps in their organization's formal structure, but also for the toxic effects of informal structures (for some early deliberations on this, see, e.g., Bucy 1991).

Attempts to influence organizational culture by means of codes of ethics and integrity campaigns are not only ineffective, they are actually often counterproductive due to the censorship effects associated with

---

244 Regarding the emergence of "special moralities" in organizations, see Luhmann 1995b, 234f.

them. But organization leaders can also use them as evidence of having done everything they could to counteract an organizational culture that encourages employees to break the law.

The pressure to demonstrate legitimacy means organizations have very limited options for self-regulating the intensity with which they want to engage in inward moralization. For example, organizations under extreme legitimization pressure following a rule deviance scandal are almost forced to demonstrate their "good moral character" by introducing codes of ethics and integrity campaigns. But these then become the organizations that have the least success addressing serious legal violations and rule deviance because of the censorship effects associated with moralization.

8.
Managing Rule Compliance and Rule Deviance: A Summary

"Would locks ever have reached their present degree of excellence had there been no thieves? Would the making of bank-notes have reached its present perfection had their been no forgers? Would the microscope have found its way into the sphere of ordinary commerce [...] but for trading frauds? Does not practical chemistry owe just as much to the adulteration of commodities and the efforts to show it up as to the honest zeal for production? [...] And if one leaves the sphere of private crime: would the world market ever have come into being but for national crime? Indeed, would even the nations have arisen? And has not the Tree of Sin been at the same time the Tree of Knowledge ever since the time of Adam?"

Karl Marx (2010b, 309f.) in
"Digression: (on productive labour)" from 1862–1863

Beyond the popular condemnation of legal violations and rule deviance following scandals, we find an initially surprising trend in the management literature, namely, the glorification of rule deviance in organizations. There is talk of "pattern breakers" who stray from an organization's set paths at great risk to themselves (Kaduk et al. 2013), "organizational rebels" who defy an organization's formal demands (Kelly and Medina 2014), and "corporate revolutionaries" who break open established structures (Peters 1988). The apparent recipe for success of the "greatest managers in the world" is that they "break all the rules" (Buckingham und Coffman 1999), and the "real creativity" that produces pioneering changes in society is supposedly always based on violating rules (Farson 1997, 103).

Stories circulate of pattern breakers, organizational rebels, and corporate revolutionaries whose rule violations were what made fundamental innovations possible in the first place. In the computer industry, heroic tales are told of programmers and engineers who developed computers—without approval from their superiors and working just on the edge of legality—that later proved to be far more advanced than the company's official developments (see Kidder 1981). In automotive companies, the stories that get told are not those in which careful planning on the part of the executive board led to the development of a new car, but rather those in which an engineer working without the knowledge of board, and in part against its explicit instructions, developed a passenger car with four-wheel drive (see Ewing 2017, 40f.). And in armies, the battles that were won thanks to the ingenuity of the senior leadership are not mythicized like those that were decided because commanders on the ground defied orders (regarding Nelson at the battle of Copenhagen, see Pope 2001).

All of the criticism of organizations exhibiting a mania for order and frenzy for regulations is accumulated in this enthusiasm for pattern breakers, organizational rebels, and corporate revolutionaries. The argument here is that bureaucratic requirements and rigid hierarchies prevent organization members from "developing initiative" and "working creatively," and that it takes courage to oppose restrictive formal structures (Bosetzky 2019, 38). Pattern breakers, organizational rebels, and corporate revolutionaries are presented as the antithesis of the pedants, nitpickers, and formalists who have dominated an organization for far too long.

It makes little sense, however, to legalistically glorify the concepts of "pattern breakers," "organizational rebels," and "corporate revolutionaries," as management literature typically does. Put simply, management literature suggests that patterns can be broken in organizations when organizational rebels gain a consensus for their approach, their carefully planned organizational revolution is reviewed for legal compliance by the organization's own lawyers, and the rebellious approach is then translated into new formal specifications so that all pattern breakers, organizational rebels, and corporate revolutionaries can be sure that they are formally on the right side. To borrow a witticism attributed to Lenin, the image here is of an organization member who first buys a train ticket before kicking off a revolution—strictly within the bounds of legality, of course.

What is overlooked here is that the pattern breakers, organizational rebels, and corporate revolutionaries glorified in the management literature not only produce innovations just on the edge of what is allowed, they also continuously violate formal rules and state laws. The way patterns get broken is not by organization members first running their ideas by the compliance department, getting the blessing of the senior management, and finally having their ideas translated into new formal rules. Instead, members experiment in the gray zone between legality and illegality, they leave their superiors largely in the dark about what they are planning, and new practices are first introduced in the shadow of the organization's existing formal structure.

8.1 Rule Compliance and Rule Deviance as Management Proverbs

Herbert A. Simon (1946, 53; 1957, 20) noted early on that the principles of management heralded up and down the land function like proverbs. For every seemingly wise saying, we can find a similarly plausible saying that claims the exact opposite. Should someone seeking a relationship follow the maxim of "birds of a feather flock together," or the principle of "opposites attract"? Is it the "early bird" who "catches the worm," or the "second mouse" who "gets the cheese"?

For every proverb pronounced by a management consultant, according to Simon, there will be a proverb from another consultant recommending the opposite (see Pfeffer and Sutton 2006, 34ff.). Should organizations follow the plausible suggestion of consultants who recommend flattening hierarchies in order to extend the spans of control of individual managers, or should they follow the recommendation to keep spans of control relatively small to ensure that managers are always accessible, even if this necessarily involves an increase in hierarchical levels?

In the management literature, the debate about rule compliance and rule breaking has largely degenerated into the propagation of one proverb over another. Some condemn the tendency to break rules as a "fundamental evil" and demand more "integrity" in organizations, while others dismiss the fixation on rule compliance as "bureaucratism" and praise the "pattern breakers" and "rebels" who intelligently ignore the rules.

In many cases, contradictory principles are demanded of the same person. Managers will often give speeches in which they express demands—in laboriously concealed terms—that their employees both comply with and deviate from the rules. On the one hand, they emphasize that members should obviously adhere to state laws and the organization's internal rules. But on the other hand, members are expected to show "personal initiative," "independent thought," and "adaptability." And they must understand that behind these terms is an expectation that to achieve the organization's goals, they will have to push against the limits of what is allowed—and sometimes go past them. "Creativity" and "flexibility" are just "pleasant-sounding formulas" for "passing on the risk of illegality further down the line" (Luhmann 1964b, 305).

This places organization members in a permanent quandary regarding rule compliance and deviance. They are supposed to intervene if they become aware of illegal practices or legal violations, but they cannot always bring a stop to the violations because these are often extremely functional for the organization. Supervisors in an airplane factory are responsible for compliance with the formal order and are therefore obligated to strictly prohibit the use of taps, but they are also supposed to ensure that their teams meet their deadlines—even if it means using a tap to do so (Bensman and Gerver 1963, 590ff.). On the one hand, a hospital board is responsible for adherence to formally specified processes, but on the other hand, it has to trust in its doctors and nurses because it cannot control every step of the treatment process. The board must rely on the doctors and nurses not to "foul their own nest," and the doctors and nurses expect in return that the hospital board will overlook the occasional useful rule deviation (Kühl 2007a, 269ff.).

Organization members will inevitably hit a wall if this decision-making quandary forces them to play only the formal card or only the informal one. If they consistently ignore seemingly constrictive rules, they will soon cross the organization's line for tolerance and be told in no uncertain terms that there are limits to creative rule interpretation. But if they consistently try to prevent rule deviance, the organization would become so inflexible that it would collapse.

In light of this quandary, organization members are in great need of guidance. In which situations should they slavishly follow the rules, and in which cases can they occasionally ignore them? Which positions in the organization must adhere to the rules, and which need to tolerate deviation? When must they strictly follow the rules, and when are there more opportunities to break them?

8.2 Rules of Thumb for Managing Useful and Non-Useful Illegality

The problem is that every decision regarding rule compliance or deviance always involves advantages and disadvantages.[245] In some respects, a willingness to break rules can be functional for an organization, even considering the calculable risks, but in others, it can prove to be dysfunctional on account of incalculable risks. Deviance that is functional for one department can cause considerable problems for another. And a legal violation that appears to be useful at one point can lead to crisis at another.

Decisions always entail a risk of damaging the organization. If it were possible to determine what was best for an organization, there would no longer be any need to make decisions. Instead, one could simply calculate the best solution from various alternatives. Although it is impossible to calculate optimal decisions, there are rules of thumb that make it easier for organizations to maneuver between following the rules and violating them.

---

245 This insight into the coexistence of functions and dysfunctions can be found even in the early functionalist literature. See, e.g., Durkheim 1982, 119ff. or Malinowski 1960, 145ff.

Factual Issues: Sensitivity to the Effects of Structural Decisions

We now know how structural decisions in organizations increase or decrease the likelihood of legal violations and rule deviance. Imposing extensive rules in an organization almost inevitably leads to the need to break more rules. For example, increased pressure to achieve goals also increases the willingness to use means that are sometimes beyond the bounds of legality.[246] Reducing buffers in the inventory of replacement parts almost inevitably leads to the creation of "shadow warehouses" because suppliers cannot count on the just-in-time delivery of spare parts.[247]

Despite this knowledge, a remarkably formalistic perspective still constrains most deliberations on structural decisions. Intensive thought is given to how a structural decision might improve efficiency, which quality effects might be achieved, and what potential there will be for innovation, but little to no consideration is given to the informal reactions and evasive maneuvers produced by these structural decisions. This robs organizations of the opportunity to systematically reflect on whether the rule compliance and deviance produced by formal structural decisions are functional for the organization or not.

Social Issues: Different Perspectives on Rule Deviance

The division of labor means that the usefulness or non-usefulness of rule deviance will be judged differently depending on one's position in an organization. Compliance, controlling, and auditing departments that are responsible for tracking down and prosecuting rule deviance

---

246 In police research, this phenomenon is discussed in terms of "performance corruption" and "task-related rule-breaking-behavior."

247 The effect of intensified pressure to fulfill goal programs has been particularly well researched. See, e.g., Wright 1979, 67f.; Yeager 1986, 110; Baysinger 1991, 359; Vardi and Wiener 1996, 160; Cressey 2001, 183f.; Anand et al. 2005, 12; Braithwaite 2009, 217; Palmer 2012, 186; Bergmann 2014, 243. How the introduction of just-in-time delivery has affected illegal warehousing has not yet been systematically studied. Armies might be an interesting field of analysis here.

generally have little sympathy for the functionality of rule violations. Products sales units and the departments responsible for providing client services in hospitals, schools, and universities, by contrast, are tolerant of rules being stretched so that the expected services can be provided. Human resources departments are responsible for attracting and (generally) keeping employees, so they have their own approach to everyday rule deviance in organizations. These departments with their different perspectives inevitably come into conflict with one another because each of them wants to assert its interests, even at the cost of other departments if necessary.[248]

Traditional management theory tends to consider these interdepartmental conflicts as problematic and thus prescribes intensive conflict management training for the parties involved. But conflicts like these are vitally important, because they are a platform for the contradictory demands of an organization's environment to be represented by different departments with their own local rationalities. Conflicts are what sensitize organizations to the contradictions and changes in their environment (regarding this argument, see Kraatz and Block 2008, 247f.; Pache and Santos 2010, 460f.). Therefore, the outcome of debates between departments must not be a "homogeneity of convictions." The danger of "overlooking" or "suppressing" signals would be too great. Instead, the aim should be to preserve the "diversity" produced by the organization in the context of a "civilized peacefulness" to be guaranteed by the organization (Luhmann 1996b, 45).

Temporal Issues: "Right" and "Wrong" Times for Rule Deviance

Whether a rule deviation comes to be viewed as generally useful or non-useful in negotiations between departments can change over time. For example, the external imposition of a growing number of rules can lead to the formation of largely tolerated patterns of controlled

---

248 These different and conflicting goals have been explored particularly in the coalition theory of Richard Cyert and James March (1963).

rule violation, while tolerance for rule violations decreases significantly following scandals or disasters caused by broken rules or laws.

Because attitudes continually change, organizations have the "right to revoke" both the tolerance and prevention of rule deviance at any time. Something that was tolerated yesterday might no longer be tolerated tomorrow. It is, therefore, necessary for "renegotiations" to take place regularly to establish just how far members are allowed to deviate from an organization's rules (Luhmann 1996b, 44).

Defining the Reference Problems

Whether a rule deviation is useful or non-useful always depends on what the reference problem is thought to be. Are individual departments supposed to optimize their performance even it involves breaking organizational rules, or are they supposed to adapt to the specifications of the organization through strict rule compliance? Does the organization aim for short-term profit maximization through aggressive tactics on the edge of legality, or for the long-term establishment of social legitimacy through strict adherence to the law?

It is hard to answer these questions because different departments and positions in an organization will necessarily identify very different reference problems. Organizations must therefore permanently negotiate which reference problems are to be considered critical. These negotiations usually take place in formally established communication settings. Workshops are held to discuss new strategic orientations, large conferences take place in which organizations position themselves between contradictory demands, and crisis meetings are called to define approaches to current problems. But what makes any discussion of the usefulness or non-usefulness of legal violations and rule deviance challenging is that such discussions evade the usual communicative methods of access and formal negotiation mechanisms.

Organizations face a fundamental dilemma. On the one hand, they need to openly discuss whether a rule deviation makes sense for the organization. This is the only way to determine whether an organizational problem can be solved through more or less intelligent rule deviation, or whether the deviation would only benefit individual people, meaning that better solutions compatible with the organization's formal structure might be found. On the other hand, one of the major weaknesses of functional rule deviance and useful illegality is that they can hardly ever be discussed openly in organizations (see Luhmann 1964b, 313). Almost everyone is aware of the functional rule deviance and useful illegalities, but in official settings it is not possible to talk about whether they should be accepted as the best solution, or if there might be more sensible approaches that are compatible with the organization's formal structure.

Despite the permanent threat of censorship effects, what options are available for discussing these issues in at least a limited way?

8.3 Addressing What Cannot be Addressed

There are good reasons for taboos to be carefully preserved by everyone involved in an interaction. Taboos prevent organizations from being communicatively overloaded because they remove items from the agenda that cannot be publicly addressed by the organization. All communication inside and outside of organizations relies on this form of structural protection, which prevents interactions from breaking apart (see Luhmann 1995b, 337).[249]

The effect of this structural protection can be tested in a simple experiment. One must simply raise the issue of an organization's central taboos in a confidential discussion, and then bring them up at a larger official gathering with participants from various departments and hierarchical levels. The need for structural protection will be apparent

---

249 This form of structural protection can be found not only in organizations, but also in protest movements, small groups, and families. For an example of the effects of breaking a taboo surrounding sexual abuse at a family gathering, see the film *The Celebration* (1998) by Thomas Vinterberg.

from the resulting awkward silence, attempts to repair the interaction, and even termination of the interaction.

What options do organizations have for occasionally neutralizing this interactional, structural protection so that taboos can be discussed in a controlled way?

Choice of Topics

In the factual dimension, it is important to carefully consider which topics might be amenable to discourse. Calling for "everything to be laid on the table" is the surest way of preventing exactly this from happening, because such a clumsy invitation tells everyone that the speaker has no sense of how taboos work in organizations. Flagging up a discussion in which rule violations will be directly mentioned usually leads to censorship mechanisms. Nowhere are the actual processes in an organization less likely to be discussed than in error culture workshops which encourage organizations to go on the offensive against everyday rule deviance.

Functional rule deviance and useful illegality must, therefore, be approached in a circuitous way. Interaction sequences must not focus on everyday rule deviance but instead on a factual issue currently of concern to the organization: How can we improve conditions for sales? What options do we have for streamlining administrative processes? How can we reduce the number of accidents in the organization? These fairly generalized topics can then lead to a discussion of everyday rule deviance without there being any direct pressure to uncover such deviance.

By euphemizing rule deviance, one can regulate how openly a topic will be discussed. "Useful illegality" is suitable as an abstract term for generating interest in the phenomenon or for relieving the pressure on organization members who feel they might be the only ones who occasionally ignore prescribed processes. "Functional rule deviance," by contrast, makes it more possible to talk about concrete violations of the rules in one's own organization. "Creative rule interpretation in the interest of the organization" will let most people know that rule violations are being discussed, but organization members can always retreat to the position that only operate within the realm of what is allowed. Phrases such as "using leeway" or "agile maneuvers" conceal the phenomenon of rule deviance to such an extent that these have become almost universally accepted value formulas for public speeches. Open questions are a means of allowing interlocutors to decide for themselves whether they want to maintain communication latency or bring up critical aspects.

The willingness of interlocutors to reveal information about rule deviance can be increased if someone carefully mediates between their discussions and mentions that juicy details have already been brought up elsewhere. The most important thing here is not just to hunt down rule deviance like a detective, but to look at the reasons for it. Why are the official processes defined by an organization not compatible with everyday practices?

Guaranteeing anonymity is critical when this information is processed further. It is important to communicatively cover one's tracks to ensure that critical content cannot be traced back to individuals. Instead of openly saying that information comes from Ms. Smith or Mr. Jones, it makes sense to use formulas such as "we've heard that..." or "it's said that...".

Choosing Interlocutors

In the social dimension, it comes down to reducing censorship mechanisms by carefully choosing the participants and setting for a discussion. Experience has shown that censorship mechanisms in organizations kick in at the latest when different hierarchical levels are together in one room. The presence of two levels of hierarchy will not necessarily trigger censorship mechanisms, but in the presence of three levels, it is almost always impossible to address sensitive topics. This is particularly apparent when senior executives "beam down" from headquarters to attend a discussion. Bringing together multiple departments can also be problematic as a first step because one department may try to keep up appearances for the others. For example, a department may openly discuss creative solutions to the conflict between fast customer delivery and high quality, but it will be understandably reticent to involve the head of quality management in this discussion.

To disable these censorship mechanisms at least occasionally, it is important to create a setting for discussions that resembles informal exchanges in the organization. What is interesting about confidential one-on-ones between co-workers, coffee breaks with colleagues, and after-work drinks at a bar is that relatively realistic descriptions of an organization can circulate without censorship effects in these informal interactions. This has to do with the fact that the pressure on the participants in these contexts is the exact opposite of formal contexts. If an administrative employee aggressively professed her commitment to the organization's current code of ethics during a coffee break, her colleagues would be extremely taken aback. If a soldier insisted during a nightly drinking bout that his unit always had to comply with the regulations, his naïve formalism would isolate him from his comrades. In brief, the act of sticking to an organization's official line is delegitimized in informal interaction settings. Instead, there is considerable pressure to demonstrate that a member knows "how things really work" in the organization.

To process and discuss taboos, it is critical to think carefully about who to involve in a discourse strategy. One-on-one discussions are most likely to generate a sense of openness. The promise of confidentiality makes it possible to talk about everyday functional rule deviations. In discussions with multiple participants, it is important for these participants to be on the same level of hierarchy if possible and from the same team or department. In this setting, signs of fatigue with the phrase-mongering accepted in more official settings will become apparent and interactional pressure to open up will be created.

The critical point is for the aspects raised in smaller settings to then be brought up in larger discussions. If an organization plans to address sensitive topics in a larger group of participants from different departments and hierarchical levels, these talks must be carefully prepared by means of exploratory conversations with individual interlocutors to identify sensitive aspects in advance and develop strategies for dealing with them. When larger discussions are carried out, safe public sub-groups should be created to address the aspects identified in the exploratory talks, the results of which can then be fed back in anonymized form to the large group. Critical comments then do not have to be presented as an individual's personal position, but rather as the joint findings from the work of the smaller group.

When these critical aspects are addressed, it can be necessary to pull in external support. This may be surprising at first glance, because the presence of consultants almost automatically triggers the usual mechanisms for smoothing over and sprucing up an organization for "non-members" (see Luhmann 1964b, 108ff.). But external support is required to make it possible to discuss taboos at all in a larger group. Since organization members always risk being informally or even formally excluded from the organization if they talk about taboos, external participants are needed who can handle being repelled by the organization's communicative immune system when taboos are discussed.

The Sequence of Interactions

The temporal dimension must also be taken into account when planning interactions. There are always points of time in organizations when, despite the most careful planning, it is not possible to discuss critical aspects. If an executive has raised his profile by restructuring an organization, it is essentially impossible to point out the undesired side effects of this restructuring—namely, new forms of rule deviance. If an organization has rebuilt its reputation so that everything is "okay again" after a scandal surrounding a legal violation, it is not possible to point out the continued existence of functional rule deviance and legal violations.

When a window does open up for a controlled discussion of functional rule deviance and useful illegalities, the timing of such interactions is important. It is generally advisable to get a feel for the situation through confidential one-on-one conversations. The sequence of these conversations can play an important role. Sometimes it makes sense to first talk with the individuals responsible for monitoring the rules to determine the formal conditions before taking a closer look at regular rule deviations in conversation with the individuals responsible for operations. But sometimes it can make sense to first identify the everyday rule violations through conversations, observation interviews, or participatory observation and then hear from the rule monitors in individual discussions.

Workshops for discussing rule deviance with multiple participants can also be productive. It is important to think about how closely spaced the workshops should be, however. Sometimes it makes sense to give the participants an opportunity to talk with each other between the workshops. But sometimes it can also make sense to conduct multiple, parallel workshops to confirm that cases of rule deviance were observed at the same time and to record evaluations of them.

8.4 Escaping the Prince of Homburg Dilemma

Organization members permanently face the same problem confronted by the Elector of Brandenburg when the Prince of Homburg disobeyed his orders: Should obvious insubordination always be punished? Or should a refusal to obey orders be ignored in light of the success of the rule-breaker (at least in the short term)? Or do organizations have options for responding that go beyond this black-and-white scenario?

One ingenious solution would be for the Elector to subsequently act as though he had secretly given the Prince of Homburg the order to attack. The advantage of this approach for the Elector is that he could wait to see the effects of his subordinate's personal initiative. If the attack failed, he could blame the prince and punish him for it. If it succeeded, the suggestion that an order had indeed been given could legitimize the attack after the fact.

Another more drastic solution would be for the Elector to praise the Prince of Homburg for his initiative and his courage but simultaneously sentence him to death for insubordination. The executed prince could then be buried with the highest award for bravery pinned to his chest—not least to placate his family. This is certainly an elegant solution for the Elector, but it carries serious personal consequences for the prince. This solution would probably effectively result in working to rule, because few would be willing to risk the death penalty just to be praised for their personal initiative.

A third, more elegant solution is available, however. The Elector could publicly sentence the prince to a relatively mild punishment but privately acknowledge his courage. Furthermore, after an acceptable period, the Elector could pardon the prince and eventually even publicly promote him. The promotion would not be officially attributed to the success of the prince's insubordination; instead, the Elector would count on his subordinates to assume that he was willing not just to tolerate rule deviance in the interest of the organization, but actually to reward it. This is the only way to explain the careers of some military figures.

Heinrich von Kleist opted for a dramatic happy ending to his play. The Elector of Brandenburg is outraged by the insubordination and has the prince arrested and sentenced to death. After a long back and forth—plays need to be certain length, after all—the prince admits he was wrong to disobey orders and accepts the death penalty. This enables the Elector to pardon him after all, because the prince's remorse has restored the legitimacy of the chain of command.

Of course, one could argue that it is the job of a senior leader to create a framework of rules which makes all forms of deviance superfluous. It is often said that the goal must be to precisely analyze rule violations, disruptions, disasters resulting from minor toxic rule deviations, and the regular subversion of orders so that a binding and functional formal framework for action can be established. This argument may be commendably idealistic, but it is also extremely naïve. Organizations operate in a complex and contradictory environment that makes it impossible to plan the "right behavior" for all situations by means of a consistent set of formal rules.

The professional skills of organization members include the ability to manage the tension between the prevention and tolerance of rule deviance. Organization members must develop a sense for which rules must be slavishly obeyed in the organization and which ones can be dealt with more "creatively." They must also determine just how far rules can acceptably be stretched or transgressed, and when such transgressions must be prevented through more or less indirect warnings. Mastering the permanent oscillation between formality and informality is ultimately what distinguishes a good organization member.

Appendix:
Theoretical and Methodological Considerations

Concept behind the Book

This book is part of a larger project on defining organizational cultures (see Kühl 2018a). Contrary to the fairly broad and breezy definition of organizational culture that currently dominates the discourse, I work with a very precise definition of organizational culture based on a systems theory perspective. Organizational cultures—or informal structures—are a complex of undecided decision premises. They comprise all of the behavioral expectations in organizations that were not established by means of decisions, but that instead slowly crept into the organization. Organizational theorists refer to this as the non-decided decision premises of an organization (see Rodríguez 1991, 140f.; Rodríguez 2001, 4f.)

Practitioners accustomed to more flowery language may find this definition of organizational culture complicated at first glance, but a closer look reveals that it is actually fairly simple (Kühl 2018b).[250]

One core tenet of organizational theory is that two fundamentally different forms of structure can develop in organizations. The first form—the already decided decision premises that are central to an organization's formal structure—comprise expectations that were previously decided on the basis of legal requirements, instructions from the head of the organization, or consultation with all members of the organization. The other form of structure—the non-decided decisions premises—comprises expectations that were not decided on, but that

---

250 Institutionalized rule deviance was previously described as a part of an organization's informal structure. Today, however, the regular evasive maneuvers in organizations tend to be considered part of the organization's culture. Regarding the use of "organizational culture" and "informal structure" as synonyms, see the detailed analysis in Kühl 2018a.

emerged through frequent repetition. This is the culture of an organization.[251]

The difference between decided and non-decided expectations is a well-established distinction in various academic disciplines. In political science, formal institutions that are set out in writing and can be meaningfully shaped and changed by actors are distinguished from informal institutions that develop organically without anything being written down (regarding this distinction, see, e.g., Lauth 1999, 64f.; Helmke and Levitsky 2004, 725ff.). In the field of legal studies, a distinction is made between positive law, which is set, and customary law, which gradually develops through repetition (regarding this distinction, see Perreau-Saussine and Murphy 2007 and the early fundamental analysis by Puchta 1828).

The basic difference between these forms of structure can be illustrated with a simple example. When a city designs a park, the municipal administration decides where to place the paths. The courses of these paths set expectations as to where visitors are supposed to walk. But visitors will quickly start to beat their own paths through the park. No one makes a decision to lay these paths—they are simply created by walkers repeatedly using them. Once they have become very well-trodden, visitors may be just as expected to use these paths as they are expected to use the "official" paths laid by the city.

The books for practitioners, presentations by managers, and concepts from consultants are dominated by a romanticized and almost naïve approach to organizational culture (for a detailed analysis, see Kühl 2019a). Organizational culture is said to be a route to ensuring that an organization can significantly boost its efficiency, produce disruptive innovations, and simultaneously be a "haven of humanity" for its employees in a world otherwise plagued by "capitalist exploitation," "bureaucratic administrative ideologies," and "alienated labor."[252] The thinking here is that if all organization members identify with the same

---

251 Regarding this, see Young 1989, 201; Alvesson 2015, 278.
252 This positive view of organizational culture was inherent in the "human relations" approach, where it was referred to as informality; for examples, see Mayo 1933; Roethlisberger and Dickson 1939, or Trist and Bamforth 1951.

values, this will produce a "strong organizational culture" that will contribute significantly to the organization's success.[253] Since organizational culture is thought to enable a "collective programming of the mind," managers believe they can counter centrifugal forces and bring their organization into line (Hofstede 1980, 13).

This overlooks the fact that while some version of organizational cultural norms may be compatible with an organization's formal structure as it aligns with state laws, in many cases these norms will contradict the organization's formal norms. Organizational cultural norms are not just the expectations of collegiality and camaraderie that are compatible with an organization's formal rules, they also comprise the frequently strong expectations placed on organization members to deviate from the formal rules. This latter aspect of organizational culture is often systematically ignored in the management literature.

Empirical Approach

One way of empirically approaching rule deviance is to conduct quantitative research. This typically involves collecting quantitative data on rule deviance and legal violations and exploring correlations with an industry, for example. Another approach particularly popular with economists is to conduct quantitative surveys on rule deviance. Their questions pertain not only to the illegal behavior of the respondents themselves, but also (and especially) to the illegal behavior they observe in others. Experiments by economists and psychologists that test people's willingness to deviate from the rules have also become increasingly important.[254] I occasionally reference these studies but do not aim to

---

253 There are countless books covering this approach; for just a few examples, see Sackmann 2006; Taylor 2015; Connors and Smith 2012.

254 The obedience experiments conducted by Stanley Milgram could be viewed as a kind of precursor to this since they measured the participants' willingness to disobey orders (see the decisive studies by Milgram 1963, 1964, 1965a, 1965b). Regarding the interpretation of Milgram's experiments as a simulation of organizations, see Kühl 2005b.

systematically incorporate them into my arguments.

Another option is to conduct qualitative studies of rule deviance. This can involve questioning individuals, but it usually entails analyzing an organization. In this book, I use empirical cases only to illustrate my theoretical arguments. This means that, at most, the empirical cases serve not to prove the theories in this book but to make them plausible. I have therefore refrained from discussing the illustrative empirical data in detail in the text and instead simply cite the works that describe the collection and analysis of this empirical evidence at length.[255]

In organizational research, there is a notion that it is difficult to conduct qualitative research into rule deviance based on case studies. This is certainly not wrong. Organizations balk when researchers ask for access in order to carry out projects focusing on functional rule deviance or useful illegality. And even in the unlikely event that access is granted, mentioning the research project tends to make one's inter-locutors reluctant to provide information (see, e.g., Mars 1973, 200f.; Szwajkowski 1986, 129; Jackall 1988, 13; Punch 1996, 43f.).

Research into rule deviance is clearly hampered by the fact that structural protection mechanisms kick in when outsiders are present. When dealing with non-members (researchers included), organization members will often attempt to present their organization in a good light at first. But despite these structural protection mechanisms, there are various ways of reconstructing cases of useful and non-useful illegality in organizations.

Publicly Accessible Cases

One way of accessing empirical data—which I have made use of—is to reconstruct cases of rule deviance after they have been made public. When rule deviance leads to a devastating accident, a civil or crimi-nal lawsuit, or a media scandal, organizations usually find themselves

---

255 My approach thus differs fundamentally from that of, e.g., Jackall 1988 or Palmer 2012, who support their arguments with detailed descriptions and analyses of multiple cases.

forced to release the details of the deviance and make them at least partially publicly accessible.

The reports of parliamentary investigative committees, indictments compiled for criminal proceedings, and even in-depth coverage by journalists often reach a level of detail not found in many empirical research studies. Insights can be gained by sociologically reinterpreting the publicly available information. The greatest compliment for an organizational researcher who has interpreted data using publicly accessible information is for someone to say that their analysis must have been based on additional insider information.

Empirical Evidence from Research Projects

Empirical studies of organizations are another source I have used. Granted, organizations are not terribly eager to let researchers directly study their functional or dysfunctional rule deviations. If a researcher asks the head of an organization for permission to systematically investigate the organization's illegalities, they will usually be told that no such illegalities exist. And even if the organization's leaders were prepared to allow such an investigation, the researcher would encounter censorship mechanisms when talking with people in the organization because they would not be sure what their information would be used for.

But researchers who study organizations for other reasons always stumble across cases of rule deviance. Studies of pioneering agile organizations reveal how shadow hierarchies, which are often safeguarded by ownership structures, form outside of an organization's formally dehierarchicalized structure (see Kühl 2020). And studies of start-ups financed by venture capital almost inevitably reveal that user numbers have been manipulated to ensure the company makes it to the next round of financing (see Kühl 2005a). The information gathered in these cases is essentially the empirical by-catch of research into entirely different issues.

Various methodological tricks can be used here to track down systematic rule deviations. In lengthy participant observation studies, organization members often find it difficult to hide their rule deviance, which is why the most interesting empirical studies of rule deviance are based on this method (for the most well-known examples, see Dalton 1959; Bensman and Gerver 1963; Jackall 1988; an interesting analysis can also be found in Analoui and Kakabadse 1992). In observation interviews, observers ask their interlocutors to precisely explain every step of a work process and, in doing so, they often encounter "workarounds" used to circumvent formal regulations. Expert interviews often only make sense if the interviewer already has a very clear understanding of the illegal practices in the organization and can confront their interlocutor with the details.

Empirical Evidence from Consulting Projects

A third approach used in this book consists of acquiring empirical data from my own consulting projects (for such approaches, see, e.g., Kühl 2007a and Kühl 2007b). Detailed consulting projects almost inevitably uncover regular deviations from an organization's formal structure, or even violations of the law. The key advantage of gaining access to organizations through consulting projects as opposed to research projects is that very different approaches to gathering empirical data are possible. The heads of organizations—whether they are secretaries of state, managing directors, or CEOS—make themselves available for discussion because they are themselves interested in the outcome of the project. Written documents that would not be accessible to researchers are provided to consultants. And the organization itself often makes it possible to also elicit the views of outsiders by questioning partners or the recipients of an organization's services.

This privileged access to the field is purchased at the cost of a smaller distance from the organization being observed. Unlike participant observation (see the early analyses by Becker and Geer 1957 and by Gold 1958), the observer in an observational participation scenario changes the situation.[256] The observer's own perceptions of success and

---

256 Regarding the tradition of this type of research and problems with methodology, also see the early pioneering studies by Whyte 1943; Warner and Low 1947; Dalton 1948; and Roy 1952.

failure can therefore distort their view of the organization.

One way of reducing this distortion is to note the details of one-on-one discussions, workshops and large conferences as precisely as possible, and to save materials produced in the form of sketches, posters, and flip charts, even if the consulting process means that the observer must break with the standard ways of storing data, such as audio and video recordings.

Empirical Data from Workshops on the Topic of Useful Illegality

Interestingly, information about functional rule deviance can be gleaned from management training workshops dealing with the approach to illegalities. The first step involves presenting the participants—all of whom will ideally be on the same level of hierarchy—with a case of successful useful illegality, such as the classic case study of the formally prohibited but informally regularly tolerated use of taps in aircraft manufacturing (Bensman and Gerver 1963), and discussing it together. In the second step, the participants break up into small groups to work through typical cases of useful illegality in their own organization. In the third step, these cases are presented and discussed within the workshop as a whole.

The orchestration of this training module partially neutralizes the censorship mechanisms that would otherwise come into play. Opening the workshop by describing a case from an unfamiliar field enables the participants to discuss the functionality and dysfunctionality of rule deviance independent of their own organization. The subsequent discussion of rule deviance in their organization is facilitated by the fact that this takes place in a small group of people who are familiar with this practice. When the findings from this discussion are then presented to the rest of the workshop participants, the group itself can decide what details they want to reveal about the rule deviation. This generally leads to a discussion of fundamental issues of rule deviance in light of the cases based on the organization members' own experiences.

Personal Experience as an Organization Member

Last but not least, one's own experience in an organization can be a source of empirical data (regarding this, see Kühl 2014). Some readers may not be able to think of any cases of functional rule deviance or useful illegality in their own field. This probably has less to do with a personal propensity to follow rules and laws, and more to do with the special nature of a few positions in organizations that relieve their members of the need to transgress rules. You could view this as a positive and praise your own organization for freeing at least some of its members from having to engage in functional rule deviance. But you could also take it as an opportunity to think about how you have wound up in a position that makes even functional rule deviance unnecessary.

On account of their overregulation, universities are among the organizations whose members can very rarely get by without functional rule deviance. University members develop a tremendous respect for the professional secretaries who are able to place urgently necessary orders despite being thwarted by rigid business management software, and for the finance employees who reimburse taxi rides for lecturers even though it is officially prohibited because they understand that lecturers have to transport their own copiers and projectors to events. They come to appreciate the fact that talented undergraduates will generally be allowed to take advanced courses even without having the officially required skills profile, and that their colleagues will count these students' achievements toward their bachelor's studies. And at graduation ceremonies, they understand why exam office employees receive the loudest applause, because without their creative interpretation of the rules, hardly any student would be able to earn a degree in a formally correct way.

Anonymization of Empirical Data

I falsified data for this book. I changed the locations of organizations, moving central European organizations to northern Europe and Asian organizations to Africa. I presented interviews as if they took place with employees in organizations other than the ones I described. And sometimes I turned two organizations into three, or three into two. This was necessary to make it impossible to reconstruct which data comes from which organizations.

Granted, one could retreat to a constructivist position and claim that there is no single reality, so every description is necessarily a falsification. Data is abbreviated even in the process of collecting and recording it, and distortions occur when empirical findings are selected for presentation. However, I am not talking about these inevitable reductions, but rather about deliberately changing information.

The Dilemma of Empirical Social Research

Social researchers face a fundamental dilemma. On the one hand, they must report their findings as precisely as possible so other scientists can reconstruct their arguments in detail. This is the only way to gauge whether their conclusions are plausible and applicable to organizations in general or only to a specific type of organization. If a researcher forgoes this concretion and leaves out specific, traceable information from the cases depicted (such as the sector, size or location of a company), then the account loses density and lacks any "feeling" for the organization.

On the other hand, it is standard scientific practice to anonymize data so that the organizations that were analyzed—and, in particular, the organization members who were observed—cannot be identified. This is especially applicable when a researcher is dealing with the informal side of organizations (as is the case here), with their gray zones and not entirely kosher practices. If it is not handled carefully, sensitive data that provides insights into the informal, not entirely representable, not entirely legitimate processes of an organization can have negative consequences both for the organization as a whole—in the form of damage to its public image—and for the employees who provided the information to the researcher. In terms of research ethics, it is imperative to avoid both situations.

Rule of Thumb - If You Don't Have to Anonymize, You Haven't Found Anything Out

Put simply, one could say that if you don't have to treat your sources of data very carefully, you haven't found anything out. You have probably just observed the display side of an organization, which is visible to everyone anyway, and therefore do not need to strictly anonymize your data.

We see this effect in practitioner magazines that place great value in identifying organizations by their actual names in their articles. As a consequence, the authors are forced to censor themselves because they have to protect the organizations they have advised or studied. This is why, if you are reading a case study that forgoes anonymization, you might learn something about the organization's front stage, but you will essentially find out nothing about its backstage.

You can almost turn this into a rule of thumb for saving time when reading articles and books. With the exception of historical organizational analyses, in which the people in question are often long dead, and investigative journalism, the very purpose of which is to reveal the backstage of a specific organization, you can safely ignore any text that fails to anonymize the organizations it discusses. At best, it might tell you something about the latest management fad, pepped up with a few success stories. At worst, it will be nothing more than a PR story by a coach, consultant, or manager disguised as an account for practitioners.

The Helpful Separation between Researcher and Subject

It is essentially impossible to resolve the tension between precision and anonymization. The more detail researchers use when describing an organization to bolster their own arguments, the easier it is to identify the organization. Sometimes all it takes is a quote from a document available on the internet to reveal an organization's name. Sometimes simply mentioning an organization's size, country, or industry hints at which organization it is. Some development banks have been described in such detail in a study that even outsiders can quickly identify the organization, and insiders can easily identify the individual project managers who are mentioned. Some pioneering companies in specific fields have been described in such detail that anyone familiar with the subject matter can name the companies and identify the individual interviewees. This is helpful to researchers because they can start out by conducting follow-up studies in the same organization, but these cases do no meet the required standards of anonymization.

Granted, in many cases this tension is not virulent because there are good reasons to let the standards of anonymization slide. The worlds of scientific and non-scientific practice are so socially separated that researchers do not need to worry that the people being researched will read the scientific article in the end. If the rumor is true that the average article in a specialist journal is read by a single person, it would be surprising for this one reader to come from the organization in question.

Researchers and their subjects routinely play this game. Before an interview, the subjects profess their interest in the research, and the researchers profess their willingness to provide feedback, and both then consciously or unconsciously forget about the promised feedback. How many doctoral studies and research reports have disappeared unread into the drawers and on the hard drives of organizations that provided access to themselves only on the condition that they would receive a copy of the findings? It would probably be possible to satisfy organizations that insist on receiving a written copy of the research results simply by sending them all the same 300-page dummy text and trusting that practitioners wouldn't read a text of that length anyway.

This also has to do with very different temporal horizons. Before scientists have even documented their findings in writing, much less published them, the organization in question has generally already forgotten that it was researched in the first place. And the material forms of presentation are often very different as well. Scientists generally opt for a language that is not immediately comprehensible to practitioners, and in doing so they protect their sources.

Even in the unlikely event that an organization not only becomes aware of the scientific findings but actually recognizes itself in them due to insufficient anonymization, the usual immune reactions generally kick in. Small, informal groups might talk among themselves about their organization being described by a researcher, but this information will not necessarily be formally communicated. Books and articles dealing with sensitive information will quietly circulate among the organization's own members without the organization as a whole having to deal with the issue.

But neither the improbability that an organization will become aware of scientific findings nor the immune system that usually functions in an organization justify negligence when it comes to strict anonymization. Scientists always have to reckon with the unlikely scenario that the organizations they study will not only become aware of their findings, but will also discuss them. Inadequate anonymization can be disastrous in this case, because the descriptions may reveal, in an uncontrolled way, structures in the organization that have been protected by communication latency for good reason.

Starting Points for Dealing with Tensions

It would be problematic to pretend that this fundamental conflict did not exist or could be resolved to everyone's satisfaction in specific cases. Granted, one could demand a description of the falsifications used to anonymize the data. It is easy enough to insert a safeguarding footnote stating that industries or organizations were changed in the text. But this does not solve the problem, because the more detailed the description of a researcher's anonymization methods, the easier it is for readers to use this information to identify the organization. For example, if an author says that they changed the country an organization is based in or slightly modified the sector in which is operates, it is easier to figure out which organization is being discussed.

When you talk with researchers, you soon realize that the deliberate falsification of data to preserve anonymity is common practice. A series of interviews with a single person might be attributed to different people so the interviewee is not identifiable. "Smokescreens" might be used in a text to prevent readers from discerning the specific organization, family, movement, or group and thus also identifying individual people. Researchers are not alone in this practice of falsification, but there are also no established professional standards to guide them in this. The literature on methodology ignores this dilemma between precision and anonymization and instead proclaims more general principles for research ethics. It is left to individual researchers to find a situationally appropriate way of dealing with the dilemma.

The Golden Standard of Successful Anonymization

From a research perspective, the greatest compliment an organization can pay to a researcher is to say that the structures, processes and effects described in scientific language are plausible—without realizing that they were based on an analysis of that very organization. For an organization to say "we've experienced the same thing"—without recognizing that one's own organization was the empirical basis of the description—is not only an expression of the plausibility of scientific analyses, it also indicates that the highest standards of anonymization have been met. But this is usually achieved at the cost of changing significant details to make it impossible to identify the organization. Anonymization, therefore, always comes at the expense of precision when empirical data is presented.

Bibliography

Abagnale, Frank W., JR., and Stan Redding. 2000. *Catch Me If You Can: The Amazing True Story of the Youngest and Most Daring Con Man in the History of Fun and Profit.* New York: Broadway Books.

Abend, Gabriel. 2014. *The Moral Background: An Inquiry into the History of Business Ethics.* Princeton: Princeton University Press.

Aichele, Alexander. 2008. "Persona Physica und Persona Moralis: Die Zurechnungsfähigkeit juristischer Personen nach Kant." *Jahrbuch für Recht und Ethik* 16: 3–23.

Alalehto, Tage. 2003. "Economic Crime: Does Personality Matter?" *International Journal of Offender Therapy and Comparative Criminology* 47 (3): 335–55.

Alatas, Syed Hussein. 1980. *The Sociology of Corruption: The Nature, Function, Causes, and Prevention of Corruption.* Singapore: Times Books.

Albini, Joseph L. 1971. *The American Mafia: Genesis of a Legend.* New York: Appleton-Century-Crofts.

Aliyev, Huseyn, and Konrad Honsel. 2015. "Netzwerke im Südkaukasus: Formen und Funktionen informeller Praktiken." *Osteuropa* 65: 181–90.

Allen, Robert F., and Saul Pilnick. 1973. "Confronting the Shadow Organization: How to Detect and Defeat Negative Norms." *Organizational Dynamics* 1 (4): 3–18

Alvesson, Mats. 2015. "Organizational Culture." In *The SAGE Handbook of the Sociology of Work and Employment*, edited by Stephen Edgell, Heidi Gottfried, and Edward Granter, 262–82. London: Sage.

Analoui, Farhad, and Andrew Kakabadse. 1992. "Unconventional Practice at Work: Insight and Analysis Through Participant Observation." *Journal of Managerial Psychology* 7 (5): 2–31.

Anand, Vikas, Blake E. Ashforth, and Mahendra Joshi. 2005. "Business as Usual: The Acceptance and Perpetuation of Corruption in Organizations." *Academy of Management Executive* 19 (4): 9–23.

Andersson, Lynne M., and Christine M. Pearson. 1999. "Tit for Tat? The Spiraling Effect of Incivility in the Workplace." *Academy of Management Review* 24 (3): 452–71.

Andreski, Stanislav. 1979. "Kleptocracy as a System of Government in Africa." In *Bureaucratic Corruption in Sub-Saharan Africa: Toward a Search for Causes and Consequences*, edited by Ekpo M., 275–90.

Anechiarico, Frank, and James Jacobs. 1994. "Visions of Corruption Control and the Evolution of American Public Administration." *Public Administration Review* 54: 465–73.

Anechiarico, Frank, and James Jacobs. 1996. *The Pursuit of Absolute Integrity: How Corruption Control Makes Government Ineffective.* Chicago: University of Chicago Press.

Anonymous. 2003. "The Good, the Bad, and Their Corporate Codes of Ethics: Enron, Sarbanes-Oxley, and the Problems with Legislating Good Behavior." *Harvard Law Review* 116: 2123–41.Arendt, Hannah. 1958. *The Origins of Totalitarism.* Ohio: Merdan Book.

Arlacchi, Pino. 1986. *Mafia Business: The Mafia Ethic and the Spirit of Capitalism.* London: Verso.

Ashforth, Blake E., and Vikas Anand. 2003. "The Normalization of Corruption in Organizations." *Research in Organizational Behavior* 25: 1–52.

Ashforth, Blake E., Dennis A. Gioia, Sandra L. Robinson, and Linda K. Treviño. 2008. "Re-Viewing Organizational Corruption." *Academy of Management Review* 33 (3): 670–84.

Aubert, Vilhelm. 1952. "White-Collar Crime and Social Structure." *American Journal of Sociology* 58 (3): 263–71.

Ayeni, Victor. 1987. "Nigeria's Bureaucratized Ombudsman System: An Insight into the Problem of Bureaucratization in a Developing Country." *Public Administration and Development* 7 (3): 309–24.

Badaracco, Joseph L., and Richard R. Ellsworth. 1989. *Leadership and the Quest for Integrity.* Boston: Harvard Business School Press.

Badaracco, Joseph L., and Allen P. Webb. 1995. "Business Ethics: A View from the Trenches." *California Management Review* 37 (2): 8–28.

Baker, Wayne E., and Robert R. Faulkner. 1993. "The Social Organization of Conspiracy: Illegal Networks in the Heavy Electrical Equipment Industry." *American Sociological Review* 58: 837–60.

Bandura, Albert. 1999. "Moral Disengagement in the Perpetration of Inhumanities." *Personality and Social Psychology Review* 3: 193–209.

Banfield, Edward C. 1975. "Corruption as a Feature of Governmental Organization." *The Journal of Law and Economics* 18 (3): 587–605.

Barkan, Joshua. 2013. *Corporate Sovereignty: Law and Government Under Capitalism.* Minneapolis: University of Minnesota Press.

Barker, Thomas, and David L. Carter. 1994. *Police Deviance.* 3rd ed. London: Routledge.

Barnard, Chester I. 1938. *The Functions of the Executive.* Cambridge: Harvard University Press.

Barnard, Chester I. 1958. "Elementary Conditions of Business Morals." *California Management Review* 1 (1): 1–13.

Barnett, Harold C. 1981. "Corporate Capitalism, Corporate Crime." *Crime & Delinquency* 27 (1): 4–23.

Barreveld, Dirk J. 2002. *The ENRON Collapse: Creative Accounting, Wrong Economics or Criminal Acts?* San Jose: Writers Club Press.

Barrile, Leo G. 1993. "A Soul to Damn and a Body to Kick: Imprisoning Corporate Criminals." *Humanity & Society* 17 (2): 176–99.

Bartlett, Christopher A., and Meg Glinska. 2001. *Enron's Transformation: From Gas Pipelines to New Economy Powerhouse.* Boston: Harvard Business School Press Case Study.

Bass, Bernard M. 1990. "From Transactional to Transformational Leadership: Learning to Share the Vision." *Organizational Dynamics* 18 (3): 19–31.

Bateman, Thomas S., and J. Michael Crant. 1993. "The Proactive Component of Organizational Behavior: A Measure and Correlates." *Journal of Organizational Behavior* 14:103–18.

Baucus, Melissa S., and David A. Baucus. 1997. "Paying the Piper: An Empirical Examination of Longer-Term Financial Consequences of Illegal Corporate Behavior." *Academy of Management Journal* 40: 129–51.

Bauschke, Rafael. 2014. "Unternehmensethik, Corporate Governance und Nachhaltigkeit - Was leistet Unternehmenskultur?" In *Einführung Unternehmenskultur: Grundlagen, Perspektiven, Konsequenzen*, edited by Norbert Homma, Rafael Bauschke, and Laila M. Hofmann. Aufl. 2014, 167–84. Wiesbaden: Springer Gabler.

Bayart, Jean-François. 1989. *L'état en Afrique: La politique du ventre.* Paris: Fayard.

Baysinger, Barry D. 1991. "Organization Theory and the Criminal Liability of Organizations." *Boston University Law Review* 71: 341–76.

Bechky, Beth A., and Gerardo A. Okhuysen. 2011. "Expection the Unexpected?: How SWAT Officers and Film Crews Handle Suprises." *Academy of Management Journal* 54: 239-61.

Becker, Franz, and Niklas Luhmann. 1963. *Verwaltungsfehler und Vertrauensschutz: Möglichkeiten gesetzlicher Regelung der Rücknehmbarkeit von Verwaltungsakten.* Berlin: Duncker & Humblot.

Becker, Gary S. 1964. *Human Capital: A Theoretical and Empirical Analysis with Special Reference to Education.* Chicago: University of Chicago Press.

Becker, Gary S. 1968. "Crime and Punishment: An Economic Approach." *Journal of Political Economy* 76 (2): 169–217.

Becker, Howard S. 1963. *Outsiders: Studies in the Sociology of Deviance.* New York: Free Press.

Becker, Howard S., and Blanche Geer. 1957. "Participant Observation and Interviewing: A Comparision." *Human Organization* 16: 28–32.

Becker, Thomas E. 1998. "Integrity in Organizations: Beyond Honesty and Conscientiousness." *Academy of Management Review* 23 (1): 154–61.

Belhoste, Nathalie, and Bastien Nivet. 2018. "Les Entreprises Et La Guerre : Vers La Responsabilité Géopolitique Des Entreprises ?" *Revue internationale et stratégique* 111:16–25.

Bensman, Joseph, and Israel Gerver. 1963. "Crime and Punishment in the Factory: The Function of Deviancy in Maintaining the Social System." *American Sociological Review* 28: 588–98.

Benson, George C. S. 1989. "Codes of Ethics." *Journal of Business Ethics* 8 (5): 305–19.

Benz, Arthur, and Wolfgang Seibel. 1992. "Statt eines Vorwortes." In *Zwischen Kooperation und Korruption: Abweichendes Verhalten in der Verwaltung*, edited by Arthur Benz and Wolfgang Seibel, 9–16. Baden-Baden: Nomos.

Berg, Nicolas. 2003. *Der Holocaust und die westdeutschen Historiker: Erforschung und Erinnerung.* Göttingen: Wallstein.

Berg, Nicolas. 2015. *The Holocaust and the West German Historians: Historical Interpretation and Autobiographical Memory.* Madison: University of Wisconsin Press.

Berger, Johannes. 1999. "Der Konsensbedarf der Wirtschaft." In *Die Wirtschaft der modernen Gesellschaft*, edited by Johannes Berger, 155–94. Frankfurt a.M./ New York: Campus.

Bergmann, Jens. 2014. "Gescheiterte Informalität am Beispiel des Korruptionsfalls Siemens." In *Scheitern: Organisations- und wirtschaftssoziologische Analysen*, edited by Jens Bergmann, Matthias Hahn, Antonia Langhof and Gabriele Wagner, 231–50.

Bergmann, Jens. 2015. "Scheiternde Rechtsnormbildung im Rahmen von Compliance-Kontrolle." *Neue Kriminalpolitik* 27: 346–58.

Bergmann, Jens. 2016. "Corporate Crime, Kriminalitätstheorie und Organisationssoziologie." *Monatsschrift für Kriminologie und Strafrechtsreform* 99: 3–22.Berliner, Joseph S. 1952. "The Informal Organization of the Soviet Firm." *The Quarterly Journal of Economics* 66 (3): 342–65.

Berliner, Joseph S. 1957. *Factory and Manger in the USSR.* Cambridge: Harvard University Press.

Berman, Bruce J. 1974. "Clientelism and Neocolonialism: Center-Periphery Relations and Political Development in African States." *Studies in Comparative International Development* 9: 3–24.

Bernstein, Carl, and Bob Woodward. 1974. *Die Watergate-Affäre.* München: Droemer Knaur.

Bernstein, Ethan S. 2012. "The Transparency Paradox: A Role for Privacy in Organizational Learning and Operational Control." *Administrative Science Quarterly* 57 (2): 181–216.

Besio, Cristina. 2013. "Uncertainty and Attribution of Personal Responsibility in Organizations." *Soziale Systeme* 19: 307–26.

Besio, Cristina. 2018. *Moral und Innovation in Organisationen.* Wiesbaden: Springer VS.

Blau, Peter M. 1964. *Exchange and Power in Social Life.* London/ Sydney: Wiley.

Blauner, Robert. 1964. *Alienation and Freedom: The Factory Worker and His Industry.* Chicago: University of Chicago Press.

Bliss, Edwin C., and Isamu S. Aoki. 1993. *Are Your Employees Stealing You Blind?* Amsterdam/ San Diego: Pfeiffer.

Bogdanov, Alexander. 1984. *Red Star: The First Bolshevik Utopia.* Bloomington: Indiana University Press.

Boltanski, Luc, and Chiapello, Ève. 1999. *Le nouvel esprit du capitalisme.* Paris: Gallimard.

Bolton, David. 1977. *The Grease Machine: The Lockheed Papers.* New York: Harper.

Bonazzi, Giuseppe. 1983. "Scapegoating in Complex Organizations: The Results of a Comparative Study of Symbolic Blame-Giving in Italian and French Public Administration." *Organization Studies* 4 (1): 1–18.

Bosetzky, Horst. 2019. *Mikropolitik: Netzwerke und Karrieren.* Wiesbaden: Springer VS.

Boulding, Kenneth E. 1963. "Towards a Pure Theory of Threat Systems." *American Economic Review* 53: 424–34.

Bourke, Joanna. 1999. *An Intimate History of Killing.* New York: Basic Books.

Bowman, James S. 1981. "The Management of Ethics: Codes of Conduct in Organizations." *Public Personnel Management* 10 (1): 59–66.

Box, Steven. 1998. *Power, Crime, and Mystification.* London: Routledge.

Braithwaite, John. 1984. *Corporate Crime in the Pharmaceutical Industry.* London: Routledge & Kegan Paul.

Braithwaite, John. 1985. "White Collar Crime." *Annual Review of Sociology* 11: 1–25.

Braithwaite, John. 1989. *Crime, Shame, and Reintegration.* Cambridge: Cambridge University Press.

Braithwaite, John. 2009. "Criminological Theory and Organizational Crime." In *Corporate Crime, Volume Two: Cases and Explanations,* edited by Hazel Croall , 214–35. London: Sage.

Braithwaite, John, and Brent Fisse. 1990. "On the Plausibility of Corporate Crime Theory." In *Advances in Criminological Theory: Volume Two,* edited by William S. Laufer, 15–38. New Brunswick/ London: Transaction Publishers.

Braithwaite, John, and Gilbert Geis. 1982. "On Theory and Action for Corporate Crime Control." *Crime & Delinquency* 28: 292–314.

Brass, Daniel J., Kenneth D. Butterfield, and Bruce C. Skaggs. 1998. "Relationships and Unethical Behavior: A Social Network Perspective." *Academy of Management Review* 23 (1): 14–31.

Braun, Andreas. 2015. *Campus Shootings: Amoktaten an Universitäten als nicht-intendierte Nebenfolgen der Restrukturierungs- und Hybridisierungseffekte der Hochschulreformen.* Bielefeld: transcript.

Braverman, Harry. 1974. *Labor and Monopoly Capital: The Degradation of Work in the Twentieth Century.* New York/ London: Monthly Review Press.

Brief, Arthur P., Robert T. Buttram, and Janet M. Dukerich. 2001. "Collective Corruption in the Corporate World: Toward a Process Model." In *Groups at Work,* edited by Marlene E. Turner, 471–99. Mahwah: Lawrence Erlbaum Associates.

Broderick, Christina Orsini. 2007. "Qui Tam Provisions and the Public Interest: An Empirical Analysis." *Columbia Law Review* 107: 949–1001.

Brown, Darryl K. 2000. "Street Crime, Corporate Crime, and the Contingency of Criminal Liability." *University of Pennsylvania Law Review* 149: 1295–1360.

Brunsson, Nils. 1986. "Organizing for Inconsistencies: On Organizational Conflict, Depression and Hypocrisy as Substitutes for Action." *Scandinavian Journal of Management Studies* 2: 165–85.

Brunsson, Nils. 1989. *The Organization of Hypocrisy: Talk, Decisions and Actions in Organizations.* Chichester: John Wiley & Sons.

Brunsson, Nils. 1993. "The Necessary Hypocrisy." *International Executive* 35: 1–9.

Brunsson, Nils. 2003. "Organized Hypocrisy." In *The Northern Lights: Organization Theory in Scandinavia*, edited by Barbara Czarniawska and Guje Sevón, 201–22. Kopenhagen/ Malmö/ Oslo: Copenhagen Business School Press.

Bryant, Donald T. 1975. *A Manager's Guide to Withdrawal from Work.* Brighton: Institute of Manpower Studies.

Buckingham, Marcus, and Curt Coffman. 2000. *First, Break All the Rules: What the World's Greatest Managers Do Differently.* New York: Simon - Schuster Business.

Bucy, Pamela H. 1991. "Corporate Ethos: A Standard for Imposing Corporate Criminal Liability." *Minnesota Law Review* 75: 1095–1184.

Burawoy, Michael. 1979. *Manufacturing Consent.* Chicago/ London: University of Chicago Press.

Burleigh, Michael. 2002. *Tod und Erlösung: Euthanasie in Detuschland 1900-1945.* Zürich/ München: Pendo.

Busch, Richard. 1933. *Grundfragen der strafrechtlichen Verantwortlichkeit der Verbaende.* Leipzig: Weicher.

Butler Committee. 2004. *Review of Intelligence on Weapons of Mass Destruction: Report of a Committee of Privy Counsellors.* London: Stationery Office.

Caiden, Gerald E., and Naomi J. Caiden. 1977. "Administrative Corruption." *Public Administration Review* 37 (3): 301-9.

Calabretta, Giulia, Boris Durisin, and Marco Ogliengo. 2011. "Uncovering the Intellectual Structure of Research in Business Ethics: A Journey Through the History, the Classics, and the Pillars of Journal of Business Ethics." *Journal of Business Ethics* 104 (4): 499–524.

Calavita, Kitty, and Henry N. Pontell. 1993. "Savings and Loan Fraud as Organized Crime: Toward a Conceptual Typology of Corporate Illegality." *Criminology* 31: 519–48.

Caldero, Michael A., Jeffrey D. Dailey, and Brian L. Withrow. 2018. *Police Ethics: The Corruption of Noble Cause.* 4th ed. Milton: Routledge.

Caminker, Evan. 1989. "The Constitutionality of Qui Tam Actions." *Yale Law Journal* 99: 341–88.

Carreyrou, John. 2018. *Bad Blood : Secrets and Lies in a Silicon Valley Startup.* New York: Knopf.

Carroll, Archie B. 1991. "The Pyramid of Corporate Social Responsibility: Toward the Moral Management of Organizational Stakeholders." *Business Horizons* 34 (4): 39–48.

Carroll, Archie B. 1999. "Corporate Social Responsibility: Evolution of a Definitional Construct." *Business & Society* 38 (3): 268–95.

Carson, W. G. 1970. "White-Collar Crime and the Enforcement of Factory Legislation." *British Journal of Criminology* 10: 383–98.

Cartier-Bresson, Jean. 1992. "Èléments D'analyse Pour Une Économie De La Corruption." *Tiers-Monde* 33: 581–609.

Cartier-Bresson, Jean. 2000. "Corruption Libéralisation Et Démocratisation." *Revue Tiers Monde* 41: 9–22.

Catanzaro, Raimondo. 1985. "Enforcers, Entrepreneurs, and Survivors: How the Mafia Has Adapted to Change." *British Journal of Sociology* 36: 34–57.

Catanzaro, Raimondo. 1988. *Il Delitto Come Impresa: Storia Sociale Della Mafia.* Padua: Liviana.

Chambliss, William J. 1989. "State-Organized Crime." *Criminology* 27: 183–208.

Chan, Janet B. L. 1999. "Governing Police Practice: Limits of the New Accountability." *The British Journal of Sociology* 50 (2): 251–70.

Chapman, Richard A. 1966. "Prismatic Theory in Public Administration: A Review of the Theories of Fred W. Riggs." *Public Administration* 44 (4): 415–34.

Chaudhary, M. Azam. 2006. "Rhineland Ethnography and Pakistani Reflexivity." *Zeitschrift für Ethnologie* 131: 1–26.

Chen, Hui, and Eugene Soltes. 2008. "Why Compliance Programs Fail—And How to Fix Them." *Harvard Business Review* 96 (2): 116–25.

Chen, Mo, Chao C. Chen, and Oliver J. Sheldon. 2016. "Relaxing Moral Reasoning to Win: How Organizational Identification Relates to Unethical Pro-Organizational Behavior." *Journal of Applied Psychology* 101 (8): 1082–96.

Clark, John P., and Richard C. Hollinger. 1983. *Theft by Employees in Work Organizations*. New York: Lexington Books.

Cleek, Margaret Anne, and Sherry Lynn Leonard. 1998. "Can Corporate Codes of Ethics Influence Behavior?" *Journal of Business Ethics* 17 (6): 619–30.

Clegg, Steward R., Martin Kronberger, and Carl Rhodes. 2007. "Business Ethics as Practice." *British Journal of Management* 18: 107–22.

Clinard, Marshall B., and Richard Quinney. 1973. *Criminal Behavior Systems: A Typology*. 2nd ed. New York: Holt Rinehart and Winston.

Clinard, Marshall B., and Peter C. Yeager. 1980. *Corporate Crime*. New York: Free Press.

Coffee, John C. 1977. "Beyond the Shut-Eyed Sentry: Toward a Theoretical View of Corporate Misconduct and Effective Legal Response." *Virginia Law Review* 63: 1099–1278.

Coffee, John C. 1980. "Corporate Crime and Punishment: A Non-Chicago View of the Economics of Criminal Sanctions." *American Criminal Law Review* 17: 419-476.

Coffee, John C. 1981. ""No Soul to Damn: No Body to Kick": An Unscandalized Inquiry into the Problem of Corporate Punishment." *Michigan Law Review* 79 (3): 386.

Coleman, James S. 1982. *The Asymmetric Society*. New York: Syracuse University Press.

Coleman, James William. 1985. *The Criminal Elite. The Sociology of White Collar Crime*. New York: St. Martin's Press.

Coleman, James William. 1987. "Toward an Integrated Theory of White-Collar Crime." *American Journal of Sociology* 93: 406–39.

Collins, Kathleen. 2006. *Clan, Politics and Regime Transition in Central Asia*. Cambridge: Cambridge University Press.

Collins, Randall. 2008. *Violence: A Micro-Sociological Theory*. Oxford/ New York: Oxford University Press.

Connors, Roger, and Tom Smith. 2012. *Change the Culture, Change the Game: The Breakthrough Strategy for Energizing Your Organization and Creating Accountability for Results*. London: Portfolio/Penguin.

Cooper, Jonathon A. 2012. "Noble Cause Corruption as a Consequence of Role Conflict in the Police Organisation." *Policing and Society* 22 (2): 169–84.

Cooper, Neil. 1981. *The Diversity of Moral Thinking.* Oxford: Clarendon Press.

Crane, Andrew. 2013. "Modern Slavery as a Management Practice: Exploring the Conditions and Capabilities for Human Exploitation." *Academy of Management Review* 38 (1): 49–69.

Cressey, Donald R. 1976. "Restraint of Trade, Recidivism, and Delinquent Neighborhoods." In *Delinquency, Crime, and Society*, edited by James F. Short, 209–38. Chicago: University of Chicago Press.

Cressey, Donald R. 1988. "Poverty of Theory in Corporate Crime Research." *Advances in Criminological Theory* 1: 31–56.

Cressey, Donald R. 2001. "The Poverty of Theory in Corporate Crime Research." In *Crimes of Privilege: Readings in White-Collar Crime*, edited by Neal Shover and John P. Wright, 175–94. New York/ Oxford: Oxford University Press.

Cressey, Donald R., and Charles A. Moore. 1983. "Managerial Values and Corporate Codes of Ethics." *California Management Review* 25 (4): 53–77.

Croall, Hazel. 1991. *Understanding White Collar Crime.* Philadelphia: Open University Press.

Croall, Hazel. 2009. "Editor's Introduction" In *Corporate Crime Volume 2: Cases and Explanations,* edited by Hazel Croall, vii-xvi. Los Angeles/ London/ New Delhi/ Singapore: Sage.

Crozier, Michel. 1963. *Le phénomène bureaucratique.* Paris: Seuil.

Crozier, Michel. 2010. *The Bureaucratic Phenomenon.* New Brunswick: Transaction Publishers.

Cunningham, Robert B., and Yasin K. Sarayrah. 1993. *Wasta: The Hidden Force in Middle Eastern Society.* Westport/ London: Praeger.

Cyert, Richard M., and James G. March. 1963. *A Behavorial Theory of the Firm.* Englewood Cliffs: Prentice-Hall.

Czarniawska, Barbara, and Bernward Joerges. 1996. "Travels of Ideas." In Translating Organizational Change, edited by Czarniawska, Barbara, and Guje Sevón, 14–48. Berlin/ New York: Walter de Gruyter.

Dabney, D. 1995. "Neutralization and Deviance in the Workplace: Theft of Supplies in Medicines by Hospital Nurses." *Deviant Behavior* 16: 313–31.

Dalton, Melville. 1948. "The Industrial Rate Buster: A Characterization." *Applied Anthropology* 7: 5–18.

Dalton, Melville. 2013. Men Who Manage: Fusions of Feeling and Theory in Administration. Brunswick: Transaction Publishers.

D'Aunno, Thomas, Robert I. Sutton, and Richard H. Price. 1991. "Isomorphism and External Support in Conflicting Institutional Environments: A Study of Drug Abuse Treatment Units." *Academy of Management Journal* 34: 636–61.

Davalos, Jorge, Mónica Delgado, and Jacobo Alban. 2018. *Guerrillereas: Testimonios De Cinco Combatientes De Las FARC.* San Sebastián de Buenavista: Nodo des saberes populares Orinoco-Magdalena.

Davenport, Thomas H., Marius Leibold, and Sven Voelpel. 2006. *Strategic Management in the Innovation Economy: Strategy Approaches and Tools for Dynamic Innovation Capabilities.* Erlangen: Publicis Corporate Publisher.

Davis, Kingsley. 1959. "The Myth of Functional Analysis as a Special Method in Sociology and Anthropology." *American Sociological Review* 24: 757–72.

Deephouse, David L., and Suzanne M. Carter. 2005. "An Examination of Differences Between Organizational Legitimacy and Organizational Reputation." *Journal of Management Studies* 42: 329–60.

Devlin, Patrick. 2009. *The Enforcement of Morals.* Indianapolis: Liberty Fund.

Díaz-Briquets, Sergio, and Jorge F. Pérez-López. 2006. *Corruption in Cuba: Castro and Beyond.* Austin: University of Texas Press.

Dobb, Maurice. 1970. *Socialist Planning: Some Problems.* London: Lawrence & Wishart.

Dombois, Rainer. 2009. "Von Organisierter Korruption zu Individuellem Korruptionsdruck? Soziologische Einblicke in die Siemens-Korruptionsaffäre." In *Der Korruptionsfall Siemens: Analysen und Praxisnahe Folgerungen des Wissenschaftlichen Arbeitskreises von Transparency International Deutschland,* edited by Peter Graeff, Karenina Schröder, and Sebastian Wolf, 131–50. Baden-Baden: Nomos.

Donaldson, Thomas, and Thomas W. Dunfee. 1994. "Toward a Unified Conception of Business Ethics: Integrative Social Contracts Theory." *Academy of Management Review* 19 (2): 252–84.

Dorn, Christopher, and Thomas Hoebel. 2013. "Mafias als organisierte Dritte." *Behemoth* 6: 74–97.

Downs, Anthony. 1967. *Inside Bureaucracy.* Boston: Little, Brown.

Dozier, Janelle Brinker, and Marcia P. Miceli. 1985. "Potential Predictors of Whistle-Blowing: A Prosocial Behavior Perspective." *Academy of Management Review* 10 (4): 823–36.

Dukerich, Janet M., Roderick Kramer, and Judi McLean Parks. 1998. "The Dark Side of Organizational Identification." In *Identity in Organizations: Building Theory Through Conversations*, edited by David A. Whetten and Paul C. Godfrey, 245–56. Foundations for organizational science. Thousand Oaks: Sage Publications.

Durkheim, Émile. 1982. *The Rules of Sociological Method.* New York: The Free Press.

Duska, Ronald F. 2007. *Contemporary Reflections on Business Ethics: Issues in Business Ethics* 23. Dordrecht: Springer.

Duster, Troy. 1970. *The Legislation of Morality: Law, Drugs and Moral Judgement.* New York/ London: Free Press; Collier-Macmillan.

Dwivedi, O. P. 1967. "Bureaucratic Corruption in Developing Countries." *Asian Survey* 7 (4): 245–53.

Eckstein, Bernd. 2018. *Brauchbarkeit und Illegalität: Abweichendes Verhalten in Heinrich von Kleists „Prinz Friedrich von Homburg".* Bielefeld: unpublished manuscript.

Edelhertz, Herbert. 1970. *The Nature, Impact, and Prosecution of White Collar Crime.* Washington, D.C.: U.S Government Printing Office.

Edelman, Lauren B. 1990. "Legal Environments and Organizational Governance: The Expansion of Due Process in the American Workplace." *American Journal of Sociology* 95: 1401–40.

Edelman, Lauren B. 1992. "Legal Ambiguity and Symbolic Structures: Organizational Mediation of Civil Rights Law." *American Journal of Sociology* 97: 1531–76.

Edelman, Lauren B., Linda H. Krieger, Scott R. Eliason, Catherine R. Albiston, and Virginia Mellema. 2011. "When Organizations Rule:

Judicial Deference to Institutionalized Employment Structures." *American Journal of Sociology* 117: 888–954.

Edelman, Lauren B., Stephen Petterson, Elizabeth Chambliss, and Howard S. Erlanger. 1991. "Legal Ambiguity and the Politics of Compliance: Affirmative Action Officers' Dilemma." *Law & Policy* 13: 73–97.

Edelman, Lauren B., and Robin Stryker. 2005. "A Sociological Approach to Law and the Economy." In *The Handbook of Economic Sociology*, edited by Neil J. Smelser and Richard Swedberg, 527–51. Princeton: Princeton University Press.

Edelman, Lauren B., and Mark C. Suchman. 1997. "The Legal Environments of Organizations." *Annual Review of Sociology* 23: 479–515.

Edelman, Lauren B., and Mark C. Suchman. 1999. "When the "Haves" Hold Court: Speculations on the Organizational Internalization of Law." *Law & Society Review* 33:941-91.

Edelman, Lauren B., and Shauhin Talesh. 2011. "To Comply or Not to Comply—That Isn't the Question: How Organizations Construct the Meaning of Compliance." In *Explaining Compliance*, edited by Christine Parker and Viebeke Lehmann Nielsen, 103–22. Cheltenham/ Northampton: Edward Elgar Publishing.

Eichenwald, Kurt. 2005. *Conspiracy of Fools: A True Story.* New York: Broadway Books.

Ellis, Allison M., Talya N. Bauer, and Berrin Erdogan. 2015. "New-Employee Organizational Socialization: Adjusting to New Roles, Colleagues, and Organizations." In *Handbook of Socialization: Theory and Research*, edited by Joan E. Grusec and Paul D. Hastings. 2nd ed., 301–24. New York: The Guilford Press.

Elster, Jon. 1990. "Merton's Functionalism and the Unintended Consequences of Action." In *Robert K. Meton: Consensus and Controversy*, edited by Jon Clark, Celia Modgil, and Sohan Modgil, 129–35. Basingstoke/ Bristol: Falmer.

Emerson, Richard M. 1976. "Social Exchange Theory." *Annual Review of Sociology* 2: 335–62.

Engels, Jens Ivo. 2019. *Alles nur gekauft? Korruption in der Bundesrepublik seit 1949*. Darmstadt: wbg Theiss.

Ekpo, Monday U. 1979. "Gift-Giving and Bureacratic Corruption in Nigeria." In *Bureaucratic Corruption in Sub-Saharan Africa: Toward a Search for Causes and Consequences*, edited by Monday U. Ekpo, 161–88. Washington: University Press of America.

Ermann, M. David, and Richard J. Lundman. 1978. "Deviant Acts by Complex Organizations." *The Sociological Quarterly* 19: 55–67.

Ermann, M. David, and Richard J. Lundman. 1982. *Corporate and Governmental Deviance: Problems of Organizational Behavior in Contemporary Society.* New York: Holt, Rinehart and Winston.

Escobar, Arturo. 1995. *Encountering Development: The Making and Unmaking of the Third World.* Princeton: Princeton University Press.

Etzioni, Amitai. 2010. "Is Transparency the Best Disinfectant?" *Journal of Political Philosophy* 18 (4): 389–404.

Ewing, Jack. 2017. *Faster, Higher, Farther: The Volkswagen Scandal.* New York: W.W. Norton & Company.

Farberman, Harvey A. 1975. "A Criminogenic Market Structure: The Automobile Industry." *The Sociological Quarterly* 16: 438–57.

Farson, Richard. 1997. *Management of the Absurd: Paradoxes in Leadership.* New York: Touchstone.

Fayol, Henri. 1916. *Administration industrielle et générale, prévoyance, organisation, commandement, coordination, controle.* Paris: Dunod.

Fernández Menéndez, Jorge, and Víctor Ronquillo. 2010. *De Los Maras a Los Zetas: Los Secretos Del Narcotráfico, De Colombia a Chicago.* 3rd ed. México City: Debolsillo.

Ferrell, O. C., and Gareth Gardiner. 1991. *In Pursuit of Ethics: Tough Choices in the World of Work.* Springfield: Smith Collins.

Filler, Louis. 1975. *The Muchrakers.* University Park: Pennsylvania State University Press.

Fischel, Daniel R., and Alan O. Sykes. 1996. "Corporate Crime." *Journal of Legal Studies* 25: 319–49.

Fiss, Peer C., and Edward J. Zajac. 2004. "The Diffusion of Ideas over Contested Terrain: The (Non)Adoption of a Shareholder Value Orientation Among German Firms." *Administrative Science Quarterly* 49: 501–34.

Fisse, Brent, and John Braithwaite. 1993. *Corporations, Crime, and Accountability.* Cambridge: Cambridge University Press.

Flynn, Sharon, Michele Reichard, and Steve Slane. 1987. "Cheating as a Function of Task Outcome and Machiavellianism." *Journal of Psychology* 121: 423–27.

Foster, Richard, and Sarah Kaplan. 2001. *Creative Destruction: Why Companies That Are Built to Last Underperform the Market and How to Successfully Transform Them.* New York: Crown Business.

Fox, Loren. 2004. *Enron: The Rise and Fall.* Hoboken: John Wiley & Sons Inc.

Frank, Björn, and Günther G. Schulze. 2000. "Does Economics Make Citizens Corrupt?" *Journal of Economic Behavior & Organization* 43 (1): 101–13.

Frank, Nancy, and Michael J. Lynch. 1992. *Corporate Crime, Corporate Violence: A Primer.* New York: Harrow and Heston.

Fred, Alford C. 2001. *Whistleblowers: Broken Lives and Organizational Power.* Ithaca: Cornell University Press.

Freedman, Jonathan L., and Scott C. Fraser. 1966. "Compliance Without Pressure. The Foot-in-the-Door Technique." *Journal of Personality and Social Psychology* 4: 195–202.

Freeman, Jo. 1972. "The Tyranny of Structurelessness." *Berkeley Journal of Sociology* 17: 151–64.

French, Peter. 1984. *Collective and Corporate Responsibility.* New York: Columbia University Press.

Frey, Bruno S., and Reto Jegen. 2001. "Motivation Crowding Theory: A Survey of Empirical Evidence." *Journal of Economic Surveys* 15: 589–611.

Friedberg, Erhard. 1997. *Local Orders: Dynamics of Organized Action.* Greenwich/ Connecticut: Jai Press.

Friedland, Roger, and Robert R. Alford. 1991. "Bringing Society Back In: Symbols, Practices, and Institutional Contradictions" In *The New Institutionalism in Organizational Analysis*, edited by Walter W. Powell and Paul J. DiMaggio, 232-66. Chicago: University of Chicago

Friedman, Andrew. 1977. *Industry and Labour.* London: Macmillan.

Friedman, Milton. 1962. *Capitalism and Freedom.* Chicago: Chicago University Press.

Friedrichs, David O. 2010. *Trusted Criminals.* 4th ed. New York: Wadsworth.

Fuchs, Peter. 2010. *Diabolische Perspektiven: Vorlesungen zu Ethik und Beratung.* Münster: Lit.

Fukukawa, Kyoko, John M. Balmer, and Edmund R. Gray. 2007. "Mapping the Interface Between Corporate Identity, Ethics and Corporate Social Responsibility." *Journal of Business Ethics* 76: 761–65.

Fuller, Lon L. 1969. *The Morality of Law.* New Haven: Yale University Press.

Furnivall, J. S. 1948. *Colonial Policy and Practice: A Comparative Study of Burma and Netherlands India.* Cambridge: Cambridge University Press.

Fusaro, Peter C., and Ross M. Miller. 2002. *What Went Wrong at Enron: Everyone's Guide to the Largest Bankruptcy in U.S. History.* Hoboken: Wiley.

Gabbioneta, Claudia, Royston Greenwood, Pietro Mazzola, and Mario Minoja. 2013. "The Influence of the Institutional Context on Corporate Illegality." *Accounting, Organizations and Society* 38 (6): 484–504.

Galperin, Bella L. 2003. "Can Workplace Deviance Be Constructive?" In *Misbehavior and Dysfunctional Attitudes in Organizations*, edited by Abraham Sagie, Shmuel Stashevsky, and Meni Koslowsky, 154–70. Basingstoke: Palgrave Macmillan.

Gambetta, Diego. 1988. "Fragments of an Economic Theory of the Mafia." *European Journal of Sociology* 29:127–45.

Gambetta, Diego. 1993. *The Sicilian Mafia.* Cambridge: Harvard University Press.

Gambetta, Diego. 2006. "Can We Make Sense of Suicide Missions?" In *Making Sense of Suicide Missions*, edited by Diego Gambetta. Reprinted., 259–300. Oxford: Oxford University Press.

Gambetta, Diego, and Peter Reuter. 2016. "Conspiracy Among the Many: The Mafia in Legitimate Industries." In *The Economic Dimensions of Crime*, edited by Nigel G. Fielding, Alan Clark, and Robert Witt, 100–121. London: Palgrave Macmillan.

Garfinkel, Harold. 1967. *Studies in Ethnomethodology.* Englewood Cliffs: Prentice-Hall.

Garoupa, Nuno. 2000. "Corporate Criminal Law and Organization Incentives: A Managerial Perspective." *Managerial and Decision Economics* 21: 243–52.

Garsten, Christina, and Monica Lindh de Montoya. 2008. "The Naked Corporation: Visualization, Veiling and the Ethicopolitics of Organizational Transparency." In *Transparency in a New Global Order: Unveiling Organizational Visions*, edited by Christina Garsten and Monica Lindh de Montoya, 79–93. Cheltenham, Northampton: Elgar.

Geis, Gilbert. 1962. "Toward a Delineation of White-Collar Offenses" in: *Sociological Inquiry* 32(2): 160-71.

Geis, Gilbert. 1995a. "A Review, Rebuttal and Reconcilation of Cressey and Braithwaite and Fisse on Criminological Theory and Corporate Crime." In *The Legacy of Anomie Theory: Advances in Criminological Theory* Volume 6, edited by Freda Adler and William S. Laufer, 399–428. New Brunswick/ London: Transaction Publishers.

Geis, Gilbert. 1995b. "White Collar Crime: The Heavy Electrical Equipment Antitrust Case of 1961." In *Contemporary Masters in Criminology*, edited by Joan McCord and John H. Laub, 139–56. New York: Springer Science+Business Media.

Geis, Gilbert. 2007a. "Crime, Corporate." In *The Blackwell Encyclopedia of Sociology*, edited by George Ritzer, 826–28. Malden: Blackwell.

Geis, Gilbert. 2007b. *White-Collar and Corporate Crime.* New Jersey: Prentice Hall.

Geis, Gilbert. 2009. "Historical Perspectives." In *Corporate Crime: Volume 1 Issues of Definition, Construction and Research*, edited by Hazel Croall, 59–75. Los Angeles/ London/ New Delhi/ Singapore/ Washington D.C.: Sage.

Gellman, Barton. 2009. *Angler: The Cheney Vice Presidency.* New York: Penguin Books.

George, Richard T. 2010. *Competing with Integrity in International Business.* Oxford/ New York: Oxford University Press.

Gerth, Hans, and C. Wright Mills. 1954. *Character and Social Structure.* London: Routledge & Kegan Paul.

Giacalone, Robert A., and Jerald Greenberg. 1997. *Antisocial Behavior in Organizations.* Thousand Oaks: Sage.

Gibney, Alex. *The Inventor: Out for Blood in Silicon Valley: Documentary,* 2019.

Gioia, Dennis A. 1992. "Pinto Fires and Personal Ethics: A Script Analysis of Missed Opportunities." *Journal of Business Ethics* 11 (5): 379–89.

Glazer, Myron. 1989. *The Whistleblowers: Exposing Corruption in Government and Indsutry.* New York: Basic Books.

Gneezy, Uri, and John A. List. 2013. *The Why Axis: Hidden Motives and the Undiscovered Economics of Everyday Life.* New York: PublicAffairs.

Gneezy, Uri, and Aldo Rustichini. 2000. "A Fine Is a Price." *The Journal of Legal Studies* 29 (1): 1–17.

Gobert, James. 2008. "The Evolving Legal Test of Corporate Criminal Liability." In *Corporate and White Collar Crime,* edited by John Minkes and Leonard Minkes, 61–80. London/ Thousand Oaks/ New Delhi/ Singapor: Sage.

Gobert, James J., and Maurice Punch. 2003. *Rethinking Corporate Crime.* Cambridge: Cambridge University Press.

Goffin, Keith, Rick Mitchell, and John Christiansen. 2017. *Innovation Management: Effective Strategy and Implementation.* 3rd ed. London, New York: Red Globe Press.

Gold, Raymond L. 1958. "Roles in Sociological Field Observations." *Social Forces* 36: 217–23.

Golembiewski, Robert T. 1965. *Men, Management, and Morality.* New York: McGraw-Hill.

Gomez Diaz, Carlos F., and Jenny K. Rodriguez Ortiz. 2005. "Four Keys to Chilean Culture: Authoritarianism, Legalism, Fatalism and Compadrazgo." *Asian Journal of Latin American Studies* 19: 43–65.

Gómez Tomillo, Manuel. 2015. *Introducción a la responsabilidad penal de las personas jurídicas.* 3rd ed. Cizur Menor (Navarra): Thomson Reuters Aranzadi.

Goode, Erich. 2007. "Deviance." In *The Blackwell Encyclopedia of Sociology,* edited by George Ritzer 2007, 1075-82. Malden: Blackwell.

Gormley, William T. 2001. "Moralists, Pragmatists, and Roges: Bureaucrates in Modern Mysteries." *Public Administrative Review* 61: 184–93.

Goscinny, René, and Albert Uderzo. 1980. *Asterix in Corsica.* London: Hodder Dargaud.

Gottfredson, Michael R., and Travis Hirschi. 1990. *A General Theory of Crime.* Stanford: Stanford University Press.

Gouldner, Alvin W. 1954a. *Patterns of Industrial Bureaucracy.* Glencoe: Free Press.

Gouldner, Alvin W. 1954b. *Wild Cat Strike.* New York: Harper.

Graham, James M. 1972. "Amphetamine Polics on Capitol Hill." *Society* 9: 14–53.

Graham, Jill W. 1986. "Principled Organizational Dissent. A Theoretical Essay." *Research in Organizational Behavior* 8: 1–52.

Graham, John R., Campbell R. Harvey, and Shiva Rajgopal. 2005. "The Economic Implications of Corporate Financial Reporting." *Journal of Accounting and Economics* 40: 3–73.

Granovetter, Mark. 2007. "The Social Construction of Corruption." In *On Capitalism*, edited by Victor Nee and Richard Swedberg, 152–72. Stanford: Stanford University Press.

Gray, Garry C., and Susan S. Silbey. 2014. "Governing Inside the Organization: Interpreting Regulation and Compliance." *American Journal of Sociology* 120 (1): 96-145.

Grayson, George W., and Sam R. Logan. 2012. *The Executioner's Men: Los Zetas, Rogue Soldiers, Criminal Entrepreneurs, and the Shadow State They Created.* New Brunswick: Transaction Publishers.

Green, Stuart P. 1993. "The Criminal Prosecution of Local Governments." *North Carolina Law Review* 72: 1197–246.

Green, Stuart P. 1997. "Why It's a Crime to Tear the Tag Off a Mattress: Overcriminalization and the Moral Content of Regulatory Offenses." *Emory Law Journal* 46: 1533–1615.

Green, Stuart P. 2004. "Moral Ambiguity in White Collar Criminal Law." *Notre Dame Journal of Law, Ethics & Public Policy* 18: 502–19.

Green, Stuart P. 2006. *Lying, Cheating, and Stealing: A Moral Theory of White-Collar Crime.* Oxford: Oxford University Press.

Greenwood, Royston, Mia Raynard, Farah Kodeih, Evelyn R. Micelotta, and Michael Lounsbury. 2011. "Institutional Complexity and Organizational Responses." *The Academy of Management Annals* 5: 317–71.

Greve, Henrich R., Donald Palmer, and Jo-Ellen Pozner. 2010. "Organizations Gone Wild: The Causes, Processes, and Consequences of Organizational Misconduct." *The Academy of Management Annals* 4: 53–107.

Groddeck, Victoria von. 2011. "Rethinking the Role of Value Communication in Business Corporations from a Sociological Perspective – Why Organisations Need Value-Based Semantics to Cope with Societal and Organisational Fuzziness." *Journal of Business Ethics* 100: 69–84.

Grüninger, Stephan, Lisa Schöttl, and Josef Wieland. 2015. *Unternehmensintegrität & Compliance - Was wirklich wichtig ist.* Berlin: Zentrum für Wirtschaftsethik.

Gutenberg, Erich. 1958. *Einführung in die Betriebswirtschaftslehre: Erster Band: Die Produktion.* Wiesbaden: Gabler Verlag.

Guthrie, Doug, David L. Wank, and Thomas Gold. 2002. *Social Connections in China: Institutions, Culture, and the Changing Nature of Guanxi.* Cambridge, New York: Cambridge University Press.

Gutterman, Ellen, and Mathis Lohaus. 2018. "What Is the "Anti-Corruption" Norm in Global Politics?" In *Corruption and Social Norms: Why Informal Rules Matter.* Vol. 31, edited by Ina Kubbe and Annika Engelbert, 241–68. New York/ Secaucus: Palgrave Macmillan.

Guzman, Lily Rueda, and Barbora Holá. 2019. "Punishment in Negotiated Transitions: The Case of the Colombian Peace Agreement with the Farc-Ep." *International Criminal Law Review* 19 (1): 127–59.

Hahn, Rüdiger. 2013. "ISO 26000 and the Standardization of Strategic Management Processes for Sustainability and Corporate Social Responsibility." *Business Strategy and the Environment* 22 (7): 442–55.

Haldane, Andrew G. 2012. *The Dog and the Frisbee.* Jackson Hole: Speech at the Economic Policy Symposium.

Hallis, Frederick. 1978. *Corporate Personality: A Study in Jurisprudence.* Aalen: Scientia Bonnensis.

Hamilton, V. Lee, and Joseph Sanders. 1992. "Responsibility and Risk in Organizational Behavior." In *Research in Organizational Behavior:* Volume 14, edited by Barry M. Staw and Larry L. Cummings, 49–90. Greenwich: JAI.

Hamilton, V. Lee, and Joseph Sanders. 1999. "The Second Face of Evil: Wrongdoing in and by the Corporation." *Personality and Social Psychology Review* 3: 222–33.

Hansen, Hans Krause. 2012. "The Power of Performance Indices in the Global Politics of Anti-Corruption." *Journal of International Relations and Development* 15: 506–31.

Hart, H. L. A. 1968. *Law, Liberty and Morality.* Oxford: Oxford University Press.

Hašek, Jaroslav. 1960. *Die Abenteuer des braven Soldaten Schwejk: Band 1.* Reinbek: Rowohlt.

Hasnas, John. 2006. *Trapped: When Acting Ethically Is Against the Law.* Washington, D.C: Cato Institute.

Hawkins, Keith. 1984. *Environment and Enforcement.* Oxford: Oxford University Press.

Hawkins, Keith. 2001. *Law as a Last Resort: Prosecution Decision-Making in a Regulating Agency.* Oxford: Oxford University Press.

Hawkins, Richard. 1984. "Employee Theft in the Restaurant Trade: Forms of Ripping Off by Waiters at Work." *Deviant Behavior* 5 (1-4): 47–69.

Heady, Ferrel. 1957. "The Philippine Administrative System a Fusion of East and West." In *Toward the Comparative Study of Public Administration,* edited by William J. Siffin, 253–77. Bloominton: Indiana University Press.

Heald, David. 2006. "Varities of Transparency." In *Transparency: The Key to Better Governance,* edited by C. Hood and D. Heald, 25–46. Oxford: Oxford University Press

Hegarty, W. Harvey, and Henry P. Sims. 1979. "Organizational Philosophy, Policies, and Objectives Related to Unethical Decision Behavior: A Laboratory Experiment." *Journal of Applied Psychology* 64: 331–38.

Heilbroner, Robert L. 1972. *In the Name of Profit.* Garden City: Doubleday.

Heimann, C. F. Larry. 1993. "Understanding the Challenger Disaster: Organizational Structure and the Design of Reliable Systems." *American Political Science Review* 87 (2): 421–35.

Heimer, Carol A. 2010. "The Unstable Alliance of Law and Morality." In *Handbook of the Sociology of Morality*. Vol. 53, edited by Steven Hitlin and Stephen Vaisey, 179–202. New York: Springer.

Helmkamp, James, Richard Ball, and Kitty Townsend. 1996. *Definitional Dilemma: Can and Should There Be a Universal Definition of White Collar Crime.* Morgantown: National White Collar Crime Center.

Helmke, Gretchen, and Steven Levitsky. 2004. "Informal Institutions and Comparative Politics: A Research Agenda." *Perspectives on Politics* 2: 725–40.

Henry, Stuart. 1978. *The Hidden Economy: The Context and Control of Borderline Crime.* London: Martin Robertson.

Henry, Stuart, and Gerald Mars. 1978. "Crime at Work: The Social Construction of Amateur Property Theft." *Sociology* 12 (2): 245–63.

Heywood, Paul M. 2014. "Introduction: Scale and Focus in the Study of Corruption." In *Routledge Handbook of Political Corruption*, edited by Paul M. Heywood, 1–14. Hoboken: Taylor and Francis.

Hilgers, Tina. 2011. "Clientelism and Conceptual Stretching: Differentiating Among Concepts and Among Analytical Levels." *Theoretical Sociology* 40: 567–88.

Hiller, Petra. 2005. "Korruption und Netzwerke. Konfusionen im Schema von Organisation und Gesellschaft." *Zeitschrift für Rechtssoziologie* 26: 57–77.

Hirsch, Jacob B., Jackson G. Lu, and Adam D. Galinsky. 2018. "Moral Utility Theory: Understanding the Motivation to Behave (Un)Ethically." *Research in Organizational Behavior* 38: 43–59.

Hirschi, Travis. 1969. *Causes of Delinquency.* Berkeley: University of California Press.

Hirschi, Travis, and Michael R. Gottfredson. 1987. "Causes of White-Collar Crime." *Criminology* 25: 949–74.

Höffling, Christian. 2002. *Korruption als soziale Beziehung.* Opladen: Leske + Budrich.

Hoffman, Andrew J. 1999. "Institutional Evolution and Change: Environmentalism and the U.S. Chemical Industry." *Academy of Management Journal* 42 (4): 351–71.

Hofstede, Geert. 1980. *Culture's Consequences: International Differences in Work Related Values.* Beverly Hills/ London: Sage.

Hollinger, Richard C., and John P. Clark. 1982. "Employee Deviance: A Response to the Perceived Quality of the Work Experience." *Work and Occupation* 9: 97–114.

Holzer, Boris. 2007. "Wie "Modern" ist die Weltgesellschaft? Funktionale Differenzierung und ihre Alternativen." *Soziale Systeme* 13: 357–68.

Holzer, Boris. 2010. *Moralizing the Corporation: Transnational Activism and Corporate Accountability.* Cheltenham: Edward Elgar.

Holzer, Boris. 2015. "The Two Faces of World Society: Formal Structures and Institutionalized Informality." In *From Globalization to World Society*, edited by Boris Holzer, Fatima Kastner, and Tobias Werron, 37–60.London: Routledge.

Hood, Christopher. 2001. "Transparency." In *Encyclopedia of Democratic Thought*, edited by Paul B. Clarke and Joe Foweraker, 863–68. Abingdon/ Oxon: Taylor and Francis.

Hood, Christopher. 2007. "What Happens When Transparency Meets Blame-Avoidance?" *Public Management Review* 9 (2): 191–210.

Hood, Christopher, Henry Rothstein, and Robert Baldwin. 2001. *The Government of Risk: Understanding Risk Regulation Regimes.* Oxford: Oxford University Press.

Horch, Heinz-Dieter. 2018. "The Intermediary Organisational Structure of Voluntary Associations." *Voluntary Sector Review* 9: 55–72.

Horning, Donald N.M. 1970. "Blue-Collar Theft: Conception of Property, Attitudes Toward Pilfering, and Work Group Norms in Modern Industrial Plant." In *Crimes Against Bureaucracy*, edited by Erwin O. Smigel and H. Laurence Ross, 46–64.New York: Van Nostrand.

Howell, Jane M., and Christopher A. Higgins. 1990. "Champions of Technological Innovation." *Administrative Science Quarterly* 35:317–41.

Huff, Kevin. B. 1996. "The Role of Corporate Compliance Programs in Determining Corporate Criminal Liability: A Suggested Approach." *Columbia Law Review* 96: 1152–1298.

Huntington, Samuel P. 1968. *Political Order in Changing Societies.* New Haven/ London: Yale University Press.

Huntington, Samuel P. 1971. "The Change to Change. Modernization, Development and Politics." *Comparative Politics* 3: 283–322.

Hutchcroft, Paul D. 1997. "The Politics of Privilege: Assessing the Impact of Rents, Corruption, and Clientelism on Third World Development." *Political Studies* 45 (3): 639–58.

Hutchcroft, Paul D. 1998. *Booty Capitalism: The Politics of Banking in the Philippines.* Ithaca: Cornell University Press.

Hwang, Hokyu, and Jeannette A. Colyvas. 2011. "Problematizing Actors and Institutions in Institutional Work." *Journal of Management Inquiry* 20: 62–66.

Idowu, Samuel O., Nicholas Capaldi, Liangrong Zu, and Ananda Das Gupta. 2013. *Encyclopedia of Corporate Social Responsibility.* Berlin: Springer.

Ilie, Alexandra. 2012. *Unethical Pro-Organizational Behaviors: Antecedents and Boundary Conditions.* Tampa: University of South Florida.

Jackall, Robert. 1988. *Moral Mazes: The World of Corporate Managers.* Oxford: Oxford University Press.

Jacobs-Jenkins, Branden. 2015. *Gloria.* New York: Dramatists Play Service.

Jacoby, Neil H., Peter Nehemkis, and Richard Eells. 1977. *Bribery and Extortion in World Business: A Study of Corporate Political Payments Abroad.* New York: Free Press.

Jakobi, Anja P. 2013. "The Changing Global Norm of Anti-Corruption: From Bad Business to Bad Government." *Zeitschrift für Vergleichende Politikwissenschaft* 7 (S1): 243–64.

Jancsics, David. 2014. "Interdisciplinary Perspectives on Corruption." *Sociology Compass* 8:358–72.

Jang, Yong Suk. 2000. "The Worldwide Founding of Ministries of Science and Technology, 1950-1990." *Sociological Perspectives* 43: 247–70.

Jarvis, Rebecca. 2018. *The Dropout:* ABC Radio.

Jenkins, Anne, and John Braithwaite. 1993. "Profits, Pressure and Corporate Lawbreaking." *Crime, Law and Social Change* 20 (3): 221–32.

Jones, Gwen E., and Michael J. Kavanagh. 1996. "An Experimental Examination of the Effects of Individual and Situational Factors on Unethical Behavioral Intentions in the Workplace." *Journal of Business Ethics* 15:511–23.

Jones, Howard. 2019. *My Lai: Vietnam, 1968, and the Descent into Darkness.* New York/ Oxford: Oxford University Press.

Jones, Thomas M. 1991. "Ethical Decision Making by Individuals in Organizations: An Issue-Contingent Model." *Academy of Management Review* 16: 355–95.

Jones, Thomas M., Will Felps, and Gregory A. Bigley. 2007. "Ethical Theory and Stakeholder-Related Decisions: The Role of Stakeholder Culture." *Academy of Management Review* 32 (1): 137–55.

Joseph, Richard A. 2014. *Democracy and Prebendal Politics in Nigeria: The Rise and Fall of the Second Republic.* Cambridge: Cambridge University Press.

Josephson, Matthew. 1995. *The Robber Barons: The Great American Capitalists, 1861-1901.* San Diego: Harcourt Brace & Company.

Jung, Jae C., and Elizabeth Sharon. 2019. "The Volkswagen Emissions Scandal and Its Aftermath." *Global Business and Organizational Excellence* 38:6–15.

Kaduk, Stefan, Dirk Osmetz, Hans A. Wüthrich, and Dominik Hammer. 2013. *Musterbrecher: Die Kunst, das Spiel zu drehen.* Hamburg: Murmann.

Kagan, Robert A., Neil Gunningham, and Dorothy Thornton. 2011. "Fear, Duty, and Regulatory Compliance: Lessons from Three Research Projects." In *Explaining Conpliance: Business Responses to Regulation*, edited by Christine Parker and Vibeke Lehmann Nielsen, 37–58. Cheltenham: Edward Elgar Publishing.

Kagan, Robert A., and John T. Scholz. 1984. "The 'Criminology of the Corporation' and Regulatory Enforcement Strategies." In *Enforcing Regulation*, edited by K. Hawkins and J. Thomas. Boston: Kluwer-Nijhoff.

Kahan, Dan. 1997. "Ignorance of Law Is an Excuse - but Only for the Virtuous." *Michigan Law Review* 96: 127-154.

Kalthoff, Herbert. 2005. "Practices of Calculation: Economic Representations and Risk Management." *Theory, Culture and Society* 22: 69–97.

Kamdar, Dishan, Daniel J. McAllister, and Daniel B. Turban. 2006. ""All in a Day's "Ork": How Follower Individual Differences and Justice Perceptions Predict OCB Role Definitions and Behavior." *Journal of Applied Psychology* 91 (4): 841–55.

Kaptein, Muel, and Martien van Helvoort. 2019. "A Model of Neutralization Techniques." *Deviant Behavior* 40:1260–85.

Karpoff, Jonathan, and John R. Lott. 1993. "The Reputational Penality Firms Bear from Committing Criminal Fraud." *Journal of Law and Economics* 36: 757–802.

Kelly, Lois, and Carmen Medina. 2014. *Rebels at Work*. Sebastopol: O'Reilly Media.

Kette, Sven. 2012. "Das Unternehmen als Organisation." In *Handbuch Organisationstypen*, edited by Maja Apelt and Veronika Tacke, 21–42. Wiesbaden: Springer VS.

Kette, Sven. 2014. "Diskreditiertes Scheitern: Katastrophale Unfälle als Organisationsproblem." In *Scheitern- Organisations- und wirtschaftssoziologische Analysen*, edited by Jens Bergmann, Matthias Hahn, Antonia Langhof und Gabriele Wagner, 159–81.Wiesbaden: Springer VS.

Kette, Sven. 2017. *Unternehmen: Eine sehr kurze Einführung*. Wiesbaden: Springer VS.

Kette, Sven. 2018a. "Unsichere Verantwortungszurechnungen: Dynamiken Organisationalen Compliance Managements." *Gesundheits-Recht* 17: 3–6.

Kette, Sven. 2018b. *Vertrauen ist gut, Kontrolle ist besser? Dysfunktionen Organisationalen Compliance Managements*. Luzern: Unveröff. Ms.

Kette, Sven, and Sebastian Barnutz. 2019. *Compliance Managen: Eine sehr kurze Einführung*. Wiesbaden: Springer VS.

Khan, Mushtaq H. 2006. "Determinants of Corruption in Developing Countries: The Limits of Conventional Economic Analysis." In

International Handbook on the Economics of Corruption, edited by Susan Rose-Ackerman, 216–46. Cheltenham: Edward Elgar.

Kidder, Tracy. 1981. *The Soul of a New Machine*. New York, Boston, London: Little, Brown & Company.

Kieserling, André. 2015. "Soziologische Ausgangspunkte für Systemi-mmanente Kritik." In *Systemtheorie und Differenzierungstheorie als Kritik: Perspektiven in Anschluss an Niklas Luhmann*, edited by Albert Scherr. Weinheim/ Basel: Beltz Juventa.

Kindler, Steffi. 2008. *Das Unternehmen als Haftender Täter: Ein Beitrag zur Frage der Verbandsstrafe im Deutschen Strafrechtssystem: Lösungswege und Entwicklungsperspektiven: De Lege Lata und De Lege Ferenda*. Baden-Baden: Nomos.

Kittler, Wolf. 1994. "Die Revolution der Revolution: Oder was gilt es in dem Kriege, den Kleists Prinz von Homburg Kämpft." In *Heinrich von Kleist: Kriegsfall - Rechtsfall - Sündenfall*, edited by Gerhard Neumann, 61–85. Freiburg i.Br.: Rombach.

Kleist, Heinrich von. 1996. "Prinz Friedrich von Homburg. Ein Schauspiel." In *Heinrich von Kleist* by Helmut Sembdner, 515-584. München/ Wien: Carl Hanser.

Klinkhammer, Julian. 2015. "Varieties of Corruption in the Shadow of Siemens: A Modus-Operandi Study of Corporate Crime on the Supply Side of Corrupt Transactions." In *Routledge Handbook of White-Collar and Corporate Crime in Europe*, edited by Judith van Erp, Wim Huisman, and Gudrun V. Walle, 318–35. London: Routledge.

Klitgaard, Robert. 1988. *Controlling Corruption*. Berkeley: University of California Press.

Kohlberg, Lawrence. 1969. "Sages and Sequence: The Cognitive-Developmental Approach to Socialization." In *Handbook of Socialization Theory and Research*, edited by David A. Goslin, 347–80. Chicago: Rand McNally.

Kölbel, Ralf. 2014. "Corporate Crime, Unternehmenssanktion Und Kriminelle Verbandsattitüde." *Zeitschrift für Internationale Strafrechtsdogmatik* 11: 552–57.

Kornberger, Martin, Stephan Leixnering, and Renate E. Meyer. 2019. "The Logic of Tact: How Decisions Happen in Situations of Crisis." *Organization Studies* 40: 239-66.

Kraakman, Reinier H. 1984. "Corporate Liability Strategies and the Costs of Legal Controls." *Yale Law Journal* 93: 857–98.

Kraatz, Matthew S., and Emily S. Block. 2008. "Organizational Implications of Institutional Pluralism." In *The SAGE Handbook of Organizational Institutionalism*, edited by Royston Greenwood, Christine Oliver, Kerstin Sahlin-Andersson, and Roy Suddaby, 243–75. Los Angeles: Sage.

Krawiec, Kimberly D. 2003. "Cosmetic Compliance and the Failure of Negotiated Governance." *Washington University Law Quarterly* 81: 487–544.

Kuchler, Barbara. 2014. "Symbiosen von Recht und Korruption." In *Vielfalt und Zusammenhalt. Verhandlungen des 36. Kongresses der Deutschen Gesellschaft ür Soziologie 2012*, edited by Martina Löw, 1–15. Frankfurt a.M./ New York: Campus.

Kühl, Stefan. 2003. *Exit. Wie Risikokapital die Regeln der Wirtschaft verändert*. Frankfurt a.M./ New York: Campus.

Kühl, Stefan: 2005a. *Exit. How Venture Capital Changes the Laws of Ecomomics*. Working Paper 3/2005

Kühl, Stefan. 2005b. "Ordinary Organizations: Simulated Brutality Reinterpreted from an Organizational Sociology Perspective." *Zeitschrift für Soziologie* 34: 90–111.

Kühl, Stefan. 2007a. "Formalität, Informalität und Illegalität in der Organisationsberatung: Systemtheoretische Analyse eines Beratungsprozesses." *Soziale Welt* 58: 269–91.

Kühl, Stefan. 2007b. "Zahlenspiele in der Entwicklungshilfe: Zu einer Soziologie des Deckungsbeitrages." In *Zahlenwerk*, edited by Andrea Mennicken and Hendrik Vollmer, 185–206. Wiesbaden: VS Verlag für Sozialwissenschaften.

Kühl, Stefan. 2011. *Organisationen: Eine sehr kurze Einführung*. Wiesbaden: VS Verlag für Sozialwissenschaften.

Kühl, Stefan. 2012. "Zwangsorganisationen." In *Handbuch Organisationstypen*, edited by Maja Apelt and Veronika Tacke, 345–58. Wiesbaden: Springer VS.

Kühl, Stefan. 2013. *Organizations: A Systems Approach*. Farnham: Gower.

Kühl, Stefan. 2014. *The Sudoku Effect: Universities in the Vicious Circle of Bureaucracy.* Wiesbaden: Springer.

Kühl, Stefan. 2015. "The Diffusion of Organizations: The Role of Foreign Aid." In *From Globalization to World Society,* edited by Boris Holzer, Fatima Kastner, and Tobias Werron, 258–78. London: Routledge.

Kühl, Stefan. 2016. *Ordinary Organizations: Why Normal Men Carried Out the Holocaust.* Cambridge: Polity.

Kühl, Stefan. 2018a. "Organisationskultur: Eine Konkretisierung aus systemtheoretischer Perspektive." *Managementforschung* 18: 7-35.

Kühl, Stefan. 2018b. *Influencing Organizational Culture: A Very Brief Introduction.* Princeton: Organizational Dialogue Press.

Kühl, Stefan. 2019a. "Jenseits von zweckrationalen Steuerungsfantasien im Management." In *Handbuch Organisationssoziologie.* Vol. 41, edited by Maja Apelt, Ingo Bode, and Raimund Hasse, 1–19. Wiesbaden: Springer Fachmedien Wiesbaden.

Kühl, Stefan. 2019b. *The Rainmaker Effect: Contradictions of the Learning Organization.* Princeton: Organizational Dialogue Press.

Kühl, Stefan. 2019c. *Work: Marxist and Systems-Theoretical Approaches.* London/ New York: Routledge.

Kühl, Stefan. 2020. *Sisyphus in Management: The Futile Search for the Optimal Organizational Structure.* Princeton: Organizational Dialogue Press.

Laabs, Dirk. 2018. *Bad Bank: Aufstieg nd Fall der Deutschen Bank.* München: DVA.

Lampert, Nicholas. 1985. *Whistleblowing in the Soviet Union: Complaints and Abuses Under State Socialism.* Studies in Soviet History and Society. London: Palgrave Macmillan.

Land, Christopher, Scott Loren, and Jörg Metelmann. 2014. "Rogue Logics: Organization in the Grey Zone." *Organization Studies* 35 (2): 233–53.

Langworth, Richard M. 2008. *Churchill by Himself: The Definitive Collection of Quotations.* Newburyport: RosettaBooks.

Larner, Justin, and Chris Mason. 2014. "Beyond Box-Ticking: A Study of Stakeholder Involvement in Social Enterprise Governance." *Corporate Governance* 14 (2): 181–96.

Lauderdale, Pat, Harold Grasmick, and John P. Clark. 1978. "Corporate Environments, Corporate Crime, and Deterrence." In *Crime, Law, and Sanctions*, edited by Marvin D. Krohn and Ronald L. Akers, 137–58. Beverly Hills/ London: Sage.

Laufer, William S. 1999. "Corporate Liability, Risk Shifting, and the Paradox of Compliance." *Vanderbilt Law Review* 52: 1341-20.

Laufer, William S. 2006. *Corporate Bodies and Guilty Minds: The Failure of Corporate Criminal Liability.* Chicago/ London: University of Chicago Press.

Laufer, William S., and Diana C. Robertson. 1997. "Corporate Ethics Initiatives as Social Control." *Journal of Business Ethics* 16 (10): 1029–47.

Lauri, Antonio de. 2013. "Corruption, Legal Modernisation and Judicial Practice in Afghanistan." *Asian Studies Review* 37 (4): 527–45.

Lauth, Hans-Joachim. 1999. "Informelle Institutionen, Politischer Partizipation und ihre Demokratietheoretische Bedeutung." In *Im Schatten Demokratischer Legitimität*, edited by Hans-Joachim Lauth and Ulrike Liebert, 61–84. Opladen: WDV.

Lauth, Hans-Joachim. 2000. "Informal Institutions and Democracy." *Democratization* 7: 21–50.

Ledeneva, Alena V. 1998. *Russia's Economy of Favours: Blat, Networking and Informal Exchange.* Cambridge: Cambridge University Press.

Ledeneva, Alena V. 2001. *Unwritten Rules: How Russia Really Works.* London: Center for European Reform.

Ledeneva, Alena V. 2008. "Blat and Guanxi: Informal Practices in Russia and China." *Comparative Studies in Society and History* 50 (01): 80.

Ledeneva, Alena V. 2011. "Open Secrets and Knowing Smile." *East European Politics and Societies* 25: 720–36.

Ledeneva, Alena V. 2018. *The Global Encyclopaedia of Informality:* Volume 1. London: UCL Press.

Lee, Frederic P. 1928. "Corporate Criminal Liability." *Columbia Law Review* 28: 1–28.

Leff, Nathaniel H. 1964. "Economic Development Through Bureaucratic Corruption." *American Behavioral Scientist* 8 (3): 8–14.

Lemarchand, René. 1972. "Political Clientelism and Ethnicity in Trop-
ical Africa: Competing Solidarities in Nation-Building." *American
Political Science Review* 66: 68–90.

Lennerfors, Thomas Taro. 2007. "The Transformation of Transparency—on the Act on Public Procurement and the Right to Appeal
in the Context of the War on Corruption." *Journal of Business Ethics*
73 (4): 381–90.

Lepper, Christoph. 2018. "Richtlinie zur Verwendung der
E-Mail-Adressfelder "An", "Cc" und "Bcc"." *Corporate Compliance
Zeitschrift* 11: 178–79.

Levi, Michael. 1998. "Perspectives on Organised Crime: An Overview."
Howard Journal of Criminal Justice 37: 335–45.

Levitt, Steven D., and Stephen J. Dubner. 2006. *Freakonomics.* New
York: HarperTorch.

Lewis, Alexandra. 2015. *Security, Clans and Tribes: Unstable Governance
in Somaliland, Yemen and the Gulf of Aden.* Basingstoke/ Hampshire:
Palgrave Macmillan.

Leys, Colin. 1965. "What Is the Problem About Corruption?" *Journal
of Modern African Studies* 3: 215–30.

Lifton, Robert Jay. 1986. *The Nazi Doctors: Medical Killing and the
Psychology of Genocide.* New York: Basic Books.

Lincoln, James R., and Michael L. Gerlach. 2004. *Japan's Network
Economy: Structure, Persistence, and Change.* Cambridge: Cambridge
University Press.

Lu, Xiaobo. 2000. "Booty Socialism, Bureau-Preneurs, and the State
in Transition: Organizational Corruption in China." *Comparative
Politics* 32 (3): 273–94.

Lübbe, Hermann. 1983. "Der Nationalsozialismus im deutschen Nach-
kriegsbewußtsein." *Historische Zeitschrift* 236: 579–99.

Lübbe, Hermann. 1998. "Kontingenzerfahrung und Kontingenzbe-
wältigung." In *Kontingenz,* edited by Gerhart Graevenitz and Odo
Marquard, 35–48. Fink: Wilhelm Fink.

Luhmann, Niklas. 1964a. "Funktionale Analyse. Methode und Systemtheorie." *Soziale Welt* 15: 1–25.

Luhmann, Niklas. 1964b. *Funktionen und Folgen formaler Organisation.*
Berlin: Duncker & Humblot.

Luhmann, Niklas. 1969. "Funktionale Methode und juristische Entscheidung." In *Archiv des öffentlichen Rechts* 94: 1–31.

Luhmann, Niklas. 1970a. "Funktion Und Kausalität." In *Soziologische Aufsätze 1: Aufsätze zur Theorie sozialer Systeme*, edited by Niklas Luhmann, 9-30. Opladen: WDV.

Luhmann, Niklas. 1970b. "Funktionale Methode Und Systemtheorie." In *Soziologische Aufsätze 1: Aufsätze zur Theorie sozialer Systeme*, edited by Niklas Luhmann, 31-53. Opladen: WDV.

Luhmann, Niklas.1972. *Rechtssoziologie*. Reinbek: Rowohlt.

Luhmann, Niklas. 1973. *Zweckbegriff und Systemrationalität*. Frankfurt a.M.: Suhrkamp.

Luhmann, Niklas. 1983. *Legitimation durch Verfahren*. Frankfurt a.M.: Suhrkamp.

Luhmann, Niklas. 1984. "Soziologische Aspekte des Entscheidungsverhaltens." In *Die Betriebswirtschaft* 44: 591–603.

Luhmann, Niklas. 1985. "Neue Politische Ökonomie." *Soziologische Revue* 8: 115–20.

Luhmann, Niklas. 1987. "Sozialisation und Erziehung." In *Soziologische Aufklärung 4: Beiträge zur funktionalen Differenzierung der Gesellschaft*, edited by Niklas Luhmann, 173–81. Opladen: WDV.

Luhmann, Niklas. 1988. "Medium und Organisation." In *Die Wirtschaft der Gesellschaft*, edited by Niklas Luhmann, 272–301. Frankfurt a.M.: Suhrkamp.

Luhmann, Niklas. 1990a. "Die Stellung der Gerichte im Rechtssystem." *Rechtstheorie* 21: 459–73.

Luhmann, Niklas. 1990b. *Paradigm Lost: Über Die Ethische Reflexion Der Moral*. Frankfurt a.M.: Suhrkamp.

Luhmann, Niklas. 1992. *Die Wissenschaft der Gesellschaft*. Frankfurt a.M.: Suhrkamp.Luhmann, Niklas. 1995a. "Kausalität im Süden." *Soziale Systeme* 1: 7–28.

Luhmann, Niklas. 1995a. "Kausalität im Süden" in: *Soziale Systeme* 1, 7–28.

Luhmann, Niklas. 1995b.: *Social Systems*. Stanford: Stanford University Press.

Luhmann, Niklas. 1996a. "Complexity, Structural Contingencies and Value Conflicts." In *Detraditionalization*, edited by Paul Heelas, Scott Lash, and Paul Morris, 59–71. Cambridge: Blackwell.

Luhmann, Niklas. 1996b. "Gefahr oder Risiko, Solidarität oder Konflikt." In *Risiko-Dialog: Zukunft ohne Harmonieformel*, edited by Roswita Königswieser, Matthias Haller, and Maas, 38–48. Köln: Deutscher Instituts-Verlag.

Luhmann, Niklas. 2000. *The Reality of the Mass Media*. Cambridge: Polity.

Luhmann, Niklas. 2002a. *Das Erziehungssystem Der Gesellschaft*. Frankfurt a.M.: Suhrkamp.

Luhmann, Niklas. 2002b. *Die Politik der Gesellschaft*. Frankfurt a.M.: Suhrkamp.

Luhmann, Niklas. 2004. *Law as a Social System*. Oxford: Oxford University Press.

Luhmann, Niklas. 2005a. "Allgemeine Theorie organisierter Sozialsysteme." In *Soziologische Aufklärung 1: Aufsätze zur Theorie sozialer Systeme*, edited by Niklas Luhmann, 48–62. Wiesbaden: VS Verlag für Sozialwissenschaften.

Luhmann, Niklas. 2005b. "Positives Recht und Ideologie." In *Soziologische Aufklärung 1: Aufsätze zur Theorie sozialer Systeme*, edited by Niklas Luhmann 2005, 224-55. Wiesbaden: VS Verlag für Sozialwissenschaften.

Luhmann, Niklas. 2008a. "Ethik als Reflexionstheorie der Moral." In *Die Moral der Gesellschaft*, edited by Niklas Luhmann, 270-61. Frankfurt a.M.: Suhrkamp.

Luhmann, Niklas. 2008b. "Gibt es in unserer Gesellschaft noch unverzichtbare Normen?" In *Die Moral der Gesellschaft*, edited by Niklas Luhmann, 228-52. Frankfurt a.M.: Suhrkamp.

Luhmann, Niklas. 2008c. "Soziologie der Moral." In *Die Moral der Gesellschaft*, edited by Niklas Luhmann, 56-162. Frankfurt a.M.: Suhrkamp.

Luhmann, Niklas. 2008d. "Verständigung über Risiken und Gefahren." In *Die Moral der Gesellschaft*, edited by Niklas Luhmann, 348-61. Frankfurt a.M.: Suhrkamp.

Luhmann, Niklas. 2008e. "Wirtschaftsethik als Ethik?" In *Die Moral der Gesellschaft*, edited by Niklas Luhmann, 196-208. Frankfurt a.M.: Suhrkamp.

Luhmann, Niklas. 2009. "Zur Komplexität von Entscheidungssituationen." *Soziale Systeme* 15: 3–35.

Luhmann, Niklas. 2010a. "Nomologische Hypothesen, funktionale Äquivalenz, Limitationalität: Zum wissenschaftstheoretischen Verständnis des Funktionalismus." *Soziale Systeme* 16: 3–27.

Luhmann, Niklas. 2010b. *Politische Soziologie*. Frankfurt a.M.: Suhrkamp.

Luhmann, Niklas. 2012. *Theory of Society*, Volume 1. Stanford: Stanford University Press.

Luhmann, Niklas. 2013. *Theory of Society*, Volume 2. Stanford: Stanford University Press.

Luhmann, Niklas. 2014. *A Sociological Theory of Law*. Oxford: Routledge.

Luhmann, Niklas. 2015. "Communication about law in interaction systems" In *Advances in Social Theory and Methodology: Toward an Integration of Micro- and Macro-Sociologies*, edited by K. Knorr-Cetina and A.V. Cicourel, 234-56. London/ New York: Routledge.

Luhmann, Niklas. 2017a. *Risk: A Sociological Theory*. Abingdon: Routledge.

Luhmann, Niklas. 2017b. *Trust and Power*. Cambridge, UK: Polity.

Luhmann, Niklas.2018a. *Organization and Decision*. Cambridge, UK: Cambridge University Press.

Luhmann, Niklas.2018b. "Verantwortung und Verantwortlichkeit" In *Schriften zur Organisation 1: Die Wirklichkeit der Organisation*, edited by Ernst Lukas and Veronika Tacke, 47–58. Wiesbaden: Springer VS.

Luhmann, Niklas. 2020. "Organization, membership and the formalization of behavioural expectations," *Systems Research and Behavioral Science* 37: 425–449.

Lundman, Richard J. 1979. "Organizational Norms and Police Discretion: An Observational Study of Police Work with Traffic Law Violators." *Criminology* 17: 159–71.

Lynch, Michael J., Danielle McGurrin, and Melissa Fenwick. 2004. "Disappearing Act: The Representation of Corporate Crime Research in Criminological Literature." *Journal of Criminal Justice* 32 (5): 389–98.

Malinowski, Bronislaw K. 1949. *Eine wissenschaftliche Theorie der Kultur und andere Aufsätze.* Zürich: Pan Verlag.

Mandeville, Bernard de. 1998. *Die Bienenfabel oder private Laster, öffentliche Vorteile.* Frankfurt a.M.: Suhrkamp.

Mangione, Thomas W., and Robert P. Quinn. 1975. "Job Satisfaction, Counterproductive Behavior, and Drug Use at Work." *Journal of Applied Psychology* 60: 114–116.

Manning, Ryann, and Michael Anteby. 2016. "Wrong Paths to Right: Defining Morality with or Without a Clear Red Line." In *Organizational Wrongdoing: Key Perspectives and New Directions,* edited by Donald Palmer, Kristin Smith-Crowe, and Royston Greenwood, 47-76. Cambridge, UK: Cambridge University Press.

Maon, François, Adam Lindgreen, and Valérie Swaen. 2010. "Organizational Stages and Cultural Phases: A Critical Review and a Consolidative Model of Corporate Social Responsibility Development." *International Journal of Management Reviews* 12 (1): 20–38.

March, James G. 1978. "Bounded Rationality, Ambiguity, and the Engineering of Choice." *Bell Journal of Economics and Management Science* 9: 587–608.

March, James G. 1991. "How Decisions Happen in Organizations." *Human-Computer Interaction* 6: 95–117.

March, James G. 2010. *The Ambiguites of Experience.* Ithaca, NY: Cornell University Press.

March, James G., and Herbert A. Simon. 1958. *Organizations.* New York: John Wiley & Sons.

Marens, Richard. 2013. "What Comes Around: The Early 20th Century American Roots of Legitimating Corporate Social Responsibility." *Organization* 20 (3): 454–76.

Maria, William de. 2008. "Whistleblowers and Organizational Protesters." *Current Sociology* 56 (6): 865–83.

Mark, Robert. 1977. *Policing a Perplexed Society.* London: Georg Allen & Unwin.

Marquette, Heather. 2011. "Donors, State Building and Corruption: Lessons from Afghanistan and the Implications for Aid Policy." *Third World Quarterly* 32 (10): 1871–90.

Marquis, Christopher, and Michael Lounsbury. 2007. "Vive La Résistance: Competing Logics and the Consolidation of U.S. Community Banking." *Academy of Management Journal* 50: 799–820.

Mars, Gerald. 1973. "Hotel Pilferage: A Case Study in Occupational Theft." In *The Sociology of the Workplace*, edited by Malcolm Warner, 200-10. New York: Halsted.

Mars, Gerald. 1974. "Dock Pilferage: A Case Study in Occupational Theft." In *Deviance and Social Control*, edited by Paul Rock and Mary Mcintosh, 209-28. London: Tavistock.

Mars, Gerald. 1982. *Cheats at Work: An Anthropology of the Workplace.* London: Routledge.

Mars, Gerald. 2013. *Locating Deviance: Crime, Change and Organizations.* Farnham/ Surrey: Ashgate.

Mars, Gerald, Donald T. Bryant, and Peter Mitchell. 1979. *Manpower Problems in the Hotel and Catering Industry.* Farnborough, Eng: Saxon House.

Mars, Gerald, and Michael Nicod. 1984. *The World of Waiters.* London: Allen & Unwin.

Martin, Bradley K. 2004. *Under the Loving Care of the Fatherly Leader: North Korea and the Kim Dynasty.* New York: Thomas Dunne Books.

Martin, John P. 1962. *Offenders as Employees.* New York: St. Martin's Press.

Marx, Gary T. 1981. "Ironies of Social Control: Authorities as Contributors to Deviance Through Escalation, Nonenforcement and Covert Facilitation." *Social Problems* 28: 221-46.

Marx, Karl. 2010a. "Capital: A Critique of Political Economy, Volume I, Book I" In *Marx & Engels Collected Works*, Volume 35, edited by Karl Marx, 45-761. London: Lawrence & Wishart.

Marx, Karl. 2010b. "Digression: on Productive Labour" In *Marx & Engels Collected Works*, Volume 30, edited by Karl Marx, 306-317. London: Lawrence & Wishart.

Masuch, Michael. 1985. "Vicious Circles in Organizations." *Administrative Science Quarterly* 30: 13–33.

Mathews, M. Cash. 1988. *Strategic Intervention in Organizations: Resolving Ethical Dilemmas.* Newbury Park: Sage.

Matsueda, Ross L. 1988. "The Current State of Differential Association Theory." *Crime & Delinquency* 34: 277–306.

Matys, Thomas. 2011. *Legal Persons - "Kämpfe" und die organisationale Form.* Wiesbaden: VS Verlag für Sozialwissenschaften.

Mauro, P. 1995. "Corruption and Growth." *The Quarterly Journal of Economics* 110 (3): 681–712.

Mayntz, Renate. 1963. *Soziologie der Organisation.* Reinbek: Rowohlt.

Mayntz, Renate, and Fritz Scharpf. 1995. "Der Ansatz des akteurzentrierte Institutionalismus." In *Gesellschaftliche Selbstregelung und politische Steuerung,* edited by Renate Mayntz and Fritz W. Scharpf, 39–72. Frankfurt a.M./ New York: Campus.

Mayo, Elton. 1933. *The Human Problems of an Industrial Civilization.* New York: Macmillan.

McBarnet, Doreen. 2006. "After Enron Will 'Whiter Than White Collar Crime' Still Wash?" *British Journal of Criminology* 46 (6): 1091-109.

McGee, Robert W. 1993. "Is Tax Evasion Unethical." *University of Kansas Law Review* 42: 411–35.

McGivern, Gerry, and Ewan Ferlie. 2007. "Playing Tick-Box Games: Interrelating Defences in Professional Appraisal." *Human Relations* 60 (9): 1361–85.

McGreal, Chris. 2018. *American Overdose: The Opioid Tragedy in Three Acts.* New York: PublicAffairs.

McLaughlin, Judith Block. 1985. "From Secrecy to Sunshine: An Overview of Presidential Search Practice." *Research in Higher Education* 22 (2): 195–208.

McLean, Bethany, and Peter Elkind. 2004. *The Smartest Guys in the Room: The Amazing Rise and Scandalous Fall of Enron.* New York: Portfolio.

McMullan, M. 1961. "A Theory of Corruption." *The Sociological Review* 9: 181–201.

McVisk, William. 1978. "Toward a Rational Theory of Criminal Liability for the Corporate Executive." *The Journal of Criminal Law and Criminology* 69: 75–91.

McWilliams, Abagail, and Donald Siegel. 2001. "Corporate Social Responsibility: A Theory of the Firm Perspective." *Academy of Management Review* 26: 117–27.

Meier, Barry. 2018. *Pain Killer: An Empire of Deceit and the Origin of America's Opioid Epidemic.* 2nd ed. New York: Random House.

Meirovich, Gavriel, and Arie Reichel. 2000. "Illegal but Ethical: An Inquiry into the Roots of Illegal Corporate Behaviour in Russia." *Business Ethics - An European Review* 9: 126–35.

Méon, Pierre-Guillaume, and Khalid Sekkat. 2005. "Does Corruption Grease or Sand the Wheels of Growth?" *Public Choice* 122: 69–97.

Méon, Pierre-Guillaume, and Laurent Weill. 2010. "Is Corruption an Efficient Grease?" *World Development* 38 (3): 244–59.

Merton, Robert K. 1936. "The Unanticipated Consequences of Purposive Social Action." *American Sociological Review* 1: 894–904.

Merton, Robert K. 1940. "Bureaucratic Structure and Personality." *Social Forces* 17: 560–68.

Merton, Robert K. 1957a. "Continuities in the Theory of Reference Groups and Social Structure." In *Social Theory and Social Structure.* 2nd ed., edited by Robert K. Merton, 281–386.Glencoe: Free Press.

Merton, Robert K. 1957b. "Manifest and Latent Functions." In *Social Theory and Social Structure.* 2nd ed., edited by Robert K. Merton, 19-84. Glencoe: Free Press.Meyer,

John W. 1992. "Institutionalization and the Rationality of Formal Organizational Structure." In *Organizational Environments: Ritual and Rationality,* edited by John W. Meyer and W. R. Scott, 261–83. Newbury/ London/ New Delhi: Sage.

Meyer, John W., and Ronald L. Jepperson. 2000. "The "Actors" of Modern Society: The Cultural Construction of Social Agency." *Sociological Theory* 18: 100–120.

Meyer, John W., Francisco O. Ramirez, and Yasemin Nuhoglu Soysal. 1992. "World Expansion of Mass Education, 1870-1980." *Sociology of Education* 65:128.

Meyer, John W., and Brian Rowan. 1977. "Institutionalized Organizations. Formal Structure as Myth and Ceremony." *American Journal of Sociology* 83: 340–63.

Meyer, Michael, and Ruth Simsa. 2018. "Organizing the Unexpected: How Civil Society Organizations Dealt with the Refugee Crisis" *Voluntas* 29, 1159–75.

Meyers, Joan M. 2013. "Alternative Organizations and Cooperatives." In *Sociology of Work: An Encyclopedia*, edited by Vicki Smith, 2–6. Los Angeles/ London/ New Delhi: Sage.

Michalowski, Raymond, and Ronald C. Kramer. 1987. "The Space Between Laws: The Problem of Corporate Crime in a Transnational Context." *Social Problems* 34: 113–21.

Michalowski, Raymond J. 1985. *Order, Law and Crime.* New York: Random House.

Miethe, Terance D., and Joyce Rothschild. 1994. "Whistleblowing and the Control of Organizational Misconduct." *Sociological Inquiry* 64 (3): 322–47.

Milgram, Stanley. 1963. "Behavioral Study of Obedience." *Journal of Abnormal and Social Psychology* 67: 371–78.

Milgram, Stanley. 1964. "Group Pressure and Action Against a Person." *Journal of Abnormal and Social Psychology* 69: 137–43.

Milgram, Stanley. 1965a. "Liberating Effects of Group Pressure." *Journal of Personality and Social Psychology* 1: 127–34.

Milgram, Stanley. 1965b. "Some Conditions of Obedience and Disobedience to Authority." *Human Relations* 18: 57-76.

Miller, Nathan. 1992. *Stealing from America: A History of Corruption from Jamestown to Reagan.* New York: Paragon House.

Miller, Philip B. 1982. *An Abyss Deep Enough: Letters of Heinrich von Kleist with a Selection of Essays and Anecdotes.* New York: E.P. Dutton.

Mills, C. Wright. 1940. "Situated Actions and Vocabularies of Motive." *American Sociological Review* 5: 904-13.

Mitchell, Basil. 1978. *Law, Morality, and Religion in a Secular Society.* Oxford: Oxford University Press.

Mokhiber, Russell. 1988. *Corporate Crime and Violence: Big Business Power and the Abuse of the Public Trust.* San Francisco: Sierra Club Books.

Molinsky, Andrew, and Joshua Margolis. 2005. "Necessary Evils and Interpersonal Sensitivity in Organizations." *Academy of Management Review* 30: 245-68.

Möllers, Christoph. 2018. *Die Möglichkeit der Normen: Über eine Praxis jenseits von Moralität und Kausalität.* Berlin: Suhrkamp.

Morris, Albert. 1934. *Criminology.* New York: Longman.

Morrison, Elizabeth W. 2006. "Doing the Job Well: An Investigation of Pro-Social Rule Breaking." *Journal of Management* 32: 5-28.

Motta, Fernando C. Prestes, and Rafael Alcadipani. 1999. "Jeitinho Brasileiro, Controle Social E Competição." *Revista de Administração de Empresas* 39 (1): 6-12.

Mühlhäuser, Regina. 2020. *Sex and the Nazi Soldier: Violent, Commercial and Consensual Encounters During the War in the Soviet Union, 1941-1945.* Edinburgh: Edinburgh University Press.

Mujtaba, Bahaudin G. 2013. "Ethnic Diversity, Distrust and Corruption in Afghanistan." *Equality, Diversity and Inclusion: An International Journal* 32: 245-61.

Müthel, Miriam. 2017. "Pro-Organisationales illegales Verhalten: Wie und warum gute Mitarbeiter dem Unternehmen schadet." *Zeitschrift Führung & Organisation* 86: 31–36.

Muzio, Daniel, James Faulconbridge, Claudia Gabbioneta, and Royston Greenwood. 2016. "Bad Apples, Bad Barrels and Bad Cellars: A "Boundaries" Perspective on Professional Misconduct." In *Organizational Wrongdoing: Key Perspectives and New Directions*, edited by Donald Palmer, Royston Greenwood, and Kristin Smith-Crowe, 141-175. Cambridge, UK: Cambridge University Press.

Myrdal, Gunnar. 1970. "Corruption as a Hindrance to Modernization in South Asia." In *Political Corruption. Readings in Comparative Analysis*, edited by Arnold J. Heidenheimer. New Brunswick: Transaction.

Myrdal, Gunnar. 1977. *Asian Drama: An Inquiry into the Poverty of Nations.* Harmondsworth: Penguin Books.

Nace, Ted. 2003. *Gangs of America: The Rise of Corporate Power and the Disabling of Democracy.* San Francisco: Berrett-Koehler Publishers.

Nader, Ralph. 1965. *Unsafe at Any Speed: The Designed-in Dangers of the American Automobile.* New York: Grossman Publishers.

Near, Janet P., and Marcia P. Miceli. 1987. "Whistle-Blowers in Organizations: Dissidents or Reformers?" *Research in Organisational Behavior* 9: 321–68.

Neckel, Sighard. 1995. "Der unmoralische Tausch. Eine Soziologie der Käuflichkeit." *Kursbuch* 120 (Juni): 9–16.

Needleman, Martin L., and Carolyn Needleman. 1979. "Organizational Crime: Two Models of Criminogenesis." *The Sociological Quarterly* 20 (4): 517–28.

New, Robert Cameron. 1994. *Are Your Employees Stealing You Blind? Answers and Solutions for Retailers and Other Small Businesses.* Amherst: Mass. HRD Press.

Neyland, Daniel. 2007. "Achieving Transparency: The Visible, Invisible and Divisible in Academic Accountability Networks." *Organization* 14 (4): 499–516.

Noonan, John T. 1984. *Bribes.* New York: Macmillan.

Nove, Alec. 1961. *The Soviet Economy.* London: Allen & Unwin.

O'Connell Davidson, Julia. 2015. *Modern Slavery: The Margins of Freedom.* Basingstoke: Palgrave Macmillan.

Olasolo, Héctor, and Jannluck Canosa Cantor. 2019. "The Treatment of Superior Responsibility in Colombia: Interpreting the Agreement Between the Colombian Government and the FARC." *Criminal Law Forum* 30 (1): 61-107.

Oliver, Christine. 1991. "Strategic Responses to Institutional Processes." *Academy of Management Review* 16: 145-79.

O'Neill, Onora. 2010. *A Question of Trust.* 5th ed. Cambridge: Cambridge University Press.

Orr, Julian E. 1996. *Talking About Machines: An Ehtnography of a Modern Job.* Ithaca: Cornell University Press.

Ortmann, Günther. 2003. *Regel und Ausnahme: Paradoxien sozialer Ordnung.* Frankfurt a.M.: Suhrkamp.

Ortmann, Günther. 2017. "Für ein Unternehmensstrafrecht: Sechs Thesen sieben Fragen, eine Nachbermerkung." *Neue Zeitschrift für Wirtschafts-, Steuer- und Unternehmensstrafrecht* 6: 241-51.

Osrecki, Fran. 2014. "Autonomie von der Abweichung her denken: Zur Wiederentdeckung einer Theoriefigur." In *Autonomie revisited: Beiträge zu einem umstrittenen Grundbegriff in Wissenschaft, Kunst und Politik*, edited by Martina Franzen, Arlena Jung, David Kaldewey, and Jasper Korte, 400-423. Weinheim: Beltz Juventa.

Osrecki, Fran. 2015. "Fighting Corruption with Transparent Organizations: Anti-Corruption and Functional Deviance in Organizational Behavior." *Ephemera* 15: 337-64.

Ott, Claus. 1977. *Recht und Realität der Unternehmenskorporation: Ein Beitrag zur Theorie der juristischen Person.* Tübingen: Mohr.

Pache, Anne-Claire, and Filipe Santos. 2010. "When Worlds Collide: The Internal Dynamics of Organizational Responses to Conflicting Institutional Demands." *Academy of Management Review* 35 (3): 455-76.

Paine, Lynn Sharp. 1994. "Managing for Organizational Integrity." *Harvard Business Review* 72 (2): 106-17.

Paine, Lynn Sharp. 2006. "Integrity." In *Business Ethics: The Blackwell Encyclopedia of Management Volume II*, edited by Patricia H. Werhane, 247-49. Malden MA:Blackwell.

Palanski, Michael E., and Francis J. Yammarino. 2007. "Integrity and Leadership." *European Management Journal* 25 (3): 171-84.

Palmer, Donald. 2008. "Extending the Process Model of Collective Corruption." *Research in Organizational Behavior* 28:107-35.

Palmer, Donald. 2012. *Normal Organizational Wrongdoing: A Critical Analysis of Theories of Misconduct in and by Organizations.* Oxford/New York: Oxford University Press.

Palmer, Donald, and Celia Moore. 2016. "Social Networks and Organizational Wrongdoing in Context." In *Organizational Wrongdoing: Key Perspectives and New Directions*, edited by Donald Palmer, Royston Greenwood, and Kristin Smith-Crowe, 203-34. Cambridge: Cambridge University Press.

Palmer, Donald, Kristin Smith-Crowe, and Royston Greenwood. 2016. "The Imbalances and Limitations of Theory and Research on Organizational Wrongdoing." In *Organizational Wrongdoing: Key Perspectives and New Directions*, edited by Donald Palmer, Royston Greenwood, and Kristin Smith-Crowe, 1-16. Cambridge: Cambridge University Press.

Parker, Christine, and Vibeke Lehmann Nielsen. 2009. "Corporate Compliance Systems: Could They Make Any Difference?" *Administration & Society* 41: 3-37.

Parker, Christine, and Vibeke Lehmann Nielsen. 2011. "Introduction." In *Explaining Compliance: Business Responses to Regulation*, edited by Christine Parker and Vibeke Lehmann Nielsen, 1–36. Cheltenham: Edward Elgar Publishing.

Parker, Christine, and Vibeke Lehmann Nielsen. 2011. *Explaining Compliance: Business Responses to Regulation.* Cheltenham: Edward Elgar Publishing.

Parker, Martin, George Cheney, Valérie Fournier, and Christopher Land. 2013. *The Routledge Companion to Alternative Organizations.* London: Routledge.

Passas, Nikos, and Neva R. Goodwin. 2004. *It's Legal but It Ain't Right: Harmful Social Consequences of Legal Industries.* Ann Arbor: University of Michigan Press.

Paternoster, Raymond, and Sally S. Simpson. 1993. "A Rational Choice Theory of Corporate Crime." In *Advances in Criminological Theory: Routine Activity and Rational Choice,* edited by Ronald V. Clarke and Marcus Felson, 37-58. New Brunswick: Transaction Publishers.

Paternoster, Raymond, and Sally S. Simpson. 2009. "A Rational Choice Theory of Corporate Crime." In *Corporate Crime, Volume 2: Cases and Explanations, edited by* Hazel Croall, 195-213. London: Sage Publications.

Pelczar, Jan. 2019. "Schlafen Über Dem Ozean." *Reportagen* 47: 18–28.

Perreau-Saussine, Amanda, and James Bernard Murphy. 2007. *The Nature of Customary Law.* Cambridge, New York: Cambridge University Press.

Perrow, Charles. 1984. *Normal Accidents.* New York: Basic Books.

Perry, Nick. 1998. "Indecent Exposures: Theorizing Whistleblowing." *Organization Studies* 19: 235–57.

Persson, Anna, Bo Rothstein, and Jan Teorell. 2013. "Why Anticorruption Reforms Fail: Systemic Corruption as a Collective Action Problem." *Governance* 26 (3): 449–71.

Peters, Tom. 1988. *Thriving on Chaos: Handbook for a Management Revolution.* New York: Harper & Row.

Pfeffer, Jeffrey, and Gerald R. Salancik. 1978. *The External Control of Organizations: A Resource Dependence Perspective.* New York: Harper & Row.

Pfeffer, Jeffrey, and Robert I. Sutton. 2006. *Hard Facts, Dangerous Half-Truths, and Total Nonsense: Profiting from Evidence-Based Management.* Boston MA: Harvard Business School Press.

Pinto, Jonathan., Carrie R. Leana, and Frits K. Pil. 2008. "Corrupt Organizations or Organizations of Corrupt Individuals? Two Types of Organization-Level Corruption." *Academy of Management Review* 33 (3): 685–709.

Piquero, Nicole Leeper, Stephen G. Tibbetts, and Michael B. Blankenship. 2005. "Examining the Role of Differential Association and Techniques of Neutralization in Explaining Corporate Crime." *Deviant Behavior* 26 (2): 159–88.

Pitt, Harvey L., and Karl A. Groskaufmanis. 1989. "Minimizing Corporate Civil and Criminal Liability: A Second Look at Corporate Codes of Conduct." *Georgetown Law Journal* 78: 1559–1654.

Pohlmann, Markus, Kristina Bitsch, and Julian Klinkhammer. 2016. "Personal Gain or Organizational Benefits: How to Explain Active Corruption." *German Law Journal* 17: 73–100.

Pope, Dudley. 2001. *The Great Gamble: Nelson at Copenhagen.* London: Chatham.

Popitz, Heinrich. 1968. Über die Präventivwirkung des Nichtwissens: Dunkelziffer, Norm und Strafe. Tübingen: J.C.B. Mohr.

Power, Michael. 1997. "From Risk Society to Audit Society." *Soziale Systeme* 3: 3-21.

Power, Michael. 2005. "The Invention of Operational Risk." *Review of International Political Economy* 12 (4): 577-99.

Power, Michael. 2007. *Organized Uncertainty: Designing a World of Risk Management.* Oxford/ New York: Oxford University Press.

Power, Michael, Tobias Scheytt, K. Soi, and Kerstin Sahlin-Andersson. 2009. "Reputational Risk as a Logic of Organizing in Late Modernity." *Organization Studies* 30: 301-24.

Prat, Andrea. 2005. "The Wrong Kind of Transparency." *American Economic Review* 95 (3): 862-77.

Prechel, Harland, and Dadao Hou. 2016. "From Market Enablers to Market Participants: Redefining Organizational and Political-Legal Arrangements and Opportunities for Financial Wrongdoing, 1930s-2000." In *Organizational Wrongdoing: Key Perspectives and New Directions*, edited by Donald Palmer, Royston Greenwood, and Kristin Smith-Crowe,77-113. Cambridge, UK: Cambridge University Press.

Price, Robert. 1974. "Politics and Culture in Contemporary Ghana: The Big-Man Small-Boy Syndrome." *Journal of African Studies* 1: 173-204.

Puchta, Georg Friedrich. 1828. *Das Gewohnheitsrecht*. Erlangen: Palm-sche Verlagsbuchhandlung.

Pufendorf, Samuel. 1998. *De Jure Naturae Et Gentium: Band 8*. Berlin: de Gruyter.

Punch, Maurice. 1996. *Dirty Business: Exploring Corporate Misconduct*. London/ Thousand Oaks/ New Delhi: Sage.

Punch, Maurice. 2008. "The Organization Did It: Individuals, Corporations and Crime." In *Corporate and White Collar Crime*, edited by John Minkes and Leonard Minkes, 102-21. London: Sage.

Puzo, Mario. 1971. *Der Pate*. Reinbek: Rowohlt.

Raine, Adrian, William S. Laufer, Yaling. Yang, Katherine L. Narr, Paul Thompson, and Arthur W. Toga. 2012. "Increased Executive Functioning, Attention, and Cortical Thickness in White-Collar-Crime." *Human Brain Mapping* 33: 2932-4290.

Ramirez, Francisco, and Phyllis Riddle. 1991. "The Expansion of Higher Education." In *International Higer Education: An Encylopedia*, edited by Philip G. Altbach, 91-106. New York: Garland Publishing.

Rapoport, Anatol, and Albert M. Chammah. 1965. *Prisoner's Dilemma: A Study in Conflict and Cooperation*. Ann Arbor: University of Michigan Press.

Rasmussen, Nicolas. 2008. "America's First Amphetamine Epidemic 1929-1971: A Quantitative and Qualitative Retrospective with Implications for the Present." *American Journal of Public Health* 98 (6): 974–85.

Reckwitz, Andreas. 2019. *Das Ende der Illusionen: Politik, Ökonomie und Kultur in der Spätmoderne*. Berlin: Suhrkamp.

Reichert, Alan K., Michael Lockett, and Ramesh P. Rao. 1996. "The Impact of Illegal Business Practice on Shareholder Returns." *The Financial Review* 31 (1): 67–85.

Reiss, Albert J. 1966. "The Study of of Deviant Behavior: Where the Action Is." *Ohio Valley Sociologist* 21: 60-66.

Reiss, Albert J., and Michael Tonry. 1993. "Organizational Crime." *Crime & Justice* 18: 1-10.

Reurink, Arjan. 2016. "White-Collar Crime: The Concepts and Its Potential for the Analysis of Financial Crime." *European Journal of Sociology* 57: 385-414.

Rhodes, Carl. 2016. "Democratic Business Ethics: Volkswagen's Emissions Scandal and the Disruption of Corporate Sovereignty." *Organization Studies* 37 (10): 1501-18.

Riggs, Fred W. 1964. *Administration in Developing Countries: The Theory of Prismatic Society.* Boston: Houghton Mifflin.

Riggs, Fred W. 1966. *Thailand: The Modernization of Bureaucratic Polity.* Honolulu: East West Center Press.

Rigi, Jakob. 2004. "Corruption in Post-Soviet Kazakhstan." In *Between Morality and the Law. Corruption, Anthropology and Comparative Society*, edited by Italo Pardo, 101-19. Aldershot: Ashgate.

Riley, Russell L. 2009. "The White House as a Black Box: Oral History and the Problem of Evidence in Presidential Studies." *Political Studies* 57 (1): 187-206.

Ringel, Leopold. 2017. *Transparenz als Ideal und Organisationsproblem. Eine Studie am Beispiel der Piratenpartei Deutschland.* Wiesbaden: Springer VS.

Ringel, Leopold. 2018. "Unpacking the Transparency-Secrecy Nexus: Frontstage and Backstage Behaviour in a Political Party." *Organization Studies* 91:705-723.

Roberts, Alasdair. 2006. "Dashed Expectations: Governmental Adaption to Transparency Rules." In *Transparency: The Key to Better Governance?*, edited by Christoph Hood and David Heald, 107-25. Oxford: Oxford University Press.

Roberts, Karlene H. 1989. "New Challenges in Organizational Research: High Reliability Organizations." *Organization & Environment* 3 (2): 111-25.

Roberts, Karlene H., and Denise M. Rousseau. 1989. "Research in Nearly Failure-Free, High-Reliability Organizations: Having the Bubble." *IEEE Transactions on Engineering Management* 36 (2): 132-39.

Robertson, Brian J. 2015. *Holacracy: The New Management System for a Rapidly Changing World.* New York: Holt.

Robinson, Paul H., and John M. Darley. 1995. *Justice, Liability, and Blame: Community Views and the Criminal Law.* Boulder: Westview Press.

Robinson, Sandra L., and Rebecca J. Bennett. 1995. "A Typology of Deviant Workplace Behaviors: A Multidimensional Scaling Study." *Academy of Management Journal* 38: 555-72.

Rochlin, Gene I. 1996. "Reliable Organizations: Present Research and Future Directions." *Journal of Contingencies and Crisis Management* 4 (2): 55-59.

Rodríguez, Darío. 1991. *Gestion organizacional: Elementos para su estudio.* Santiago de Chile: Pontificia Universidad Católica de Chile.

Rodríguez, Darío. 2001. *Cultura organizacional.* Santiago de Chile: Pontificia Universidad Católica de Chile.

Roethlisberger, Fritz Jules, and William J. Dickson. 1939. *Management and the Worker: An Account of a Research Program Conducted by the Western Electric Company, Hawthorne Works, Chicago.* Cambridge: Harvard University Press.

Rose-Ackerman, Susan. 1978. *Corruption: A Study in Political Ecoomy.* New York: Academic Press.

Ross, H. Laurence. 1960. "Traffic Law Violation: A Folk Crime." *Social Problems* 231: 231-42.

Ross, Jeffrey Ian. 2003. *The Dynamics of Political Crime.* Thousand Oaks: Sage.

Rothwell, Gary R., and J. Norman Baldwin. 2007. "Whistle-Blowing and the Code of Silence in Police Agencies." *Crime & Delinquency* 53 (4): 605-32.

Rottenburg, Richard. 1994. "Orientierungsmuster afrikanischer Bürokratien. Eine Befragung modernisierungstheoretischer Ansätze." In *Systematischer Völkerkunde*, edited by Matthias S. Laubscher, 217-32. München: Akademischer Verlag München.

Rottenburg, Richard. 1995. "Formale und informale Beziehungen in Organisationen." In *Organisationswandel in Afrika*, edited by Achim v. Oppen and Richard Rottenburg, 19-36. Berlin: Verlag Arabisches Buch.

Rottenburg, Richard. 1996. "When Organization Travels: On Inter-cultural Translation." In *Translating Organizational Change,* edited by Barbara Czarniawska and Guje Sevón, 191-240. Berlin/New York: Walter de Gruyter.

Rottenburg, Richard. 2000. "Accountability for Development Aid." In *Facts and Figures,* edited by Herbert Kalthoff, Richard Rottenburg, and Hans J. Wagener, 143-73. Marburg: Metropolis.

Rottenburg, Richard. 2009. *Far-Fetched Facts: A Parable of Development Aid.* Cambridge: MIT Press.

Rotter, Frank. 1968. *Zur Funktion der juristischen Person in der Bundes-republik und in der DDR.* Karlsruhe: Moeller.

Roy, Donald F. 1952. "Quota Restriction and Goldbricking in a Machine Shop." *American Journal of Sociology* 57: 427-42.

Saam, Nicole J. 2002. *Prinzipale, Agenten und Macht: Eine machttheore-tische Erweiterung der Agenturtheorie und ihre Anwendung auf Interak-tionsstrukturen in der Organisationsberatung.* Tübingen: J.C.B. Mohr.

Sachs, Wolfgang. 1990. "The Archaeology of the Development Idea." *Interculture* 23 (4): 1-37.

Sachs, Wolfgang. 1992. *The Development Dictionary.* London: Zed Books.

Sackmann, Sonja A. 2006. *Success Factor: Corporate Culture: Developing a Corporate Culture for High Performance and Long-Term Competit-iveness.* Gütersloh: Verlag Bertelsmann Stiftung.

Sahlin-Andersson, Kerstin. 1996. "Imitating by Editing Success. The Construction of Organization Fields." In *Translating Organizational Change,* edited by Barbara Czarniawska and Guje Sevón, 69-92. Berlin/New York: Walter de Gruyter

Saleilles, Raymond. 2003. *De La Personnalité Juridique: Histoire Et Théories.* Paris: Éditions la Mémoire du droit.

Sallaz, Jeffrey J. 2009. *The Labor of Luck: Casino Capitalism in the United States and South Africa.* Berkeley: California University Press.

Salter, Malcolm S. 2008. *Innovation Corrupted: The Origins and Legacy of Enron's Collapse.* Cambridge, Mass. Harvard University Press.

Santiesteban, Ángel. 2017. *Wölfe in der Nacht: 16 Geschichten aus Kuba.* Frankfurt a.M.: S. Fischer.

Savigny, Friedrich Carl von. 1884. *Jural Relations, Or, The Roman Law of Persons as Subjects of Jural Relations: Being a Translation of the Second Book of Savigny's System of Modern Roman Law*. London: Wildy.

Scahill, Jeremy. 2011. *Blackwater: The Rise of the World's Most Powerful Mercenary Army*. London: Profile.

Schäfers, Mark. 2018. *Legitimation und Vertrauen: Prozesse und Mechanismen der Einführung in bestehende Praktiken Brauchbarer Illegalität*. Bielefeld: seminar paper.

Schauer, Frederick F. 1991. *Playing by the Rules: A Philosophical Examination of Rule-Based Decision-Making in Law and in Life*. New York/ Oxford: Clarendon Press; Oxford University Press.

Schmidt, Karl, and Christine Garschagen. 1978. "Korruption." In *Handwörterbuch Der Wirtschaftswissenschaft*, edited by Willi Albers, Karl E. Born, Ernst Dürr, Helmut Hesse, Alfons Kraft, Heinz Lampert, Klaus Rose, 565–73. Stuttgart/ New York/ Tübingen/ Göttingen/ Zürich: Gustav Fischer; J.C.B. Mohr; Vandenhoeck & Ruprecht.

Schneider, Anthony. 2004. *Tony Soprano on Management: Leadership Lessons Inspired by America's Favorite Mobster*. New York: Berkley Books.

Schöttl, Lisa, and Robert Ranisch. 2016. "Compliance- und Integrity-Ansätze in der Unternehmensethik: Normenorientierung ohne Werte oder Werteorientierung ohne Normen?" *Zeitschrift für Wirtschafts- und Unternehmensethik* 17: 311-26.

Schrager, Laura Shill, and James F. Short. 1978. "Toward a Sociology of Organizational Crime." *Social Problems* 25 (4): 407-19.

Schreyögg, Georg. 1984. *Unternehmensstrategie: Grundfrage einer Theorie strategischer Unternehmensführung*. Berlin/ New York: Walter de Gruyter.

Schröder, Thomas. 2019. "Corporate Crime, the Lawmaker's Options for Corporate Criminal Laws and Luhmann's Concept of "Useful Illegality"." *International Journal of Law, Crime and Justice* 57: 13–25.

Schünemann, Bernd. 1979. *Unternehmenskriminalität und Strafrecht: Eine Untersuchung der Verantwortlichkeit der Unternehmen und ihrer*

Führungskräfte nach geltendem und geplantem Straf- und Ordnungswidrigkeitenrecht. Köln: Carl Heymann.

Schünemann, Bernd. 1999. "Criticising the Notion of a Genuine Criminal Law Against Legal Entities" In *Criminal Responsibility of Legal and Collective Entities,* edited by Albin Eser, Günter Heine, and Barbara Huber, 225-33. Freiburg: edition iuscrim.

Schütz, Marcel, Richard Beckmann, and Heinke Röbken. 2018. *Compliance-Kontrolle in Organisationen.* Wiesbaden: Springer Gabler.

Schwartz, Mark S. 2001. "The Nature of the Relationship Between Corporate Codes of Ethics and Behaviour." *Journal of Business Ethics* 32 (3): 247-62.

Scott, Alan. 2003. "Organisation zwischen charismatischer und bürokratischer Revolution." In *Menschenregierungskünste: Anwendungen poststrukturalistischer Analyse auf Management und Organisation,* edited by Richard Weiskopf. 1. Aufl., 304-18. Wiesbaden: Westdt. Verl.

Scott, James C. 1969a. "Corruption, Machine Politics, and Political Change." *The American Political Science Review* 63: 1142-58.

Scott, James C. 1969b. "The Analysis of Corruption in Developing Nations." *Comparative Studies in Society and History* 11: 315-41.

Scott, W. Richard. 1982. "Managing Professional Work: Three Models of Control for Health Organizations." *Health Services Research* 17: 213-40.

Seibel, Wolfgang, Kevin Klamann, and Hannah Treis. 2017. *Verwaltungsdesaster: Von der Loveparade bis zu den NSU-Ermittlungen.* Frankfurt/ New York: Campus Verlag.

Selznick, Philip. 1948. "Foundations of the Theory of Organization." *American Sociological Review* 13: 25–35.

Selznick, Philip. 1949. *TVA and the Grass Roots.* Berkeley: University of California Press.

Senturia, Joseph J. 1931. "Corruption, Political (General)" In *Encyclopedia of the Social Sciences, Volume 4,* edited by Edwin R.A. Seligman and Alvin Johnson, 448-52. New York: Macmillan.

Shapiro, Susan P. 1983. "The New Moral Entrepreneurs: Corporate Crime Crusaders." *Contemporary Sociology* 12 (3): 304–7.

Sharp, Walter R. 1957. "Bureaucracy and Politics. Egyptian Model." In *Toward the Comparative Study of Public Administration*, edited by William J. Siffin, 145-81. Bloomington: Indiana University Press.

Shleifer, Andrei, and Robert W. Vishny. 1993. "Corruption." *The Quarterly Journal of Economics* 108 (3): 599–617.

Shover, Neal, and K. M. Bryant. 1993. "Theoretical Explanation of Corporate Crime." In *Understanding Corporate Criminality*, edited by M. Blankenship, 141–76. New York: Routledge.

Shover, Neal, and Andy Hochstetler. 2002. "Cultural Explanation and Organizational Crime." *Crime, Law and Social Change* 37 (1): 1–18.

Shrivastava, Paul. 1987. *Bhopal: Anatomy of a Crisis*. Cambridge: Ballinger.

Sidhu, Karl. 2009. "Anti-Corruption Compliance Standards in the Aftermath of the Siemens Scandal." *German Law Journal* 10 (8): 1343–54.

Simon, Herbert A. 1946. "The Proverbs of Administration." *Public Administration Review* 6: 53–67.

Simon, Herbert A. 1957. *Administrative Behavior.* 2nd ed. New York: The Free Press.

Simpson, Sally S. 2002. *Corporate Crime, Law, and Social Control.* Cambridge studies in criminology. Cambridge: Cambridge University Press.

Sims, Ronald R. 2003. *Ethics and Corporate Social Responsibility: Why Giants Fall.* Westport: Greenwood.

Sjoberg, Gideon. 1960. "Contradictory Functional Requirements and Social Systems." *Journal of Conflict Resolution* 4: 198–208.

Skolnick, Jerome. 2002. "Corruption and the Blue Code of Silence." *Police Practice and Research* 3 (1): 7–19.

Smigel, Erwin O., and H. Laurence Ross. 1970. "Introduction." In *Crimes Against Bureaucracy*, edited by Erwin O. Smigel and H. Laurence Ross, 1–14. New York: Van Nostrand.

Smith-Crowe, Kristin, and Danielle E. Warren. 2014. "The Emotion-Evoked Collective Corruption Model: The Role of Emotion in the Spread of Corruption Within Organizations." *Organization Science* 25 (4): 1154–71.

Snider, Laureen. 2000. "The Sociology of Corporate Crime: An Obituary (Or: Whose Knowledge Claims Have Legs?)." *Theoretical Criminology* 42: 169–206.

Snook, Scott A. 2002. *Friendly Fire: The Accidental Shootdown of U.S. Black Hawks over Northern Iraq.* 4th ed. Princeton: Princeton University Press.

Solomon, David, and Eugene Soltes. 2015. "What Are We Meeting for? The Consequences of Private Meetings with Investors." *The Journal of Law and Economics* 58:325–55.

Soltes, Eugene. 2016. *Why They Do It: Inside the Mind of the White-Collar Criminal.* New York: PublicAffairs.

Spreitzer, Gretchen M., and Sscott Sonenshein. 2003. "Positive Deviance and Extraordinary Organizing." In *Positive Organizational Scholarship*, edited by Kim S. Cameron, Jane E. Dutton, and Robert E. Quinn, 207–24. San Francisco: Berrett-Koehler.

Srivastva, Suresh C. 1988. *Executive Integrity: The Search for High Human Values in Organizational Life.* San Francisco: Jossey-Bass.

Stark, Johanna. 2019. *Law for Sale: A Philosophical Critique of Regulatory Competition.* Oxford/ New York: Oxford University Press.

Staw, Barry M., and Eugene Szwajkowski. 1975. "The Scarcity-Munificence Component of Organizational Environments and the Commission of Illegal Acts." *Administrative Science Quarterly* 20: 345.

Stinchcombe, Arthur L. 2001. *When Formality Works: Authority and Abstraction in Law and Organizations.* Chicago: University of Chicago Press.

Stoddard, Ellwyn R. 1968. "Informal Code of Police Deviancy: a Group Approach to Blue-Coat Crime." *Journal of Criminal Law, Criminology & Police Science* 59: 201–13.

Stokes, Susan S. 2007. "Political Clientelism." In *The Oxford Handbook of Comparative Politics*, edited by Charles Boix and Susan S. Stokes, 604–27. Oxford: Oxford University Press.

Stone, Christopher D. 1975. *Where the Law Ends: The Social Control of Corporate Behaviour.* New York: Harper & Row.

Stone, Christopher D. 1980. "The Place of Enterprise Liability in the Control of Corporate Conduct." *Yale Law Journal* 90: 1–77.

Stone, Joseph, and Tim Yohn. 1992. *Prime Time and Misdemeanors: Investigating the 1950s TV Quiz Scandal.* New Brunswick: Rutgers University Press.

Sullivan, Bilian Ni, Pamela Haunschild, and Karen Page. 2007. "Organizations Non Gratae? The Impact of Unethical Corporate Acts on Interorganizational Networks." *Organization Science* 18 (1): 55–70.

Sutherland, Edwin H. 1939. *Principles of Criminology.* 3rd ed. Philadelphia: Lippincott.

Sutherland, Edwin H. 1940. "White-Collar Criminality." *American Sociological Review* 5: 1–12.

Sutherland, Edwin H. 1945. "Is "White Collar Crime" Crime?" *American Sociological Review* 10: 132–39.

Sutherland, Edwin H. 1947. *Principels of Criminology.* 4th ed. Philadelphia: Lippincott.

Sutherland, Edwin H. 1949. *White Collar Crime.* New York: Holt, Rinehart & Winston.

Sutherland, Edwin H. 1983. *White Collar Crime: The Uncut Version.* London: Yale University Press.

Sykes, Gresham, and David Matza. 1957. "Techniques of Neutralization: A Theory of Delinquency." *American Sociological Review* 22: 664–70.

Szwajkowski, Eugene. 1986. "The Myths and Realities of Research on Organizational Misconduct." *Research in Corporate Social Performance and Policy* 8: 121–47.

Tappan, Paul W. 1947. "Who Is the Criminal?" *American Sociological Review* 12: 96–120.

Taylor, Carolyn. 2015. *Walking the Talk: Building a Culture for Success.* London: Random House Business Books.

Taylor, Frederick W. 1967. *The Principles of Scientific Management.* London: Norton.

Tekleab, Amanuel G., Riki Takeuchi, and M. Susan Taylor. 2005. "Extending the Chain of Relationships Among Organizational Justice, Social Exchange, and Employee Reactions: The Role of Contract Violations." *Academy of Management Journal* 48 (1): 146–57.

Teubner, Gunther. 1987a. "Juridification - Concepts, Aspects Limits, Solution." In *Juridification of Social Spheres: A Comparative Analysis in the Areas Ob Labor, Corporate, Antitrust and Social Welfare Law*, edited by Gunther Teubner, 3–48. Berlin: de Gruyter.

Teubner, Gunther. 1987b. "Unternehmenskorporatismus: New Industrial Policy und das "Wesen" der Juristischen Person." *Kritische Vierteljahresschrift für Gesetzgebung und Rechtswissenschaft* 2: 61–85.

Thompson, James D. 1967. *Organizations in Action.* New York: McGraw-Hill.

Thornton, Partricia H., William Ocasio, and Michael Lounsbury. 2012. *The Institutional Logics Perspective: A New Approach to Culture, Structure, and Process.* Oxford/ New York: Oxford University Press.

Tidd, Joseph, and John R. Bessant. 2014. *Strategic Innovation Management.* Chichester: Wiley.

Tignor, Robert L. 1971. "Colonial Chiefs in Chiefless Societies." *The Journal of Modern African Studies* 9:339–59.

Tilly, Charles. 1985. "War Making and State Making as Organized Crime." In *Bringing the State Back in*, edited by Peter B. Evans, Dietrich Rueschemeyer, and Theda Skocpol, 169–86. Cambridge/ New York: Cambridge University Press.

Tolk, Janice Newquist, Jaime Cantu, and Mario Beruvides. 2013. "High Reliability Organization Research: A Literature Review for Health Care." *Engineering Management Journal* 27 (4): 218–37.

Treiber, Hubert. 1973. *Wie man Soldaten macht: Sozialisation in „kasernierter Vergesellschaftung".* Düsseldorf: Bertelsmann.

Treviño, Linda K. 1986. "Ethical Decision Making in Organizations: A Person-Situation Interactionist Model." *Academy of Management Review* 11 (3): 601–17.

Treviño, Linda K., Gary R. Weaver, David G. Gibson, and Barbara Ley Toffler. 1999. "Managing Ethics and Legal Compliance: What Works and What Hurts." *California Management Review* 41 (2): 131–51.

Treviño, Linda K., and Stuart A. Youngblood. 1990. "Bad Apples in Bad Barrels: A Causal Analysis of Ethical Decision-Making Behavior." *Journal of Applied Psychology* 75: 378–85.

Trist, Eric, and Ken W. Bamforth. 1951. "Some Social and Psychological Consequences of the Longwall Method of Coal Getting."
Human Relations 4: 3–38.

Tucker, James. 1989. "Employee Theft as Social Control." *Deviant
Behavior* 10: 319–34.

Turk, Austin. 1982. *Political Criminality.* Newbury Park: Sage.

Twining, William L., and David Miers. 2010. *How to Do Things with
Rules: A Primer of Interpretation.* 5th ed. Cambridge: Cambridge
University Press.

Umphress, Elizabeth E., and John B. Bingham. 2011. "When Employees Do Bad Things for Good Reasons: Examining Unethical Pro-Organizational Behaviors." *Organization Science* 22 (3): 621–40.

Umphress, Elizabeth E., John B. Bingham, and Marie S. Mitchell.
2010. "Unethical Behavior in the Name of the Company: The
Moderating Effect of Organizational Identification and Positive
Reciprocity on Unethical Pro-Organizational Behavior." *Journal of
Applied Psychology* 95 (4): 769–80.

Vadera, Abhijeet K., Michael G. Pratt, and Pooja Mishra. 2013. "Constructive Deviance in Organizations: Integrating and Moving Forward." *Journal of Management* 39: 1221–76.

van de Walle, Nicolas. 2009. "Meet the New Boss, Same as the Old
Boss? The Evolution of Political Clientelism in Africa." In *Patrons,
Clients and Policies: Patterns of Democratic Accountability and Political Competition*, edited by Herbert Kitschelt and Steven I. Wilkin-
son, 50–67. Cambridge: Cambridge University Press.

van Dyne, Linn, Jill W. Graham, and Richard M. Dienesch. 1994.
"Organizational Citizenship Behavior: Construct Redefinition,
Measurement, and Validation." *Academy of Management Journal*
37 (4): 765–802.

van Maanen, John. 1991. "The Smile Factory: Work at Disneyland."
In *Reframing Orgnizational Culture*, edited by Peter J. Frost, Larry
F. Moore, Meryl R. Louis, Craig C. Lundberg, and Joanne Martin,
58–76. Newbury Park: Sage.

Vandekerckhove, Wim. 2006. *Whistleblowing and Organizational Social
Responsibility: A Global Assessment.* Aldershot,/ Burlington: Ashgate.

Vardi, Yoav, and Yosh Wiener. 1996. "Misbehavior in Organizations: A Motivational Framework." *Organization Science* 7: 151–65.

Vaughan, Diane. 1980. "Crime Between Organizations." In *White-Collar Crime: Theory and Research*, edited by Gilbert Geis and Ezra Stotland, 77–97. Beverly Hills/ London: Sage.

Vaughan, Diane. 1981. "Recent Development in White-Collar Crime Theory and Research." In *The Mad, the Bad, and the Different: Essays in Honor of Simon Dinitz*, edited by C. R. Huff and Israel L. Barak-Glantz. Lexington: Lexington Books.

Vaughan, Diane. 1998. "Rational Choice, Situated Action, and the Social Control of Organizations." *Law & Society Review* 32 (1): 23–61.

Vinterberg, Thomas. 1998. *Das Fest:* Film.

Wagner, Gerhard. 2016. "Sinn und Unsinn der Unternehmensstrafe: Mehr Prävention durch Kriminalisierung." *Zeitschrift für Gesellschaftsrecht* 45: 112–52.

Walker, Nigel. 1980. *Punishment, Danger and Stigma: The Morality of Criminal Justice.* Totowa: Barnes and Noble Books.

Waller, James E. 2002. *Becoming Evil: How Ordinary People Commit Genocide and Mass Killing.* 2nd ed. Oxford/ New York: Oxford University Press.

Walsh, Charles J., and Alissa Pyrich. 1994. "Corporate Compliance Programs as a Defense to Criminal Liability: Can a Corporation Save Its Soul." *Rutgers Law Review* 47: 605–91.

Ward, John William. 1964. "The Ideal of Individualism and the Reality of Organizations." In *The Business Establishment*, edited by Earl F. Cheit, 37–76. New York: Wiley.

Wardi, Yoav, and Ely Weitz. 2004. *Misbehavior in Organizations: Theory, Research, and Management.* Mahwah: Erlbaum.

Warner, William Lloyd, and Josiah Orne Low. 1947. *The Social System of the Modern Factory,* New Haven: Yale University Press.

Warren, Danielle E. 2003. "Constructive and Destructive Deviance in Organizations." *Academy of Management Review* 28: 622–32.

Weaver, Gary R. 1984. "Corporate Codes of Ethics: Purpose, Process and Content Issues." *Business & Society* 32 (1): 44–58.

Weaver, Gary R., Linda K. Treviño, and Philip L. Cochran. 1999. "Corporate Ethics Practices in the Mid-1990's: An Empirical Study of the Fortune 1000." *Journal of Business Ethics* 18 (3): 283–94.

Weber, Max. 1976. *Wirtschaft und Gesellschaft.* Tübingen: J.C.B. Mohr.

Weber, Max. 1978. *Economy and Society: An Outline of Interpretive Sociology.* Berkeley: University of California Press.

Weber, Max. 2011. *The Protestant Ethic and the Spirit of Capitalism.* New York: Oxford University Press.

Weick, Karl E. 1988. Enacted Sensemaking in Crisis Situations. *Journal of Management Studies* 25: 305–317.

Weick, Karl E., and Kathleen M. Sutcliffe. 2007. *Managing the Unexpected: Resilient Performance in an Age of Uncertainty.* 2nd ed. San Francisco: Jossey-Bass.

Weiner, Myron. 1962. *The Politics of Scarcity.* Chicago: University of Chicago Press.

Wells, Celia. 2005. *Corporations and Criminal Responsibility.* 2nd ed. Oxford: Oxford University Press.

Westley, William A. 1956. "Secrecy and the Police." *Social Forces* 34 (3): 254–57.

Wheeler, Stanton. 1982. "The Problem of White-Collar Crime Motivation." In *White Collar-Crime Reconsidered*, edited by Kip Schlegel and David Weisburd, 108–23. Boston: Northeastern University Press.

Wheeler, Stanton, and Mitchell Lewis Rothman. 1982. "The Organization as Weapon in White-Collar Crime." *Michigan Law Review* 80, 1403–26.

Whyte, William Foote. 1943. *The Street Corner Society.* Chicago: University of Chicago Press.

Whyte, William H. 1956. *The Organization Man.* New York: Simon & Schuster.

Wieland, Josef. 2010. "Ethics and Economic Success: A Contradiction in Terms?" *Zeitschrift für Psychologie / Journal of Psychology* 218: 243–45.

Williams, Colin C., and Junhong Yang. 2017. "Evaluating the Use of Personal Networks to Circumvent Formal Processes: A Case Study of Vruzki in Bulgaria." *South East European Journal of Economics and Business* 12:57–67.

Williams, David E., and Glenda Treadaway. 1992. "Exxon and the Valdez Accident: A Failure in Crisis Communication." *Communication Studies* 43 (1): 56–64.

Williams, Robin M. 1970. *American Society: A Sociological Interpretation.* 3rd ed. New York: Knopf.

Wilson, James Q. 1989. *Bureaucracy: What Government Agencies Do and Why They Do It.* New York: Basic Books.

Wilson, Larry C. 1979. "The Doctrines of Wilful Blindness." *University of New Brunswick Law Journal* 28: 175–94.

Winslow, Don. 2017. *The Force.* New York: William Morrow and Company.

Wright, J. Patrick. 1979. *On a Clear Day You Can See General Motors: John Z. De Lorean's Look Inside the Automotive Giant.* Grosse Pointe: Wright Enterprises.

Xin, Katherine K., and Jone L. Pearce. 1996. "Guanxi: Connections as Substitutes for Formal Institutional Support." *Academy of Management Journal* 39:1641–58.

Yeager, Peter Cleary. 1986. "Analyzing Corporate Offenses: Progress and Prospects." In *Research in Corporate Social Performance and Policy: Vo. 8*, edited by James Post, 93–120. Greenwich: JAI Press.

Yeager, Peter Cleary. 2007. "Understanding Corporate Lawbreaking: From Profit Seeking to Law Finding." In *International Handbook of White-Collar and Corporate Crime*, edited by Henry N. Pontell and Gilbert Geis, 25–49. New York: Springer Science + Business Media.

Young, Ed. 1989. "On the Naming of the Rose: Interests and Multiple Meanings as Elements of Organizational Culture." *Organization Studies* 10 (2): 187–206.

Zeitlin, Lawrence R. 1971. "A Little Larceny Can Do a Lot for Employee Morale." *Psychology Today* (5): 22-64.

Ziegleder, Diana. 2007. "Business and Self-Regulation: Results from a Comparative Study on the Prevention of Economic Crime." *Zeitschrift für Rechtssoziologie* 28: 203–13.

Znoj, Heinzpeter. 1994. "Der Intime Staat: Korruption aus ethnologischer Sicht." *Reformatio* 43: 143–50.

Zuckmayer, Carl. 2004. *Der Hauptmann von Köpenick: Ein deutsches Märchen in drei Akten.* Fischer 7002. Frankfurt a.M.: Fischer.

Zum-Bruch, Elena Isabel. 2019. *Polizeiliche Pro-Organisationale Devianz: Eine Typologie.* Wiesbaden: Springer VS.

www.ingramcontent.com/pod-product-compliance
Lightning Source LLC
Chambersburg PA
CBHW020249030426
42336CB00010B/678